Montana Fishing and C

Glacier to Yellowstone

An informative guide to camping and fishing from Glacier National Park to Yellowstone National Park.

David Archer

Photographs by the author

First Edition

Published by: www.glaciertoyellowstone.com
David Archer
5311 Leaning Tree, Florence, Montana 59833

Website: www.glaciertoyellowstone.com
Email: darcher@glaciertoyellowstone.com

Note: Emailed suggestions, corrections or additions are welcome.

Printed in the United States
ISBN: 0-9670806-0-6

Maps by GeoData Services, Inc
104 South Ave. E., Missoula, MT 59801

INTRODUCTION

Having been an English teacher for 25 years and a fly fishing guide in western Montana for 15 years, I initially set out to write a few articles on fishing creeks in my own backyard for our community newspaper. I just kept writing. After all these years, I still marvel at the wonderful fishing opportunities to be found in the feeder streams and canyon creeks. Raised in a small village perched in the eastern Sierra Nevada Mountains, I have always had a fondness for small creeks. My first fishing memories are with my mother as we picnicked on Pine Creek. Fly fishing was not an option at age five, and bait was generally a piece of hot dog or a wadded up chunk from a peanut butter and jelly sandwich.

In this book I have included only creeks, rivers and lakes that can be reached from a passenger vehicle or a short day hike. My focus is on the intimacy of small lakes and streams, and I have selected what I consider to be the best options as you travel between Glacier National Park and Yellowstone National Park. The book is not a comprehensive guide that covers all the fishing waters stretching between the two parks, but I haven't overlooked much. As a river guide for 15 years, I have also included detailed information for the rivers in Montana from Glacier to Yellowstone. The maps that are included are not drawn to scale, nor do they reflect all the dangerous obstacles that come and go with each passing run-off.

As much as possible, I have combined the Montana highway system with the major rivers and tributaries. The focus, naturally, is on fishing, but I include almost all of the state and federal campgrounds as well as mentioning those unimproved campsites which are slowly disappearing. I have utilized the mile-markers signs you see at every mile along the highways and secondary roads throughout western and southwestern Montana. The mile-marker signs run from west to east and from south to north. **Mile 0** is typically placed at the west or south state line.

Many of the Montana fly-fishing books on the market are detailed in fishing techniques and prescribed fly patterns to use on a particular water. I decided against this prescriptive format for the simple reason that after 35 years of being a fly fisherman and 15 years as a guide I have yet to make a study of aquatic entomology, nor am I a master fly tier. Secondly, since a great deal of redundancy exits in the hatches in western and southwestern Montana, I have instead chosen to include a section on fly patterns and the major hatches at the end of the book. Mother Nature rarely consults with an author's hatch charts.

My goal for this book is quite simple. I want to guide you to as many waters as you can fish during your visit to Montana. I want to help you prioritize your fishing choices, keep you from getting lost or wasting time, and I want to help those fishers who like to camp along the way. If you are new to fly fishing, be sure to read my comprehensive primer, "Mastering the Basics of Fly Fishing", at www.glaciertoyellowstone.com. You may also email me and offer any corrections or additions you think would be important for a book revision or an update for the website.

Acknowledgments: I would like to acknowledge Dick Konizeski's book, The Montanans' Fishing Guide that I purchased over 20 years ago when I moved from Jackson Hole to the Bitterroot Valley. Although initially overwhelmed by the comprehensiveness of the book (Mary's Frog Pond), the book has served me well. I would also like to thank the fly shop owners and outfitters who have contributed their expertise to this book. I would like to thank Rick VanderKnyff, my brother-in-law, and Pauline Delano for helping me proofread the text.

I dedicate this book to my two sons who both plan to leave Montana in pursuit of "the big bucks!" All their lives I reminded them how lucky they were living in Montana. This book's for you, fellows. When you come back for visits, be sure to bring your fly rods.

The author enjoying a fall day on the Blackfoot River.

Table of Contents

Western Montana

Southwestern Montana

Southwest Montana

Glacier National Park to Yellowstone National Park

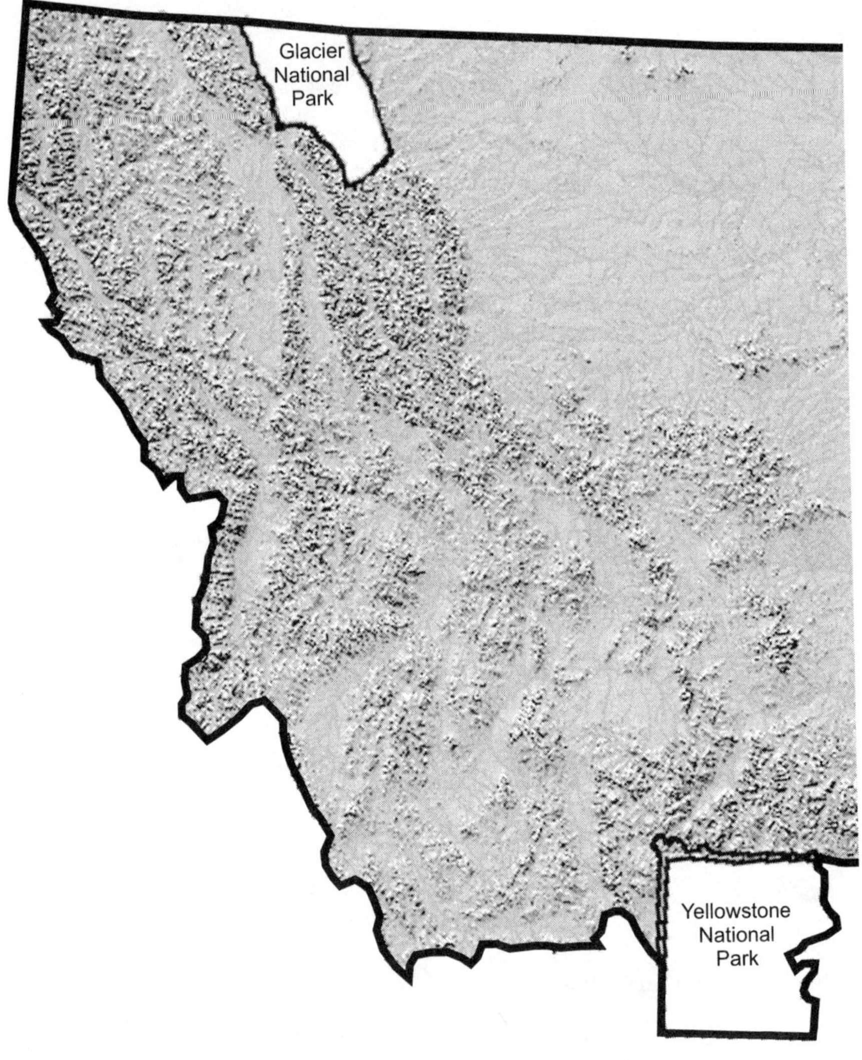

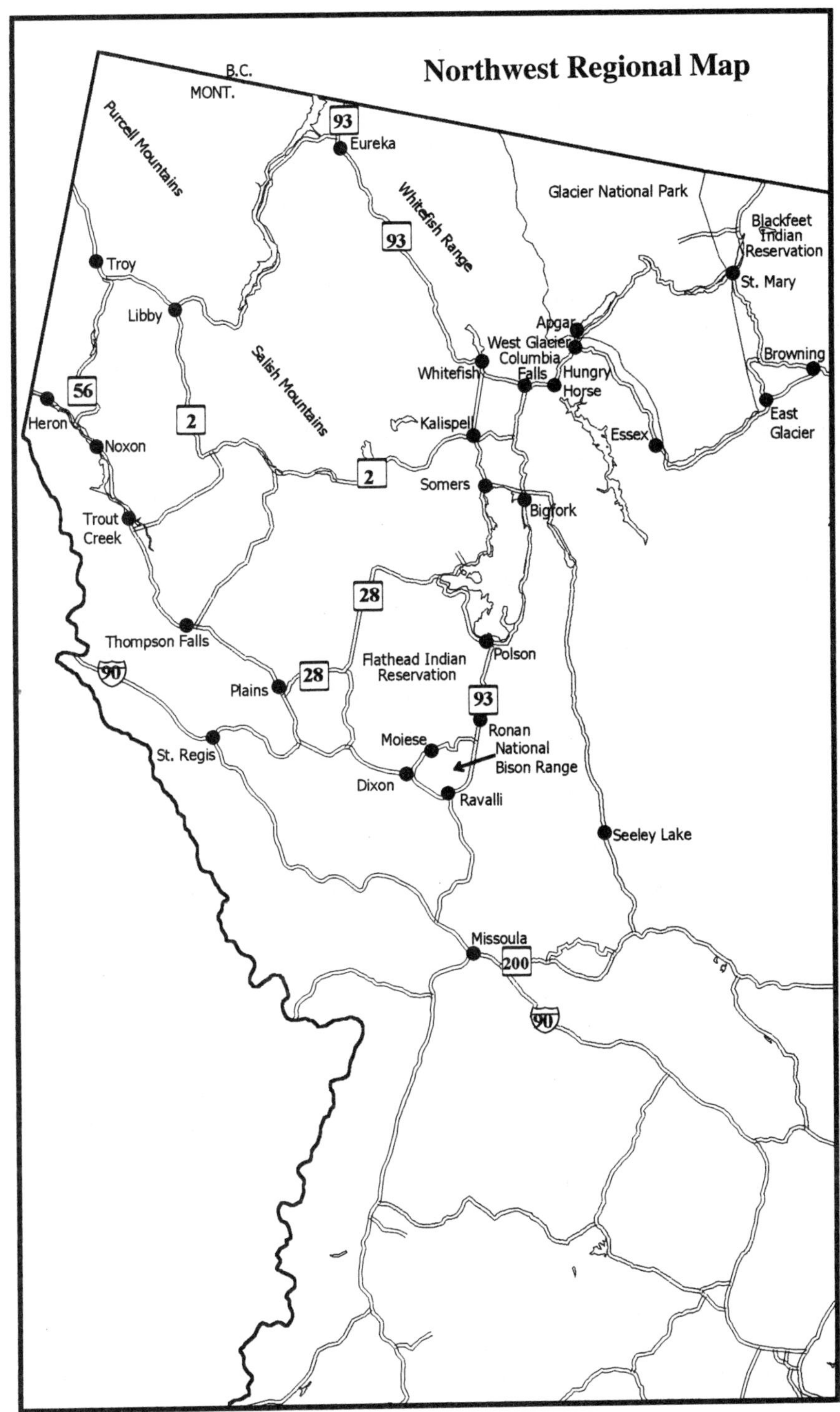
Northwest Regional Map
B.C.
MONT.
Purcell Mountains
93
Eureka
Whitefish Range
93
Glacier National Park
Blackfeet Indian Reservation
St. Mary
Troy
Libby
Salish Mountains
Apgar
West Glacier
Columbia Falls
Hungry Horse
Whitefish
Browning
East Glacier
56
Heron
Noxon
2
Kalispell
Essex
2
Somers
Bigfork
Trout Creek
28
Thompson Falls
Polson
90
28
Flathead Indian Reservation
Plains
93
Ronan
Moiese
National Bison Range
St. Regis
Dixon
Ravalli
Seeley Lake
Missoula
200
90

Northwestern Montana
Accommodations and Services

The northwest region is vast. I have included only accommodations that are reasonably close to good fishing. For a complete regional listing and descriptions of accommodations and services, request a free travel planner from Travel Montana, Department of Commerce, P.O. Box 200533, Helena, Montana 59620-0533, or telephone1 800 847-4868. For Travel Montana Internet Information: http://travel.mt.gov

Columbia Falls Private Campgrounds

Big Creek Campground, 1 800-416-6992 / Boat launch and rentals

Columbia Falls RV Park, 1000 3rd Ave East, Columbia Falls, MT 59912
Telephone: (406) 892-1122 / Tepees, playground

Glacier Peaks RV Park, 3185 Highway 40, Columbia Falls, MT 59912
Telephone: (406) 892-2133 (800) 268-4849; Pull through sites; cable available
http://www.digisys.net/rvs/

La Salle RV Park & Campground, 5618 Hwy. 2 West, Columbia Falls, MT 59912 Telephone: (406) 892-4668

Western Inns Glacier Mountain Shadows; Telephone: 1 800-766-1137
Playground, volleyball court, pull-throughs

Eureka Private Campground: Blue Mountain RV Park, (406) 889-3868
Six new cabins, café and bar on site.

Kalispell Fly Shops and Sporting Goods

Snappy Sport Center, 1400 Hwy. 2 East, Kalispell, MT 59901 (406) 257-7525
Sportsman & Ski haus, 40 East Idaho, Kalispell, MT 59901 (406) 755-6484

Kalispell Private Campgrounds

Glacier Pines RV Park, 1850 Hwy. 35 E., Kalispell, MT 59901 (406) 752-2760
Trout pond, river access, playground, clean restrooms

Greenwood Village Campground: Telephone (406) 257-7719
Pool; forested setting; near town; paved roads

Lake Blaine Resort: Telephone (406) 854-2744
Swimming, playground, skating, boating, fishing; cabins

Rocky Mountain "Hi" RV Park: (406) 755-9573; playground, cabins, cable TV; swimming, canoeing

Spruce Park RV, 1985 Hwy. 35, Kalispell, MT 59901 (406) 752-6321
Fishing, boat tours, playground; family rates

White Birch RV, 17 Shady Lane, Kalispell, MT 59901 (406) 752-4008

Libby Fly shops and Sporting Goods Stores:

Libby Sport Center, 204 West 9th Street, Libby, Montana 5992 (406) 293-4641

Kootenai Angler, 13546 Highway 37, Libby, Montana 59923 (406) 293-7578

Libby Private Campgrounds:

Big Bend RV Park, 13 miles from Libby on Highway 37, (406) 293-4536
10 acres on river; restaurant, bar and casino

Koocanusa Resort, 23 miles from Libby on Highway 37, (406) 293-7548
Lounge, store, cabins, marina, boat rentals and trail rides

Meadowlark RV Park, Libby; Telephone: (406) 293-8323 grassy sites, trees, shade, close to shopping

Sportsman's RV Park, 11741 Highway 37, Libby, MT 59923 (406) 293-2267
Next to national forest; good hunting and fishing

Woodland RV Park, Libby, (406) 293-8395 Creek, trees, grassy sites; golf

Noxon Private Campground: Cabinet Gorge RV Park, PO Box 1485, Noxon, MT 59853 Telephone: (406) 847-2291 Fish and boat dock

Thompson Falls Private Campgrounds:

Birdland Bay RV, 171 Blue Slide Road, Thompson Falls, MT 59873
(406) 827-4757 Boat docks, fishing; next to golf course

The Riverfront RV Park and Cabins: (406) 827-3460; large group fire pit, fishing access, antiques, gift shop

Troy Private Campgrounds:

Kootenai River Campground, 2898 Hwy. 2 N, Troy, MT 59935 (406) 295-4090 Playground, rentals, cabins

Glacier Campground, 12070 Hwy. 2 W, West Glacier, MT 59936 (406) 387-5689 Playground, volleyball, cabins

Lake Five Resort: Hwy. 2 three miles west of West Glacier (406) 387-5601 Lake swimming, boat rentals, barbecue pits

San-Suz-Ed RV Park & Campground: 2.5 miles from West Glacier entrance 1 800-562-3313: Pies, cinnamon rolls and bread is our specialty

West Glacier KOA, 355 Half Moon Flats Road, West Glacier, MT 59936 1 800-562-3313: Kamping Kabins, game rooms, breakfast, and dinner

Whitefish Fly Shop: Lakestream Fly Fishing Shop, 15 Central Avenue, Whitefish, MT 59937 (406) 862-1298

Whitefish KOA & Chuckwagon: 5121 Hwy 93 S., Whitefish, MT 59937-8502 Telephone: 1 800-562-8734; 10 Kabins; chuckwagon suppers

Northwestern Montana

Kootenai River / Lake Koocanusa

The Kootenai River from Libby Dam seventeen miles down river to Libby is another great tailwater fishery for Montana. After years of pressure from fishermen, biologists and local concerned citizens, the days of wild fluctuations have come to an end. Posing danger to fishermen and floaters, the erratic rise and fall of the river also posed a threat to the insect larva stranded high and dry by the whims of a dam army corps engineer. With current standards for water draw down, insect larva have a chance to retreat into deeper, receding water. With consistent yearly insect survival, the Kootenai gets better every year.

Sitting in the Kootenai Angler, I overheard Dave's exuberant announcement to a local fisherman that Green Drakes had appeared in the river, possibly washed down from the Fisher River. Being one of the first fly fishing guide service on the Kootenai, Dave and his guides are intimately acquainted with all the nuances and fluctuations of this tailwater fishery. In his 1998 newsletter (email kangler@libby.org), Dave talks about the genetic verification of native redband trout in the Kootenai River. Indigenous to the Columbia River drainage, redband trout are noted for having larger spots and a darker background. Dave reports that they are both acrobatic and strong fighters. In addition to a healthy population of trout averaging 2400 per mile below the dam, one advantage to this large, tailwater marvel is the extended season.

Dave reports that the cold waters of March and April provide fishing opportunities for Rainbows during the spawning period. Although the water can be off-colored, fishermen can experience some good nymphing and streamer fishing. During May and June the water begins to warm, precipitating the emergence of caddis and the Western March Brown. Dry fly fishing heats up, and by far the most important hatch is the PMDs ranging in seize 14 to 16 in the early summer to seize 18 in the latter part of summer. July and August may bring the heat to the fishermen, but the warmer water activates fish feeding for both dry flies and hoppers. The fall brings forth both foliage change and clarity to the river. With lots of mid day hatches, trout are eager to store up fat reserves for the winter. But winter is a long time coming on the Kootenai River according to Dave. The Kootenai season is extended with warm water releases in the 50's, and the fish are still active all the way into December. Like the Bitterroot River, the Kootenai River is Whirling Disease free.

Wade fishing is best from 8,000 cfs to 12,000 cfs. It is next to impossible during high water releases of over 15,000 cfs. When the water rises, guides and float fishermen head for the side channels as do the larger trout. Popular float trips originate at the dam with the final take-out in the town of Libby. The 17-mile section can be broken up into a number of potential float trips depending how much time you would like to spend on the water. Below Libby are the Kootenai Falls which are deadly. Powerboat operators fishing below the Libby Bridge should first confer with a local expert. Although the world record rainbow at 33 pounds one ounce was caught at the outlet of the dam, the average catch of the day will be around 10-14 inches with plenty of 18+ inch trout to challenge everyone. Overlooked for years by the fly fishing public plying the waters of the Madison and Missouri, people in the know are looking to the northwest. A tour of the Clark Fork drainage rivers and then a sampling of the Kootenai could provide some of the best trout fishing in the lower 48!

Lake Koocanusa

Straddling the border with 48 miles in Montana and 42 miles in British Columbia, Lake Koocanusa was formed with the creation of the Libby Dam in 1971. Alice Beers of Rexford, Montana, coined the name of the lake. The name combines the first part of the Kootenai, the second part "can" representing Canada and the last three letters being "USA". The lake is immense and offers very marginal shore fishing. The principal draw is the prodigious numbers of kokanee salmon that range from 11 to 14 inches. Large kamloop rainbows lure boat fishermen from all around the region. Boaters will find plenty of water to fish with over 46,000 surface acres. Campground and boat launches are spread evenly around the lake.

MM 0: Idaho Stateline / Highway 2

MM 1.9: Fishing access to the Kootenai River: The access is right next to a residence. Drive one mile to a parking place, but do not drive the last .02 of a mile to the old bride. The road is a bumpy, unmaintained road to a closed bridge. Upriver from the bridge is a long bank with shallow water. Park .2 of a mile up from the bridge and follow the trail down to the river. This should be a good evening spot prior to the summer heat.

MM 3: Junction with Route 508 to Yaak, Montana (Two bars facing each other across the street)

(Side trip) Route 508 / Yak River: The Yaak is a fair sized tributary of the Kootenai River and enters the river at the Yaak Campground. The Yaak splits the campground. The campground provides good access to both rivers as well as a boat launch. The Yaak River has two distinct types of water. Below the falls by the Yaak Falls campground (non-fee), the river quickly drops in elevation, which provides lots of holding water down through a steep canyon gorge. A haven to some big bull trout, the canyon is difficult to access and much of it is posted. After a long hike down the canyon during a heat spell, I caught a few fish in the 12-inch range, but most of the ones I caught were 8-10 inches, which is more typical of the river in general. Above the falls a ways is some nice water, but a good portion of it flattens out and heats up as well. Above and below the town of Yaak, the river looks like a slough, and most of it runs through private property. This valley section is home to a lot of small brookies, rainbows and a few small cutthroats. The Yaak Falls Campground offers seven campsites, toilets, and it is a non-fee area. It offers a great swimming hole if you are hot and driving through the area. At mile marker 27 the Yaak picks up some speed.

Seventeen Mile Creek: A few miles above the Yaak Falls Campground, Seventeen-Mile Creek Road is closed and gated due to flood damage. It is also a wildlife security. The lower stretch of the creek can be accessed at the first right turn which provides an access over the bridge. The area is posted so stay in the creek. Take Seventeen-Mile Creek 4.5 miles to the gate and hike into a great little creek. This would be a good creek to ride in on a mountain bike as the closed road parallels the creek. The first 4.5 miles of the creek is blocked by private property.

MM 15.6: Red Top Recreation (5 primitive camping sites)

MM 20.9: Bridge access to the south fork

MM 24.1: Whitetail Campground: 12 campsites, water, toilets, fee area, right on the river.

MM 26.8: Pete Creek Campground: 12 campsites, water, toilets, fee area.

Return to Highway 2 east towards Troy and Libby

MM 6.2: Yaak Campground / Boat Launch: 44 campsites, pull-throughs, water, toilets, fee area.

MM 7.8: Fishing access: The turn around offers a jeep trail which follows the river downstream offering great access to the river.

MM 10: Fishing access / boat launch: Follow Forest Drive and then Beachward Trail .5 miles to a nice boat launch.

MM 10: Kilbrennan Lake (9.2 miles): Kilbrennan Lake is a 59-acre lake, and it is deep in the middle. At the far end of the lake is a non-fee campground and a boat launch. The lake is full of perch and bullhead, but boat fishermen can catch good numbers of brook trout on the side of the lake opposite of the road. Locals tend to fill up this campground Thursday through Sunday. Seven campsites, toilets, non-fee.

MM 11.8: Bridge crossing

MM 14: Troy, Montana: Kootenai River Boat Launch: Turn on Third Street and go .4 of a mile, and then turn left on Riverside Drive .4 of a mile to the launch.

MM 15: Callahan Creek Road: Callahan Creek is not accessible in its lower reaches in Troy, and then it is not accessible as the road climbs up the mountain for a number of miles. To fish this creek you will need to drive all the way back to the bridge by the south fork and north fork. From this point you can fish the main stem of the creek or the forks. The creek is boulder strewn, however, so the going is rough for small cutthroats. The road is paved all the way but the last mile and a half. From the highway to the bridge is 7.5 miles.

MM 16.5: Lake Creek Road / Spar Lake: Affording little access due to private property, Lake Creek surely has some bragging rights for the prettiest creek in the area. Nonetheless, bridge crossing and a few non-posted spots provide a sampling of this beautiful creek. I came upon one couple who were fishing right from the side of the road. The wife had just killed a 16" rainbow dragging a night crawler through a small hole next to the road. Hopefully the landowners are more sensitive. The Lake Creek Road is actually a loop connecting Highway 56. The road changes to Chase Cutoff and leads to Spar Lake. The upper road is gravel all the way with a few washboard sections. From the highway to the lake is 17.4 miles.

Spar Lake Campground: Eight campsites, water, toilets, non-fee.

MM 21: Kootenai Falls Scenic Trail

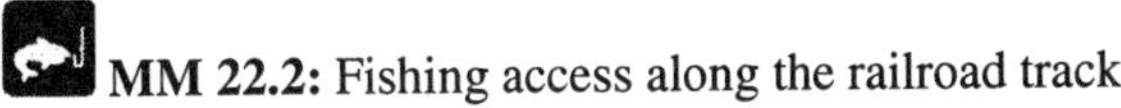

MM 22.2: Fishing access along the railroad track

MM 23: Fishing access (rapids)

MM 30: Libby, Montana

Side Trip: Route 68 toYaak, Montana

(Side trip) Cut-off road to Yaak, Montana via Route 68 and Pipe Creek: Follow California Street and cross the Kootenai River (boat launch just by the bridge). California Street changes to Route 567. Take Route 567 to Yaak, a distance of 37 miles. (Pipe Creek Road) Pipe Creek gets fairly small during the summer. Nonetheless, it offers good fishing for small trout. The East Fork of Pipe Creek is a tiny, brushy creek holding a lot of small brookies.

The only lake worth fishing is **Rainbow Lake** at Mileage Marker 22. Rainbow Lake is reached on road 4712. The road is a bit bumpy and narrow, and it is a second gear pull in places. A little over 30 acres, the lake is a small circular lake with a grassy lined shoreline. You can not drive to the lake. From the small parking area, you have to follow a trail three minutes down to the lake. This is a great lake for a canoe or belly boat. It offers fair catches of cutthroats. **Vinal Lake**: (Road 746 MM 32.3) Vinal Lake is about eight miles on Road 746 that forks north. You will need to hike a half-mile to the lake. Easily fished from the shoreline, this 18-acre lake fishes well for 12 inch rainbows. Continuing on Route 68 to Yaak, the road follows the south fork of the Yaak River. The south fork is very small and posted.

Continuing on Highway 2 from Libby to Kalispell

MM 30: Libby, Montana

MM 44: Howard Lake Loop: Libby Creek, Howard Lake and East Fisher Creek and exiting again on Highway 2 at MM 56.8: A small 34-acre lake 14 miles from the highway, Howard Lake is popular for rainbows from 8 to 14 inches. The lake has a popular campground with nine campsites, water, toilets, small boat launch, and it is a fee area. Libby Creek follows the highway a number of miles outside of Libby, but it offers only fair fishing. The Howard Lake outlet creek and East Fisher Creek are tiny creeks holding little trout.
MM 56.8: Howard Lake Loop returning to MM 44MM 60.5: Taking the Silver Butte Road #148 will both lead you to another fork of the Fisher River

which provides creek type fishing as well as a junction with Highway 200 near Trout Creek. The road is narrow and winding.

MM 63.4: Pleasant Valley Campground (Pleasant Valley Fisher River Section)

MM 65.8: Lyons Spring Campground (St. Regis Company)

MM 69: Mckillop Road #535: This paved road leads north to the main stem of the Fisher River and exits out on Highway 37 fourteen miles above Libby and just a few miles from the Libby Dam. The road is 32 miles long, and the first eight miles are narrow and winding high up on the side of the mountains. Called the Mckillop Road, it intersects with the Fisher River Road #763.

MM 69 to MM 86: Thompson Chain of Lakes: The Thompson Chain of Lakes, stretching along Highway 2 for 17 miles between Libby and Kalispell, quite possibly offers more fishing variety than any other stretch of highway in Montana. Nineteen lakes ranging in size from three acres to 1,300 acres, the chain boosts both warm water fish and cold water trout, along with a number of campgrounds. Perch, pumpkinseeds, largemouth bass and northern pike cruise through Crystal, Horseshoe, Lavon, Little Loon, Little McGregor, Loon, Lower Thompson, Middle Thompson and Upper Thompson. Rainbows, Eastern brook and cutthroats can be located together or isolated in Banana, Bootjack, Cad, Cibid, Leon, Lilly Pad, Little Loon, Little McGregor, Loon, Lower Thompson, Middle Thompson, Myron, Rainbow, Topless and Upper Thompson.

Add in kokanee salmon and brown trout to some of the lakes, and you have enough variety and challenges to last a life time, all of which is compressed in a 17-mile stretch. Best of all, some of the lakes hold huge lake trout in the 10 to 20 pound range; however, with the illegal introduction of pike to some of the lakes, trout and bass numbers have declined in some of the lakes. What follows is a listing of the lakes starting with Loon Lake and progressing towards McGregor Lake, 28 miles from Kalispell.

MM 70: Loon Lake: (238 acres / 114 feet maximum depth): yellow perch, rainbow, largemouth bass, Eastern brook trout.

Little Loon Lake (south of Loon Lake, 11.6 acres / 38 feet maximum depth): cutthroat, largemouth bass, and smallmouth bass

Leon Lake (southwesterly tip of Loon Lake, 15 acres / 22 feet): cutthroat

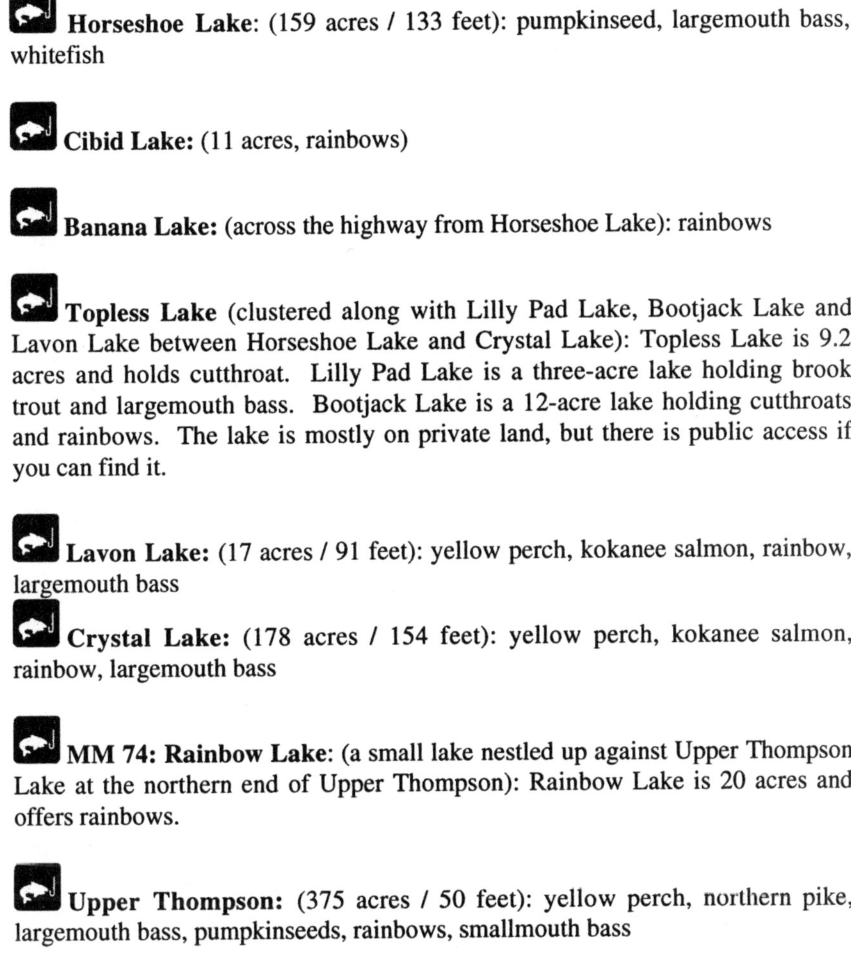

Horseshoe Lake: (159 acres / 133 feet): pumpkinseed, largemouth bass, whitefish

Cibid Lake: (11 acres, rainbows)

Banana Lake: (across the highway from Horseshoe Lake): rainbows

Topless Lake (clustered along with Lilly Pad Lake, Bootjack Lake and Lavon Lake between Horseshoe Lake and Crystal Lake): Topless Lake is 9.2 acres and holds cutthroat. Lilly Pad Lake is a three-acre lake holding brook trout and largemouth bass. Bootjack Lake is a 12-acre lake holding cutthroats and rainbows. The lake is mostly on private land, but there is public access if you can find it.

Lavon Lake: (17 acres / 91 feet): yellow perch, kokanee salmon, rainbow, largemouth bass

Crystal Lake: (178 acres / 154 feet): yellow perch, kokanee salmon, rainbow, largemouth bass

MM 74: Rainbow Lake: (a small lake nestled up against Upper Thompson Lake at the northern end of Upper Thompson): Rainbow Lake is 20 acres and offers rainbows.

Upper Thompson: (375 acres / 50 feet): yellow perch, northern pike, largemouth bass, pumpkinseeds, rainbows, smallmouth bass

MM 77: Middle Thompson Lake: yellow perch, northern pike, largemouth bass, pumpkinseeds, rainbows and smallmouth bass. **Logan State Park Campground:** Logan has 39 campsites and trailer spaces up to 40 feet.

Lower Thompson Lake: yellow perch, rainbow, largemouth bass, pumpkinseeds, kokanee salmon, northern pike, brown trout

Little McGregor Lake (north side of the highway, 40 acres): brook trout, cutthroat, yellow perch, largemouth bass

MM 85: McGregor Lake: (1,328 acres): lake trout, rainbow, yellow perch, whitefish. McGregor Lake Campground has 15 campsites accommodating trailer space up to 32 feet.

MM 100.7: Little Bitterroot Lake: Almost three miles long and a half-mile wide, the lake is a recreational lake with summer homes and boating activities. Nonetheless, the lake fishes well for perch, kokanee salmon and nice size rainbows

MM 105: Ashley Lake: Another large recreation lake, Ashley Lake offers good fishing for kokanee salmon and nice size rainbows.

MM 110: Smith Lake: A marshy, shallow 300 acre lake, Smith Lake has one state access site to launch a boat. The lake fishes well for perch and bass.
MM 120: Kalispell, Montana

Highway 37

Highway 37 from Libby to Eureka, Montana via Lake Koocanusa: Highway 37 passes the Libby Dam via Lake Koocanusa 66 miles to Eureka and then into Canada on Highway 93 to Banff and Jasper National Parks in British Columbia. Parallel to this highway is a paved road on the other side of the lake that intersects with the highway at the Koocanusa Bridge, a distance of 45 miles. Take California Street to the bridge crossing and the city boat launch. At about a half of a mile is the turn-off to Pipe Creek and Yaak. (See page 25.)

MM 1: Ranger Station (Information). MM 13: Canoe Gulch Ranger Station (USFS information on camping and boating facilities).

MM 8.9: Boat launch on the Kootenai River
MM 14: Junction with the Fisher River and the Fisher River Road #763: The Fisher River is more like a creek and offers fair fishing.

(Side trip): Fisher River / Short-cut to Highway 2 connecting Kalispell and Libby: The Fisher River access is at mileage marker 14 on Highway 37 a few miles below the Libby Dam. The Fisher River is only fair fishing for small rainbows and whitefish. The road is paved and runs 24 miles to meet Highway 2. The road is narrow in places. Primitive campsites may be found all along the Fisher River.

MM 13: Dunn Creek Recreation Campground – US Army Corp of Engineers (non-fee) Alexander Creek Campground, Dunn Creek Flats Campground, Blackwell Flats Campground.

MM 15: Libby Dam: The dam road can be crossed to **Souse Gulch** adjacent to the dam, which provides picnicking as well as a boat launch. You may follow this road downstream to Blackwell Flats Campground. Both Blackwell and Dunn Creek Flats provide boat launches. Along Lake Koocanusa are a series of campgrounds and marinas. Lake Koocanusa is a popular lake for boaters.

MM 23.8: Koocanusa Resort and public boat launch

Rocky Gorge Campground: 120 campsites, water, toilets, fully developed boat launch, fee area.

MM 48.8: Peck Gulch: 75 camping sites, picnicking and boat launch, water, toilets, fee area.

MM 61.5: Rexford, Montana / Rexford Bench Complex: Campground with 54 campsites, water, flush toilets, fee area; Boating site: 33 campsites, water, flush toilets, fully developed boat launch, fee area. Kamloops Terrace: 50 campsites, water, flush toilets, fee area.

MM 64: Fishing access to Tobacco River

MM 64.8: Eureka airport, Tetrault Lake, Sophie Lake and fishing access on Lake Koocanusa: Tetrault is periodically stocked with Arlee rainbows and is a popular lake with the locals. Bill Myra of Green Mountain Sports reported that the lake is scheduled for poisoning sometime in 1998 so that the lake can be managed as a trophy trout lake. Sophie Lake offers a full range

of fish species. This 200- acre lake has recently been stocked with kamloop rainbows.
MM 66.8: Junction with Highway 93, a mile from Eureka

Highway 200 beginning at the Idaho border traveling east to Highway 93 north of Missoula

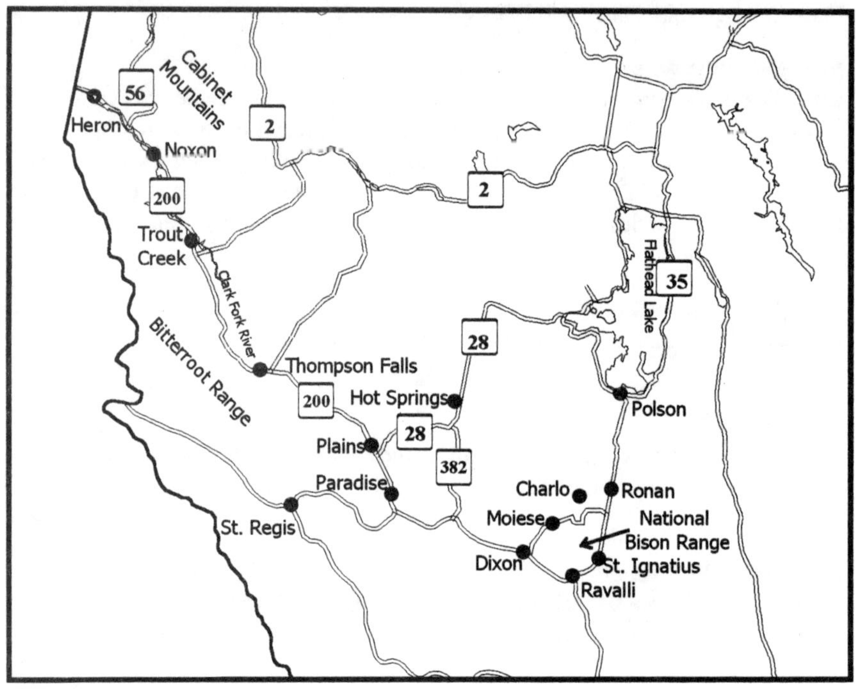

MM 0: Highway 200: Idaho Border

MM 3.7: Heron, Montana

MM 10.5 Junction with Montana State Highway 56 to Troy, Montana
(See page 35 for Highway 56.)

MM 11: Bull River Campground: 26 campsites, 2 pull-throughs, water, flush toilets, fully developed boat launch, fee area.

MM 14: Gas and store

MM 15.5: Noxon, Montana

MM 18.5: Noxon Rapids Dam

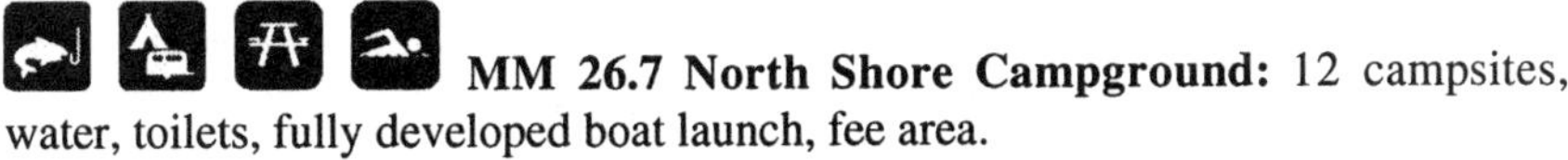 **MM 26.7 North Shore Campground:** 12 campsites, water, toilets, fully developed boat launch, fee area.

MM 27: Cabinet Ranger Station

MM 28: Vermillion River: The lower section of the river is slow fishing, but above the falls about 11 miles from the highway, the river (creek) provides good fishing for creek-size cutthroats and brookies. If you arrive in the fall, cross your fingers that you will find and entice a big brown up from the Clark Fork.

MM 29-30: Trout Creek, Montana

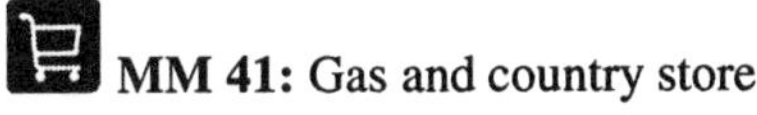 **MM 41:** Gas and country store

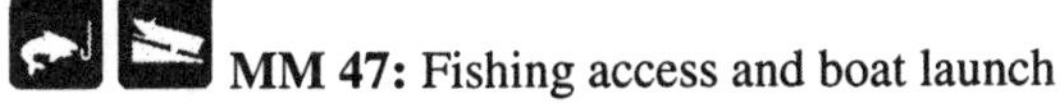 **MM 47:** Fishing access and boat launch

 **MM 49.5: Thompson Falls State Park:** 17 campsites, 55' trailer space.

MM 50-52: Thompson Falls, Montana
MM 56: Thompson River / Junction with Thompson River Road which follows the river and intersects with Highway 2 to Libby or Kalispell

Thompson River

The Thompson River flows from the Thompson Lake chain to the Clark Fork. Considered one of the best streams in the area, the Thompson River is pounded by catch-and-eat fishermen who have easy access to the river along Thompson River Road #56 and the private logging road on the east side of the river. Road #56 parallels the river for almost 40 miles. If you plan on camping and fishing, Copper King Campground (USFS) offers a nice campground right on the river four miles from the junction with highway 200. Offering five sites, the campground has no drinking water. Above the campground the road begins a single lane dirt and gravel road with a number of intersecting logging roads. The Thompson River is worth the dusty ride as the stream and road winds up through wooded mountainsides and canyons to the meadow section. A free flowing stream, the Thompson River produces healthy populations of 10 to 12 inch rainbows along with some hefty browns and bull trout in the lower section. Small cutthroats and brook trout are the staple in the upper river.

The Thompson River kicks off in the spring with a healthy salmon fly hatch and an abundance of Grannom caddis. Late summer brings out the hoppers, drakes and Baetis hatches all the way into the fall. The Thompson is just fun to fish. For the most part, fly fishers need only present an attractor pattern on a short cast to hungry trout!

The river is easily fished with lightweight spinning rods and fly rods. It offers a little bit of everyone's favorite type of water, from small riffles and pools to long glides and deep pockets in the canyon section. During late summer and early fall, large stonefly nymphs such as the Bitch Creek and Woolly Buggers are the choice patterns of fly fishers searching for the early browns and bulls heading up from the Clark Fork to spawn.

MM 63: Big Horn Sheep Viewing Area

MM 75: Plains, Montana

MM 77: Junction with Highway 28 to Elmo, Montana and Highway 93

MM 81.7: Paradise, Montana

MM 85: Junction with Highway 135 to St. Regis, Montana (Interstate 90)

MM 96: Junction with Highway 382 cutoff north to Hotsprings, Montana

MM 109: Dixon, Montana: Dixon has a boat launch on the Flathead River which is popular with local pike fishermen. Floating down to the Perma Bridge is almost 17 miles so plan on a long day. This would be a great stretch for a canoeist or family float. However, don't forget to purchase a tribal use permit.

MM 110.2: Junction with Route 212 to the National Bison Range, Charlo, Montana and the Ninepipe Wildlife Refuge on Highway 93.

MM 116: Bridge over the Jocko River (Flathead Indian Reservation)

Junction with Highway 93 north to Flathead Lake.

Highway 56 North

MM 0: Junction with Highway 56 a few miles west of Noxon, Montana

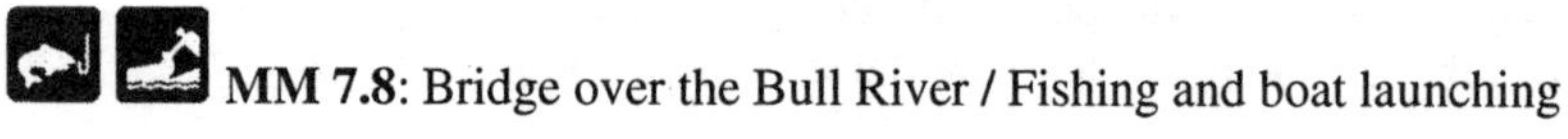

MM 7.8: Bridge over the Bull River / Fishing and boat launching

Bull River: Warning: The last four miles of the Bull River runs down through a canyon to meet the Clark Fork. During spring this section offers some nasty whitewater, and during the summer the same stretch calls for dragging your raft or canoe over a lot of shallow, rocky stretches. With the exception of a few lurking bull trout, the Bull River hosts 8-12 inch rainbows and cutthroats. Mostly the river meanders through bottomland that is posted. The "river" is narrow, slow, clear and deceptively deep in places. Once summer arrives, the trout have less cover and tend to hide in or around grassy tendrils along the bottom of the stream, as well as those shady banks afforded by willow and tag alder. Floating access is at the bridges.

MM 8.9: East Fork Bull River / St. Paul Lake Trailhead: At 1.3 miles the road forks left to the north fork and the St. Paul Lake trailhead, which is six miles from the highway. St. Paul Lake is a three-mile hike. Although it lacks in scenery, the lake fishes well for 10 to 14 inch cutthroats. Below the trailhead the creek is small and offers good fishing for typical creek size trout. You have to look for a pullout and scramble down to the creek. Plan on heavy brush and pocket water. At 1.3 mileage turn right and proceed one mile, and you will come to a historic ranger station and a great spot to fish the lower creek.

MM 11.6: Pull out / access and boat launching access

MM 13.8: Fishing access

MM 15: Fishing access and canoe launch

MM 16: South Fork Bull River (too small to be worthwhile)

MM 16.8: Ross Creek Cedar Picnic Site and Bad Medicine Campground: 17 campsites, water, toilets, fully developed boat launch, fee area.

MM 21: Dorr Skeels Campground: Seven campsites, toilets, fully developed boat launch, non-fee.

MM 29.4: Spar Lake Campground / Chase Cutoff (Seep.24, Highway 2, MM 16.5)

MM 32.4: Savage Lake: A relatively small lake of about 100 acres, Savage Lake is surrounded by summer homes with only one public access right off the highway. Belly boaters have fun on this lake for both cold and warm water species.

MM 35: Junction with Highway 2 (West to Troy and East to Libby)

Highway 93 from Missoula to Eureka

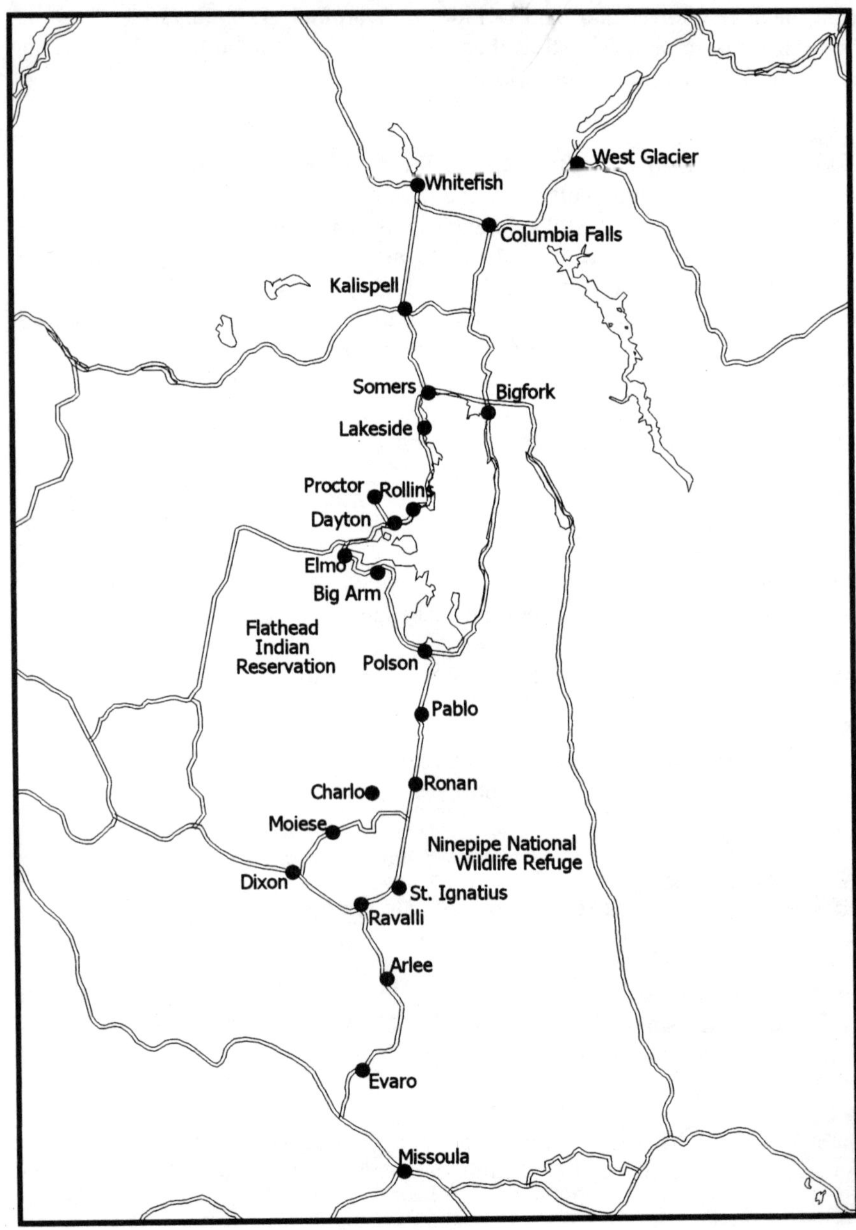

Highway 93 North from Missoula to Kalispell

Highway 93 continues west of Missoula from Exit 96 on Interstate 90. From Interstate 90 it is 17 miles to Arlee, 27 miles to the junction with Highway 200, and 112 miles to Kalispell. Highway 93 from Missoula to the Canadian border covers almost 188 miles through some of the most beautiful country in western Montana. Leaving Interstate 90 onto Highway 93 north, you will travel through the Flathead Indian Reservation towards Flathead Lake.

The Mission Mountains rise straight up from the valley floor as you pass through the towns of Arlee, St. Ignatius, and Polson. A few miles north of Polson, visitors will come to a crest and be struck by the size and beauty of Flathead Lake, the largest natural lake west of the Great Lakes. Highway 93 follows the east shore of the lake to Kalispell, or you may choose to take Highway 35 to Bigfork and then connect with Highway 93 at the top end of the lake.

From Kalispell, travelers to Glacier National Park may route themselves on Highway 93 to Whitefish, take the mid-way Highway 2 or pick up Highway 35 which turns into Route 206 to Columbia Falls. By the time you reach the border, you will have traveled through the Mission Valley, the Flathead Valley and the Tobacco Plains in the Eureka area.

Flathead Indian Reservation: Established July 16, 1885, as part of the Hellgate Treaty, the Salish and Kootenai tribes were forced on what is known as the Flathead Indian Reservation. Encompassing 1.2 million acres, the reservation has as its northern boundary the Flathead Lake, which is almost 27 miles long and 16 miles wide at its widest point. To the east the reservation is bordered by the majestic Mission Mountains. Across the rolling pothole country to the west, the reservation is bordered by the Cabinet Mountains. Although originally including portions of the Bitterroot Valley, those lands were lost in subsequent revisions of the treaty, which was typical of Indian treaties in general. Fishing on the reservation requires a special tribal stamp and a recreation permit. The reservation offers excellent angling opportunities for both warm water species such as perch, bass and pike as well as all the major trout species.

The reservation offers alpine lakes, streams, ponds and reservoirs. Tribal wildlife managers continually work to upgrade the quality of riparian habitat for enhancement of native salmonids. The Jocko River is testimony to their efforts, providing good fishing for browns, cutthroats and rainbows. Local fishermen boast that Kicking Horse and Ninepipe Reservoir offer some of the best largemouth bass fishing in the region. And there is always the prospect of landing a 20-pound pike on the lower Flathead River or hiking into the Mission Mountains for native westslope cutthroats, brook trout and rainbows. The Flathead Reservation offers over a million acres of fishing opportunities. The best source of information for fishing the reservation is Rob Shrider at Ronan Sports and Western in Ronan, Montana.

The southern half of Flathead Lake is part of the reservation. During the past 15 years a number of changes have impacted the lake, most notably the introduction of mysis shrimp that precipitated the decline of the kokanee salmon. Preyed upon by lake trout, native cutthroats, bull trout and kokanee salmon have declined steadily during the past 10 years.

Many local-experts believe that a growing balance between species does not necessitate over-harvesting the lake trout. The average lake trout is 20 inches, and 20 pounds is not uncommon. The best fishing is from October to December when lake trout are spawning in the shallows along the lake. Most experienced fishing guides boast large catches of these prodigious lunkers with jig type lures.

MM 16.7: Jocko River Road: The Jocko Road winds up the headwaters of the Jocko River over the divide and down into the Seeley Lake area past Lake Placid. A reservation fishing permit is required on tribal lands.

MM 17: Arlee, Montana

MM 19: Crossing the Jocko River

MM 27: Ravalli, Montana

MM 27.5: Junction with Highway 200 to Thompson Falls (See page 32 for Highway 200)

MM 32.5: St. Ignatius, Montana

MM 39: McDonald Lake

MM 40.4: Ninepipe Reservoir

MM 42: Charlo, Montana / National Bison Range
Kicking Horse Reservoir (dirt road to the right)

MM 44: Picnic Site with shaded tables, toilets

MM 46: Ronan, Montana

MM 52.5: Pablo National Wildlife Refuge

MM 59: Junction Highway 35 to Bigfork / Kalispell

MM 59.5: Polson, Montana / Polson Recreation Park

MM 61: Riverside Park / city boat launch

MM 71.5: Walstad Memorial State Recreation Area: Fishing access, boat launch, picnic area.

MM 73: Big Arm Resort and Marina

MM 74.4: Big Arm Campground and Picnic Area

MM 77: Elmo Store / gas

MM 77.3: Junction with Highway 28 to Hotsprings, Montana

MM 82.8: Lake Mary Ronan State Park: Lake Mary Ronan is a large recreational lake encompassing almost 1,500 acres. It provides good fishing for Kokanee, Rainbow and bass. 27 campsites, 35 foot trailer spaces, water, fee area.

MM 85: Northern boundary for the Flathead Indian Reservation

MM 92.8: Westshore State Campground / boat launch: 26 campsites, water, toilets, fee area.

MM 97.5: Lakeside, Montana

MM 102.5: Somers Fishing Access / boat launch and picnic site

MM 103: Somers, Montana

MM 104.2: Junction with Highway 82 to Bigfork, Montana

MM 110: Kalispell, Montana (Information Center)

MM 112: Kalispell, Montana

MM 113: Junction with Highway 2 to Whitefish and Glacier National Park

MM 125: Whitefish, Montana / Columbia Falls and Glacier National Park: The cut-off to Glacier National Park from Whitefish is 24 miles.

Highway 93 from Whitefish to the Canadian Border

Stillwater River: The Stillwater is just that – still. The mid-section often intersects Highway 93, and access points are found at bridge crossings, pullouts and dirt roads. Slow water and willow lined stream banks host good populations of brook trout, rainbows and cutthroats. Some sections are floatable.

MM 129: Whitefish Lake State Park: 1.1 mile from Highway 93 in the town of Whitefish. Shaded and beautiful, the campground is close to a golf course as well!

MM 132: Tally Lake: (See MM 139.)

MM 135: Beaver Lake: Four miles. Beaver Lake, Little Beaver Lake, Murray Lake, Rainbow Lake, Woods Lake, Dollar Lake: Beaver Lake is a beautiful lake with just a small turn-around provided by the state. The lake is bordered by private property. The access site has one picnic site. Canoeists will have to slide their canoes down an embankment to the lake. Beaver Lake is a popular fishing lake for rainbows. Coming into the area, you will find a sign showing the location of all the little lakes. The roads are bumpy and narrow, and some of them, like the road to Little Beaver Lake, definitely need the high clearance of a truck. Little Beaver Lake has one public access spot to launch a boat, but you probably will need a 4x4.

I personally would pass up Little Beaver Lake as the last two tenths of a mile is on a rutted, boggy road, and when I pulled up to the lake there were already two families camped in a one family site. I walked down to Dollar Lake and met a teenage boy and his friend who said the lake has always fished well for them, but some of the lakes have been over-populated with Flathead minnows and as such are scheduled for rehabilitation. I would stick with Beaver Lake if you have a car-topper boat, a canoe or a belly boat.

MM 139: Tally Lake Campground / Sheppard Creek / Sylvia Lake Campground: Take the Star Meadow road about 10 miles to the turn-off to Tally Lake. Tally Lake is a large 1,300-acre lake, and it is the deepest lake in Montana at 492 feet. Tally Lake is a recreation lake and popular with water skiers. The campground is on the north shore and has 39 campsites, water, toilets, and boat launch as well as an RV dump station and a swimming area. (Fee area.)

If you continue to Star Meadows, consult the Flathead National Forest Visitor's Map for mileage. On the way to Sylvia Lake, you will pass Sheppard Creek, a brushy little creek holding typical creek-size trout. Sylvia Lake is a 20-acre lake, and it is stocked with grayling.

MM 144.2: Good Creek / Martin Lake and access to the Stillwater River: The road to Good Creek is an easy drive to a good creek. At .4 miles you will cross a bridge over the Stillwater River, which provides fishing access. At 3.2 miles there is a turn-off road to Martin Lake, which is a fair fishing lake for smaller rainbows. The pavement ends at 6.1 miles, and there is a turn-off to Star Meadows at 15 miles and Sylvia Lake at 23 miles.

At 8.6 miles Good Creek is not visible, but the distance to the creek is less than a mile. At mile 9.3 you will have your first sighting of the creek. Further up the road the creek meanders through thick willow and tag alder. The creek holds lots of small brook trout and cutthroats.

MM 145.6: Upper Whitefish Lake and Red Meadow Lake: Both lakes can be driven to on a fairly good dirt road. The first lake, Upper Whitefish Lake, is 13.5 miles.

Upper Whitefish Lake is in the Stillwater State Forest and offers a campground and fishing for small cutthroats. Red Meadow Lake is about six miles further and offers camping on a picturesque 19-acre lake along with fair fishing for cutthroats and grayling.

MM 151.5: Upper Stillwater Lake and Lagoni Lake: Upper Stillwater Lake is unseen from the highway, but it is only 1.3 miles away. This 630-acre lake offers a campground and fair fishing for brook trout, pike, perch and the occasional cutthroat. Above Upper Stillwater Lake is Lagoni Lake, a small 20-acre lake offering the same type of fishing.

MM 158.8: Bull Lake / Stryker Lake (Fish Lake): Both lakes lie side-by-side just a few miles from the community of Stryker and offer good fishing for cutthroat and brook trout. These are native trout, but be sure you have a Montana State Land Permit before you fish!

MM 159.8: Picnic spot on South Dickey Lake – Day use only.

MM 161: Dickey Lake: Dickey Lake is a summer recreation lake with a pot pourri of specie offerings, none of which get very big.

MM 163.3: Dickey Lake Campground:
25 campsites, 50 foot trailer spaces, toilets, water, boat launch, fee area.

MM 165.1: Murphy Lake Ranger Station

MM 165.8: Murphy Lake: Murphy Lake is a popular 163-acre, warm water fishery for largemouth bass, perch and pike. Murphy Lake also offers camping.

MM 170.2: Grave Creek (Campground), Blue Sky Creek, Weasel Lake, Lake Therriault (Little and Big) and the 10 Lakes Scenic Area:

For the fishermen and camper in the Eureka area, this is your access! Grave Creek has the largest volume of water of any creek in the area. Just a few miles from the highway, Grave Creek Campground offers a number of campsites right on the creek, but the campground is not practical for larger RV's or trailers. In fact, I found only three sites suitable for smaller trailers. The short access road into the campground makes a tight turn, and the road is bumpy.

Grave Creek, a tributary of the Tobacco River, is a very good fishing creek for 10-12 inch rainbows and cutthroats. The bottom section is private, and there is a small area of private land near the campground, but above that is national forest land with a number of miles of creek to fish.

Above Grave Creek is Blue Sky Creek, a tributary of Grave Creek. The creek is small and the small fish are plentiful, but the creek is closed to protect spawning runs of cutthroats and bulls as of July 31. Before you reach Therriault Lakes, the road goes by Weasel Lake. Weasel Lake is a pretty little lake with small fish.

Therriault Lakes are about 28 miles from the highway. Both lakes offer camping and good fishing for 10 to 12 inch cutthroats. The big lake is 55 acres, and the smaller lake 26 acres. Little Therriault Lake is the trailhead for the 10 Lakes Scenic Area.

When I spoke to Bill Myra, owner of Green Mountain Sports Center in Eureka, Bill became passionate in describing the 10 Lake Area. Having spoken about my home waters with the same enthusiasm, I know I will have to spend a couple of days exploring the region on my next trip. Bill said to plan on a full day hike to these high elevation lakes, where you can expect great beauty and feisty 10-12 inch native trout. Some of the lakes are barren so you might want to check in with Bill to plan your hike.

MM 174: Glen Lake: Glen Lake is surrounded by residences, and the fishing is fair to poor.

MM 178: Eureka, Montana

MM 180: Junction with Highway 37 to Libby via Lake Koocanusa

Glacier Fed - Three Forks of the Flathead River

The three forks of the Flathead River testify to the raw force of nature and qualify as part of the National Scenic River Act. Essentially a migratory fishery out of Flathead Lake, all of the forks testify to the power of carved, glacial drainages and unspoiled beauty. One look at the high water marks and the scrubbed riverbed, and a fisherman will know immediately why he or she is sharing the river with white water rafters and kayakers.

Basically the force of spring run-off in glaciated country dooms the forks to a nutrient-deficient environment which impacts the insect hatches and limits the opportunity for resident trout populations. For the wade fisherman, all three forks have limited accessibility due to steep canyons and private property on the North Fork and the Middle Fork.

Rafters should have white water experience before they attempt float fishing any one of the three forks. Some of the coldest river water in the state is found on the South Fork and the North Fork. Rafters need to be properly equipped, experienced and prepared. Although low water levels appear by mid-August, each of the forks offers class II and III spots that can sneak up on rafters intent on catching fish.

The International Scale for River Difficulty grades water based on the characteristics and action of the water as well as how much maneuvering is called for in a given passage. The North Fork, after high water, is generally a Class II water. The Middle Fork offers Class IV and V in certain stretches during high water. The South Fork below Spotted Bear is generally rated Class II and III. For a great booklet (sectional maps) on rafting all three forks, purchase "3 Forks of the Flathead River – Floating Guide" published by the Glacier Natural History Association in cooperation with the Flathead National Forest and Glacier National Park.

International Scale for River Difficulty

Class	Skill Level	Characteristics
I	Very easy	Class I water provides small, regular waves with few obstacles. Very little maneuvering is necessary.
II	Easy skills	Class II water requires some maneuvering, but the water is essentially easy rapids which are easy to read.
III	Medium skills	Class III water offers numerous waves, narrow passages and precise maneuvering. Scouting may be required.
IV	Difficult	Class IV challenges rafters with difficult rapids, abrupt bends, narrow passages, and precise maneuvering. Scouting is usually required.
V	Very Difficult	Class V water clearly raises the level of risk with long rapids, wild turbulence and extremely congested routes. Complex maneuvering requires scouting.
VI	Limits of Navigation	Nearly impossible and a definite hazard to life

Note: A detailed, spiral-bound series of maps of all three forks may be purchased at the following information centers. Glacier View Ranger District, 774 Railroad Street EN, Columbia Falls, MT 59912
Information: 406-892-4372

Hungry Horse Ranger District
Box 340
Hungry Horse, MT 59919
Information: 406-387-5243

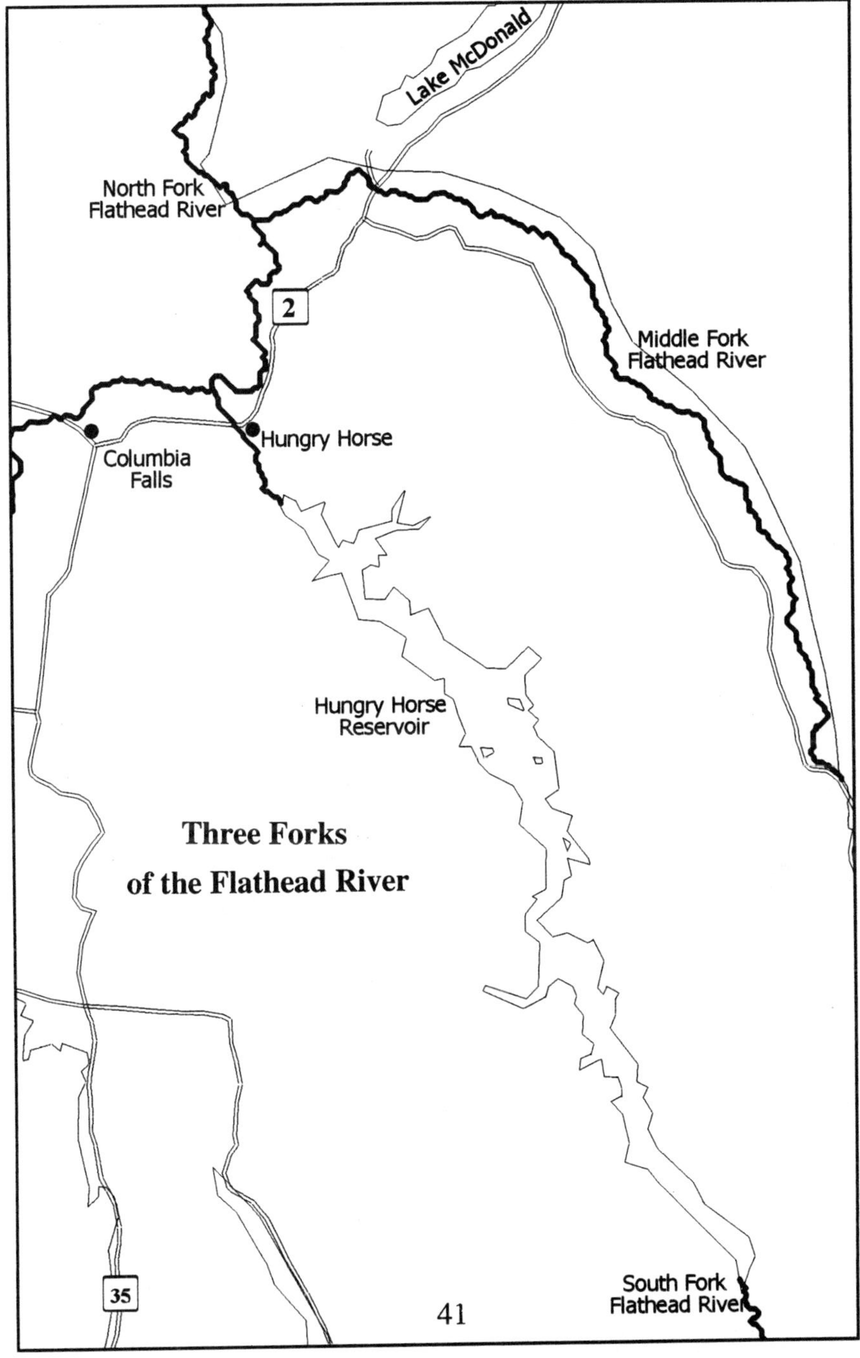

North Fork of the Flathead: The North Fork originates in Canada, with the east shore being the border of Glacier National Park. Access for the wade fisherman is somewhat limited as the road parallels the river high up the mountainsides in places. Although the North Fork is home to some huge Bull trout, the majority of the trout will be migratory cutthroats from 8 to 10 inches moving down river. The North Fork is heavily silted and appears more turquoise in color than the Middle Fork and the South Fork. To reach the North Fork, turn onto Nucleus Street, the business district of Columbia Falls. Follow the signs to Glacier National Park, a distance of 22 miles.

Access above the park entrance is limited due to private property. Access points are limited with the first float section from the border to Ford Access, a distance of 14 miles with a Class II rating. From the Ford Access to Polebridge is 11 river miles and is rated Class II. From Polebridge to Big Creek is 18 miles and is rated as Class II. The next float, from Big Creek to Glacier Rim, is probably the most popular float among the local guides. It is 12 miles and rated Class II and III. The last float, a short four miles, is from Glacier Rim to Blankenship Bridge and is Class I. Blankenship Bridge turn-off is before the Glacier Rim Access. The bridge is located just below the confluence of the North Fork and the Middle Fork. On one side of the bridge is a boat launch, and on the other side is a county, non-fee campground. Blankenship Bridge may also be reached from Highway 2 above Coram. (Look for mileage marker 148. Take the second left after the marker (148.3). When you reach a hairpin turn, bear left and head down the mountain. From the highway to the bridge is 3.8 miles.)

The only campground on the North Fork is Big Creek Campground, a few miles before the Camas Creek entrance to Glacier National Park and 25 miles north of Columbia Falls. The campground is a fee campground and includes a non-fee picnic site and a boat launch. The campground offers 22 campsites, toilets, water, RV dump station and a swimming area.

Middle Fork of the Flathead River: The one thing that the Middle Fork has in common with the North Fork is limited access. Like the North Fork, the highway often leaves the river or is high above it. It differs from the North Fork in that it provides much more challenging sections even during mid-summer. The road departs from the Middle Fork at the Bear Creek Access which is about 33 miles from the Glacier Park entrance. From this point the Middle Fork leaves the highway corridor and enters the Great Bear Wilderness. Floating from Bear Creek to Paola Access is 10 miles and rated Class III-IV. From the Paola Access to Cascadilla is 12 miles and rated Class III-IV. Cascadilla Access to Moccasin Creek is seven miles. It is an area noted for serious logjams. Moccasin Creek to West Glacier is 9 miles and rated Class II-IV. The shortest run, and popular with the local guides, is from West Glacier to Blankenship Bridge which is only 5.5 miles and designated Class III water. Although the

Middle Fork produces healthy populations of 8 to 12 inch cutthroats, 14 to 16 inch catches are not uncommon. For the dry fly purist, bigger is better.

The only campground in the area is the non-fee campground, Devil Creek Campground. The campground is 38 miles from the entrance to the park and about five miles above the Bear Creek Access.

Middle Fork of the Flathead River

By Steve Smith

When was the last time you fished a river and a grizzly bear swam in front of your boat? Or you came away from the day amazed that fish would live in such fast water, let alone able to see and rise to your fly as it sped by them? Or you wondered whether you had fished during a white water trip or shot some rapids while fishing? And maybe at the end of the day you exclaim, "Holy cow, it has been such a great day, it wouldn't have mattered if we didn't catch a fish at all." (Even though you wouldn't really mean that).

The Middle Fork of the Flathead River punches its way through the mountains of northwest Montana. From its beginnings in the Great Bear Wilderness area, the Middle Fork offers a unique blend of scenery, wildlife and fishing in uncrowded and pristine surroundings. From Bear Creek, where the river leaves the Great Bear 45 miles downstream to Blankenship Bridge, the river separates Glacier National Park and the Bob Marshall Wilderness Complex (of which the Great Bear is a component). Highway 2 and the Burlington Northern Railway run through the canyon cut by the river, though they seldom impose on it.

The Middle Fork is a freestone stream. Freestone streams are not overly rich in nutrients, so the Middle Fork doesn't boast prolific insect hatches or even predictable ones. What it lacks in numbers of insects, it makes up for by supporting one of the most diverse arrays of aquatic insects in the lower 48 states. Understanding this is the key to success on the Middle Fork.

The fish on the Middle Fork, primarily native west slope cutthroat trout, and a growing wild rainbow population, thrive in the cool, clear and fast water of the river. They are accustomed to seeing all sorts of insects shooting by them in the current at a high rate of speed.

Envision a native cutthroat lying on the bottom just downstream of a fast riffle waiting for the current to wash feed down to it. The trout snatches up a stonefly nymph, scrambling along the bottom. Next, an emerging mayfly suspended mid depth floats by and is devoured. Then an adult caddis fly, bobbing along in the choppy water on top, goes flashing by, and the cutthroat goes for it. What the trout may not distinguish, in its rush to swallow whatever feed the current delivers, is that the caddis fly is a number 12 elk hair caddis on the end of your tippet. The fish, forever famished, doesn't have the luxury of an in-depth analysis on the Middle Fork. Chuck out a high riding dry fly into choppy water, mend like crazy and pay attention.

West slope cutthroat trout are indigenous to the river. The higher up the river, the more you will find. The rainbow trout population is self sustaining now and is considered to be "wild." The rainbows and cutthroats can interbreed, resulting in the "cuttbow" hybrid. Bull trout also are native to the river. Sadly, sediments from logging roads have destroyed spawning habitats and heavy

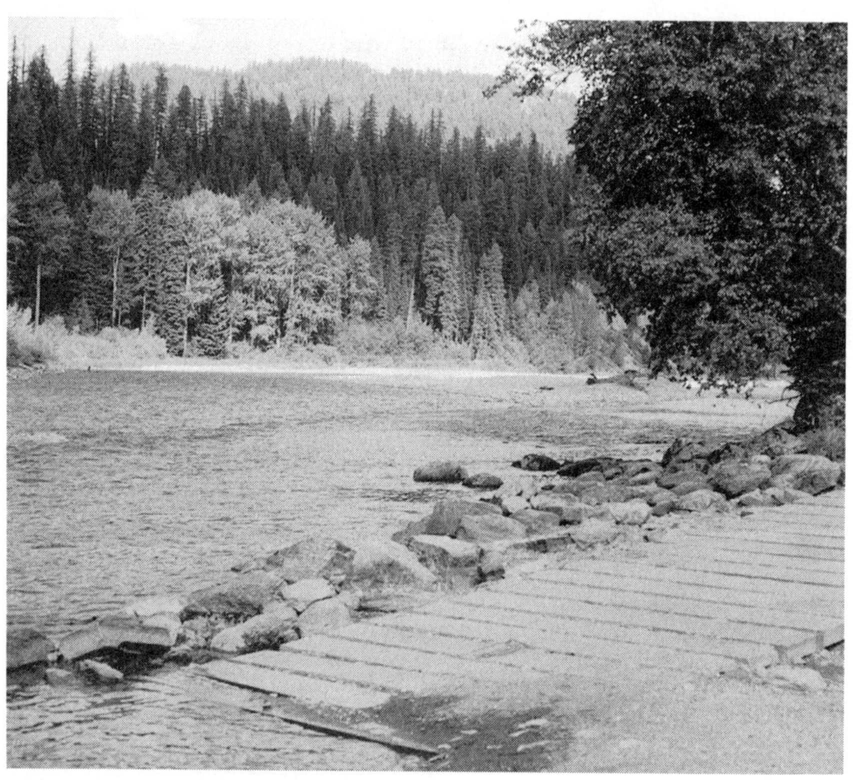

Middle Fork of the Flathead River with Glacier National Park on the other bank.

fishing pressure has combined to dwindle the reserves of this fishery so that it is now illegal to even fish for bull trout. Care must be exercised to properly identify fish caught on the Middle Fork. Bull trout are often mistaken for brook and lake trout that also inhabit these waters.

The Middle Fork is included in the wild and scenic river system and so is looked after by the US Forest Service. Remember that the right bank of the river is the boundary of Glacier National Park, which has a separate set of regulations concerning camping and other activities.

Access to the river is good, although a four-wheel drive vehicle is handy for some boat launches. Bear Creek is the highest access point along Highway 2. Below that is a rough, sandy access by the bridge at Walton. Paola Creek access is downstream, followed by Cascadilla Creek access, Moccasin Creek access (the beginning of the eight mile class III white water section and the most heavily used), then the West Glacier access and finally, Blankenship Bridge, where the Middle Fork joins the North Fork of the Flathead River. An excellent map of the entire Flathead River system is available at the Forest Service station in Hungry Horse.

Wade fishing the Middle Fork, while possible, is limited by fast water and deep pools between the runs. The best way to fish it is to cover some water, and for this there is no finer boat than the McKenzie River boat. Whatever craft you choose (don't even think about a canoe), be advised that even outside of the white water section, the Middle Fork is a fast, powerful, cold and remote river. Blind bends, rock-choked chutes and numerous downed trees make the river pilot's job a demanding and serious one.

The river is frequented by a variety of big game animals, and some of them have fangs and claws. Be aware this is bear country, and mountain lions have also been sighted along and in the river. Seeing them safely from a McKenzie boat (remember rafts can pop) is a memorable addition to any fishing trip.

The Middle Fork is a great but relatively unknown river. The combination of the Middle Fork's scenery, wildlife, fishing opportunities and uncrowded conditions rarely is seen in one place all at once. Kindly give plenty of room to other people fishing; there is plenty of it on the Middle Fork.

Seasons: The Middle Fork can fish well in April and early May when spawning runs of cutthroat enter the river from Flathead Lake. High water generally occurs mid May through late June. After July 1, the fishing continues on into October. Local inquiry of river conditions or hazards is recommended.

Fly selections: This is easy. Anything will catch fish on the Middle Fork as long as it is well presented. If you are unable to make a good presentation, try dragging a nymph in front of the boat, or let your dry fly draw under the water at the end of your drift. While anathema to the purist, these techniques are godsends to the novice or flustered fishing guide. It ain't pretty, but it works.

About the Author: Smith is an advocate of small tippets, large calibers, V-8 engines, and Labrador retrievers. He aspires to one day harpoon a jet ski. He spends the summers rowing fly fishers on the Middle Fork near West Glacier, Montana. He and the other fine fly fishing guides of Glacier Wilderness Guides may be reached at:

Glacier Wilderness Guides
Box 535
West Glacier, MT 59936
1-800-521-7238

South Fork of the Flathead River: Top off your gas tank if your are heading up the South Fork. Follow Highway 2 to the town of Hungry Horse at mileage marker 143.4. Follow the signs to Hungry Horse Dam. Cross the dam and follow the West Side South Fork Road. The mileage markers start at the dam. Spotted Bear Campground, a few miles above the inlet to Hungry Horse Lake, is 55 miles from the dam, and most of it is dirt road. If you are pulling a trailer, plan on cruising 35 mph. Draining the Bob Marshall Wilderness, the South Fork is the crown jewel of northwestern Montana. From the Spotted Bear Campground, access is by trail or plane into the designated Wild River section. A good portion of this wilderness encompasses the Jewell Basin Hiking Area. (To reach the trailheads to the Jewell Basin, look for Wounded Buck Road, West Fork Clayton Creek Road, Clayton Creek Road, Graves Creek Road or Wheeler Creek Road. (For more information on the Jewell Basin Hiking Area, see page 133.)

Unlike the other forks, the South Fork fishery is not a migratory fishery after the completion of Hungry Horse Dam in 1952. Expect to catch cutthroats averaging 8-to-10 inches. Bull Trout, although plentiful, have been protected since 1993. One of the guides I spoke to said that some days the river offers many 14 to 16 inch trout. Again, access is limited. The primary floating section that can be reached by road is from Cedar Flats River Access to a launch access just below Spotted Bear Campground. The guides in this country work very hard for their wages. Guiding in western Montana all those years, the toughest launch I can think of consisted of dragging my raft maybe 30 yards to the water. I kept thinking there must be a mistake when I got out of my truck at Cedar Flats. I walked a narrow trail about 50 yards until the trail plunged down a cliff. Standing high up on the ridge, I couldn't even hear the water below. Later I talked to a local guide who told me he has to completely break his raft down, and depending on the willingness of his clients, he could count on a minimum of four trips up and down the steep trail. From Cedar Flats to the Spotted Bear Access point is eight miles and rated Class II water. Above Cedar Flats is a gorge rated Class V to VI. From Spotted Bear Campground Boat Launch to the next access, Twin Creeks is 6.5 miles and rated Class III. Although I swear there are some Class IV spots, probably a perspective view sitting in my 9 1/2 foot one-man drift boat.

Numerous non-fee primitive campsites may be found during the last few miles along Hungry Horse Lake. In addition to the Spotted Bear Campground, Crossover campground can be easily found on the east side of the lake a couple of miles below Twin Creeks. When you are headed to the Spotted Bear Ranger Station, you will cross the river on the South Fork Bridge and come to a T intersection. If you turn left the road will head you back down the lake on the east side to the town of Hungry Horse. Crossover Campground is a few miles down this road and provides a boat launch to the lake.

Spotted Bear River: The Spotted Bear Campground, ranger station and river all come together 55 miles from the dam. Spotted Bear River is indeed a river during spring run-off, but by summer it drops to creek size. The river is excellent for 10-to-14 inch cutthroats, but once again access is difficult in all but a few places. From the confluence with the South Fork to Beaver Creek Campground is 9.4 miles, with only the lower stretch accessible by just parking your vehicle and walking down to the river. Two miles above the Beaver Creek Campground (non-fee) the road is blocked. The access roads in the upper half are not access roads! The first three access roads in the lower half of the road will get you right to the river or very close; in between you have to park and hike down the mountain. The hike back up the mountain would be tough for me, but the biggest challenge for me would be on deciding the question do I walk up the road looking for my rig or walk down?

When I took the first access road that led to a primitive camping site on the river, I ran into what I consider a real "Old Timer." I had just stopped to fish a section of the river and caught three fat cutthroats from 10 to 12 inches. I worked one riffle and one hole, but in truth I had to fish these two spots hard and smart to bring them up from the bottom. I was a bit disappointed, but it was almost 90 degrees so even the usual greedy little ones were sulking from the heat. As I pulled out, I drove past a primitive campsite and spotted an older man sitting in a lawn chair reading a novel.

I leaned out of my truck window and asked him about the typical size for this section. Pat Hardin smiled. Wearing a white, brimmed hat and red suspenders, Pat looked like the friendly grandfather type. His kind eyes and easy smile marked him as a soft touch for grand kids.

"Depends when you're here," he said.

"Well, I just caught three over there and the largest was 12 inches. What kind of size do you generally catch."

"Depends on when I was here. The first time was 1928. That was 70 years ago."

Without even hesitating I asked, "Could I get out of this truck and talk to you?"

"Grab a chair and join me in this patch of shade," he said.

What a story he had to tell. Twenty minutes later I regretted not asking all of the questions I would have liked to ask. I wished I were a newspaper writer. With some credibility as a writer I might have probed into his story for all the rich details. Pat's parents were ranchers in the Columbia Falls area. Both were avid outdoors people, and both his mom and dad hunted in the fall for elk. Pat said they'd hitch up a wagon with a team of horses and head up Hungry Horse Creek and camp and hunt until they both shot their elk.

Pat recalled his first trip up the South Fork to the Spotted Bear Ranger Station in 1928. The rough road paralleled the river, and the going was rough for a Model T Ford. It took them two days to travel the 60 miles from Hungry Horse. They'd stop and fish when they needed to stretch their legs. Pat remembered the excitement of arriving at the ranger station, which at that time was fairly new. He was seven years old on his first visit to the South Fork.

As a little kid he most enjoyed fishing the little feeder creeks, which produced some very nice size cutthroats. Fourth of July on the South Fork was tradition for a number of local ranching families. Years later after the dam was built, Pat noticed a decline in the numbers of fish just above the lake to Spotted Bear although above Spotted Bear the river maintained its richness. As the popularity of floating increased on the South Fork, noticeable declines in numbers and size alarmed Pat and other folks who had fished the South Fork for years. Pat joined a committee and helped to establish the Wilderness Limit, which limits a fisherman to three fish all less than 12 inches. Pat now feels the South Fork is rebounding.

Just as I was getting up to leave, Pat confided that you can catch them up to 18 inches if you know what you are doing. "My old holes on the South Fork and Spotted Bear are just about as good as they ever were." Maybe the good old days are now.

Pat's final comment for me to include in this book was to encourage campers to have a fish fry without any guilt. "Whitefish," he asserted, "are as good eating as a trout, maybe better." The cold waters of the South Fork produce some of the best eating whitefish in Montana. With incredibly generous limits of 50 a day and in possession, Pat suggests filleting them or just skinning them. The flaky white meat just falls off the bones.

Mileage Markers for the West Side Road of the South Fork

MM 0: Hungry Horse Dam

Doris Boat Landing: Located eight miles from the dam, the Doris Boat Landing is reached by a paved road.

MM 5: Lost Johnny Campground: Five campsites, water, toilets, limited space for large trailers or RVs. Fee area.

MM 5.6: Lost Johnny Point Campground: 21 campsites, water, trailer space for 26 foot camper trailers, concrete launch site to 45-foot drawdown. Fee area.

MM 8.3: Lid Creek Campground: 23 campsites, toilets, concrete boat ramp serving full pool to 31-foot drawdown. Fee area.

MM 19: Lakeview Campground: Five campsites, no water.

MM 28.9: Graves Bay Campground: 10 campsites, no water.
Graves Creek: Graves Creek may be accessed along the road to Handkerchief Lake and above the lake and then by trail into the Jewell Basin. The creek fishes well for 8-to-10 inch cutthroats.

MM 28.9: Handkerchief Lake Campground:
Handkerchief Lake is 32 acres and can be reached within a couple hundred yards of the campground. The fishing is good for cutthroats and grayling. The campground is also the trailhead for the **Jewell Basin.** **(See page 121)**

MM 55: Spotted Bear Campground: 13 campsites, toilets, water, RV dump facility. Just short of the campground is an access road for launching rafts, although during mid-summer plan on carrying your boat about 40 yards over rocks.

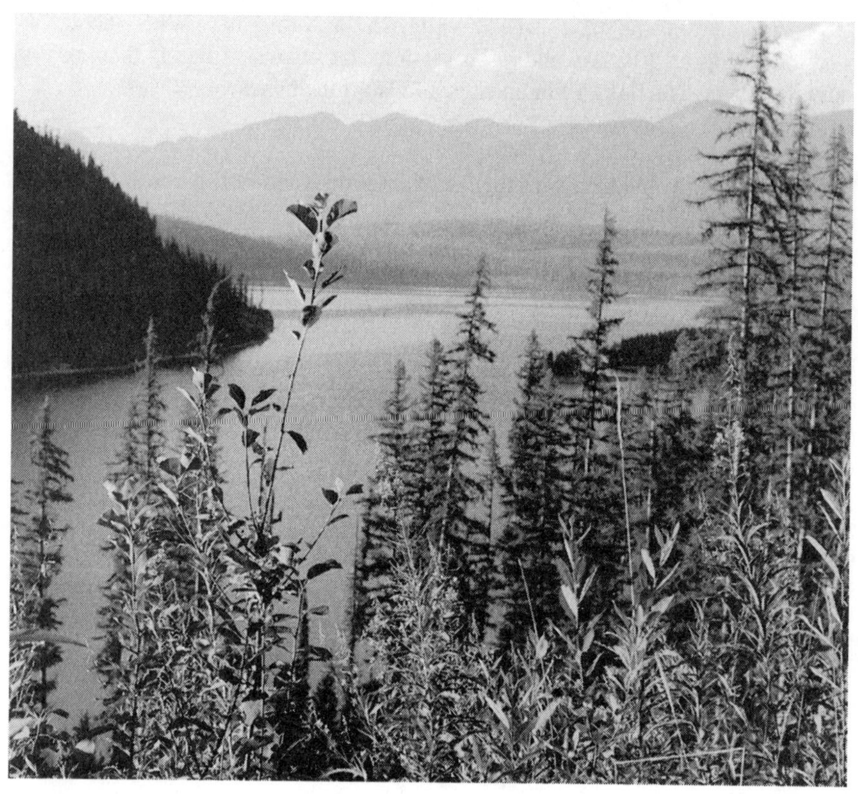

A view of Hungry Horse Reservoir

Beaver Creek Campground: Beaver Creek Campground is 9.4 miles above the ranger station on Spotted Bear Road. Three sites, outhouses, loading ramp and feed bunks for horses.

Hungry Horse Lake, Eastside Road
MM 0: Martin City

MM 5: Emery Bay Campground: 26 campsites, toilets, water, concrete boat ramp serving full pool to 35 foot. Fee area.

MM 22.2: Murray Bay Campground: 18 campsites, water, toilets, boat ramp to drawdown level 20 feet.

MM 37.4: Devil's Corkscrew Campground: Four campsites, toilets, cement boat ramp.

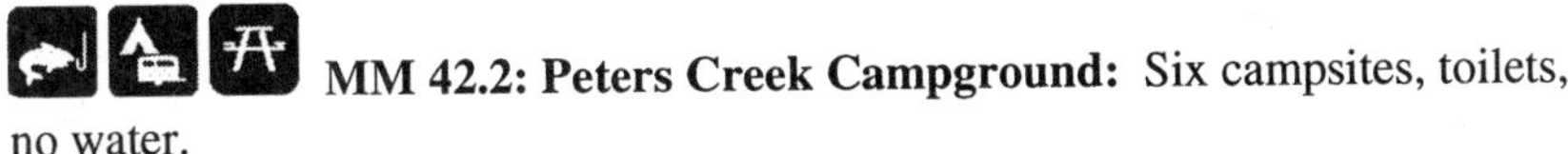

MM 42.2: Peters Creek Campground: Six campsites, toilets, no water.

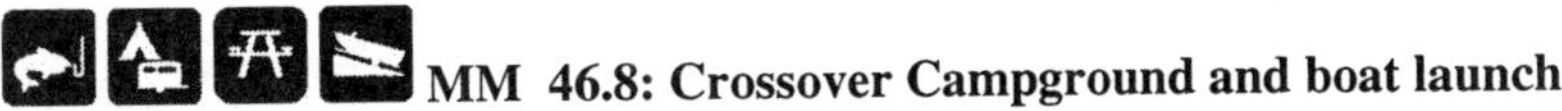

MM 46.8: Crossover Campground and boat launch

Glacier National Park

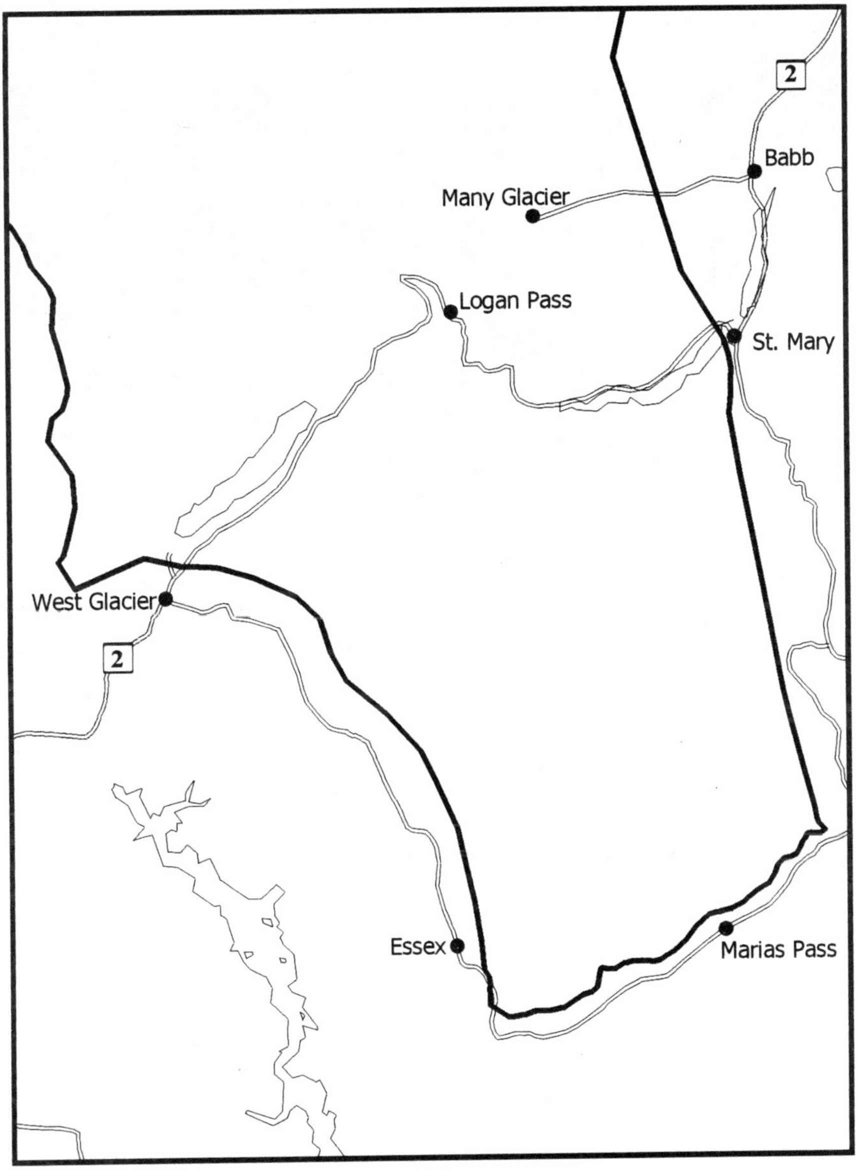

Fishing in Glacier National Park

Unlike Yellowstone National Park, which is a mecca for fly fishers from all around the country, Glacier National Park renders no great piscatorial praise. Nonetheless, if I were flying into the area just to visit the park, my on-board luggage would include a camera and a travel rod. Although the fishing does not compare to Yellowstone National Park, good fishing opportunities abound for those fishers who are willing to trek three to six miles into the interior lakes. When a river is off and the fishing is slow, the reasons are readily forthcoming. "We are in between hatches. We had a late run-off. Last year's drought hurt the hatches. The hot weather has made for slow fishing." When a lake offers up slow fishing, it sometimes defies logic. Consider a good day of fishing a bonus to a scenic hike into the wilderness.

Most of the park's smaller lakes are home to brook trout, cutthroats and bull trout. Cutthroat will generally cruise along the shoreline during the day, providing opportunities for the fly fisher. With the approach of dusk, however, the spin fisher will have the advantage by tossing a water-filled bubble far out into the lake and slowly reeling in a small nymph such as a Gold-Ribbed Hare's Ear, a Zug Bug, a bead-head Prince or a drowned Elk Hair Caddis. Backpacks with strapped downed belly boats and flippers provide greater opportunities for the fly fisher. If you are a spin fisher, small popular lures such as Mepps, Thomas Cyclone, Rappala and Daredevils are park standards like most small trout lakes.

If you are new to fly-fishing on a lake, I would suggest carrying an assortment of size 16 and 18 dry flies such as yellow Humpies, parachute Adams, Royal Wulffs, Renegades and Elk Hair Caddis. If you are fishing the outlet of a lake, be sure to have some ant and beetle patterns for late in the summer. Finally, be sure your fly box has a few Girdle Bugs and streamers. The goal of this guide is to include only lakes that can be reached on a day hike. Keep in mind that Glacier National Park does provide excellent cutthroat fishing in the North Fork of the Flathead and the Middle Fork of the Flathead. Both forks serve as the park's boundaries.

Be sure to read the fishing regulations carefully. Keep in mind that your best source of fishing information is often the park rangers as Glacier has no stocking programs, and lake populations are adversely impacted by harsh winters. Trails are often closed due to bear activity. Regarding the grizzly bear, your chances of being attacked by a bear are about one in a million. The odds are greater that you will be struck by lighting while hiking in the park. But when there is lightning in the area, I don't stand around until I smell the ozone before I take precautions. Read all the park advisories on avoiding bears. Here are some suggestions taken from the Waterton-Glacier Guide that each park visitor receives.

"If you surprise a bear, here are a few guidelines to follow that may help:

5. Talk quietly or not at all; the time to make loud noise is before you encounter a bear. Try to detour around the bear if possible.
6. Do not run! Back away slowly, but stop if it seems to agitate the bear.
7. Assume a non-threatening posture. Turn sideways, or bend at the knees to appear smaller.
8. Use peripheral vision. Bears appear to interpret direct eye contact as threatening.
9. Drop something (not food) to distract the bear. Keep your pack on for protection in case of an attack.
10. If a bear attacks and you have pepper spray, use it!
11. If the bear makes contact, protect your chest and abdomen by falling to the ground on your stomach, or assuming a fetal position to reduce the severity of the attack. Cover the back of your neck with your hands. Do not move until you are certain the bear has left....
12. If you are attacked at night or if you feel you have been stalked and attacked as prey, try to escape. If you can not escape, or if the bear follows, use pepper spray, or shout and try to intimidate the bear with a branch or rock. Do whatever it takes to let the bear know you are not easy prey."

Bearing that in mind, what follows are some suggested day hikes to Glacier's popular backcountry lakes.

East Entrance: Highway 89 from Browning, Montana turning south on Highway 49 to Two Medicine Campground.

Oldman Lake: Beginning at the Two Medicine Campground, hike seven miles for cutthroats. **Two Medicine Lake:** Drive to the lake for brook trout and rainbows. **Upper Two Medicine Lake:** Follow the trail 5.5 miles or take a two-mile trail if you begin at the upper boat landing on Two Medicine Lake. The lake contains both brook trout and rainbows.

East Entrance: Highway 89 from Browning, Montana to the Saint Mary Visitor Center and then to Rising Sun Campground on the Going-to-the Sun Road.

Otokomi Lake: Beginning at Rising Sun Campground, the trail climbs rather steeply six miles to the lake. The trout are said to be finicky but fat. Continuing on the Going-to-the Sun Road towards Logan Pass, stop at the Jackson Glacier Overlook. The trail leads six miles to **Gunsight Lake.** The hike is rated as moderate, and the fishing is generally good for rainbows and cutthroats. Along the way you can fish the St. Mary River if you are so inclined to leave the trail. Arriving at Logan Pass, follow the Hidden Lake Nature Trail three miles to **Hidden Lake** for Cutthroats**.** Be alert, as this is bear country.

East Entrance: Highway 89 from Browning, Montana to Saint Mary Visitor Center and then to Babb, Montana: From Babb enter the park through the Many Glacier Entrance past Lake Sherrburne to the **Many Glacier Campground**. **Lake Sherrburne** is basically a pike fishery. The Many Glacier area offers a number of short hikes to good fishing lakes. **Swiftcurrent Lake** is near the end of the road and is good fishing for brook trout. Above Swiftcurrent Lake, and a short 1.5-mile hike, is Josephine Lake which has a good supply of brook trout as well. **Grinnel Lake** is above Josephine Lake four miles from the trailhead and offers both brook trout and rainbows.

A short distance from Swiftcurrent Lake, and at the end of the road, is the trailhead to Red Rock Lake. The hike to Red Rock Lake is three miles, and the lake provides fishing for brook trout. A third trail from Many Glaciers leads to Fisher Cap Lake, Iceberg Lake and Ptarmigan Lake. **Fishercap Lake** is a five-mile hike from Swiftcurrent Campground and provides fishing for brook trout and rainbows. Pass up Iceberg Lake, as it is barren, and plan on a hard five-mile hike to **Ptarmigan Lake**, which could very well reward you with good fishing for cutthroat and brook trout.

East Entrance: Follow Highway 89 to the junction with Highway 17, Chief Mountain International Highway. Follow this highway until you enter Canada and proceed to the Belly River Campground. The **Belly River** is good fishing for brook trout, rainbows and grayling.

West Glacier: Highway 2 from Columbia Falls: The most famous road in Montana is the Going-to-the Sun Road in Glacier National Park. Above Lake McDonald, you will drive past McDonald Creek. It is beautiful, but it is generally bereft of trout with the exception of a few migratory fish. Following this famed road to Logan Pass, turn left at the top end of McDonald Lake and head south. Look for the trailhead to Rogers Lake and Trout Lake. Rogers Lake is approximately 4.5 miles, and Trout Lake is four miles. Both lakes have populations of cutthroats, but Trout Lake is restricted to fly-fishing only. Returning to the Going-to-the Sun Road, the next stop is Avalanche Creek Campground. Follow the trailhead two miles to Avalanche Lake for cutthroat fishing. At the Logan Pass Visitor Center, take the Hidden Lake Nature Trail to Hidden Lake, which is a little more than three miles. Hidden Lake offers cutthroats.

West Glacier: Apgar Visitor Center to Bowman Lake via the North Fork Road: Camas Creek is a small creek draining Rogers Lake and holds small cutthroats; the first trailhead is to **Logging Lake**, a long skinny lake which holds small cutthroats. The hike into the lake is about four miles. The next lake is Bowman Lake and campground, which you can drive to. **Bowman Lake** offers fair fishing for cutthroats and bull trout. From Bowman Lake Campground, follow the trail four miles to **Lower Quartz Lake** and another two miles to Middle Quartz Lake and Quartz Lake. Fishing is generally good in all three lakes for cutthroats. The North Fork Road ends at **Kintla Lake** and campground. The lake is fair fishing for cutthroats, lake trout, and bull trout. Above Logging Creek the best access to wade fish the North Fork of the Flathead is from inside the park on the North Fork Road.

Saga: I Don't Mess with Moose

About a half of a mile up the creek from the Mill Creek Trailhead, the Forest Service sign warned of an aggressive bear in the area. I had heard that the bear had been feeding on a dead moose. I decided to take my chances with the aggressive bear. If it had been a warning of an aggressive moose, however, I would have hastily left the area.

When I had taught in Jackson, Wyoming, almost 20 years ago, I had a student walk in late to my first period class with a note from his mother. I had assumed he was a town kid as he wore a baseball hat, a satin jacket promoting a local business and Nike shoes, not exactly the attire I attributed to a ranch kid. Later I found out that the kids in school with the cowboy attire lived out on 5-to-10-acre spreads west of town. The note read: "Dear Mr. Archer, Bill is late to class this morning because he was trapped under his truck by a mean tempered cow moose."

You're kidding, I said. "Nah," the teenager drawled. "The worst part was when I dashed out to warm up the truck. I forgot to put on my coat. The moose charged, I dove under my truck, and she kept me there for about 40 minutes until my mom came out and shooed it away."

For the rest of the class period in sophomore English, harrowing moose stories prevailed. Years later while floating on Rock Creek, I had a bull moose charge into the creek right after we silently floated past him. After some quiet reflection, my clients and I concurred that his stopping point would have been right in the middle of my raft had he decided to charge when we were abreast of him. And then a few years later I experienced my brush-with-death moose story.

If you recall the movie The Ghost and the Darkness about two man-eating lions, you will recall the line from the white hunter when he says to the young engineer after he has had a close encounter with a lion: "You got knocked down. Now you got to stand up and decide what you're going to do about it." I got knocked down too, but I don't want a rematch!

Unlike the brave engineer, moose will forever intimidate me. Pauline and my sons and I were camped out at the second hog back on Rock Creek during Memorial Day weekend. I was fishing alone on an island with Shadow, my black Labrador. When I came to a spot on the creek that was too deep to wade, I pulled myself up on the grass bank and pushed my way through the dense willow thicket. The creek was still to my left as I entered a small opening. I walked a couple of paces, and suddenly a cow moose struggled up from her bed scattering dust like a cowpoke's pickup truck on a Saturday night.

I froze. Shadow froze. The moose pawed the ground. I let out a startled whoop and took off running. I saw an opening in the brush and jumped into the creek. I heard the snorts and grunts from the moose directly behind me. At any moment I was expecting a hoof to split me in two. The creek was only a foot deep when I landed. Unlike the protagonist in the adolescent novel, Hatchet, the water was not going to help me.

Across the narrow creek I observed a rock cliff with no trees. Down I went on the slippery rocks. I heard a terrible commotion in the brush. I turned around just in time to see the pawing moose chasing my lab in circles around a thin willow bush. Poor Shadow. Her tail was tucked under her belly, her ears were drooped, and she was running around the willow in a sideways motion with her head turned towards the moose in askance. Shocked silent, she never let out a bark. Finally, the cow charged off, and Shadow meekly joined me at my side in the creek. She had silently stood her ground and saved my life as I ran away.

My sons accused me of story embellishment, but Shadow and I know. The following year two fishermen barely escaped a charging moose in the same area. Their dog stood his ground and was injured. Later that same summer a cow moose killed a man as he crossed the street in a small town in Washington. I don't mess with moose.

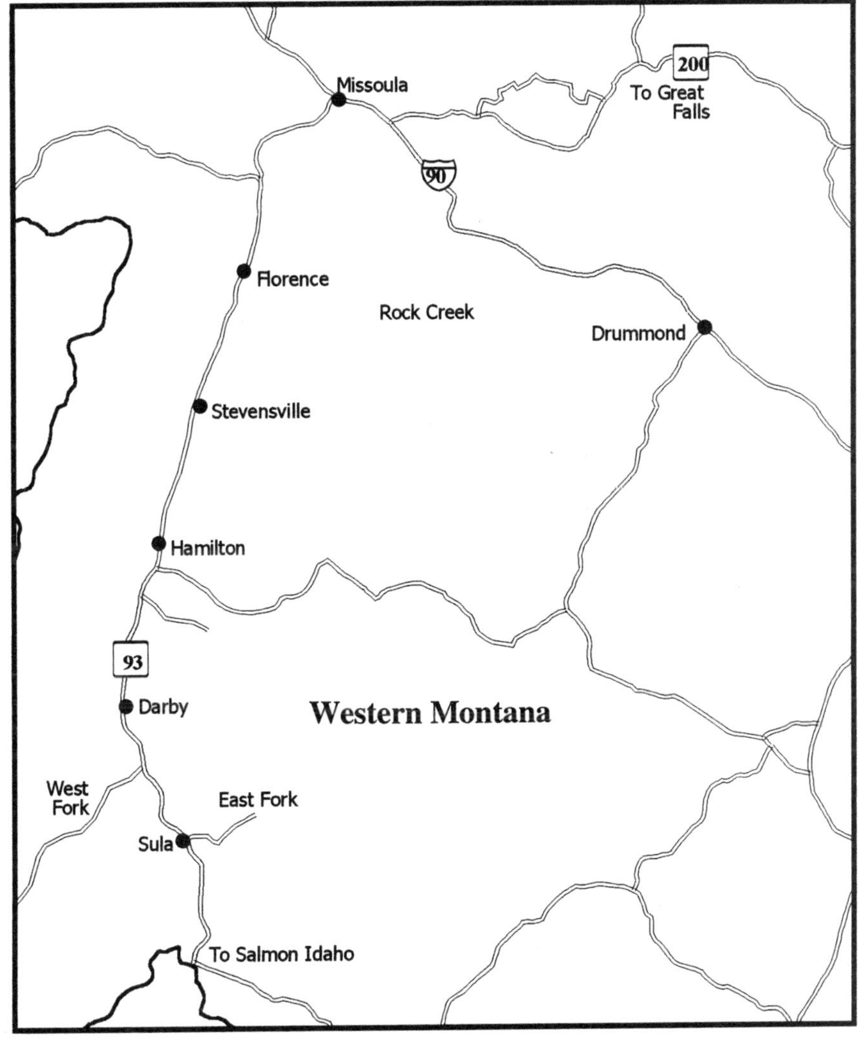

Western Montana Accommodations and Services

The western region is quite large. I have included only accommodations that are reasonably close to good fishing. For a complete regional listing and descriptions of accommodations and services, request a free travel planner from Travel Montana, Department of Commerce, P.O. box 200533, Helena, Montana 59620-0533, or telephone: 1 800-847-4868. For Travel Montana Internet Information: http://travel.mt.gov.

Hamilton Area Fly Shops and Sporting Goods:

Angler's Roost, 815 Hwy 93. S., Hamilton, MT 59840 (406) 363-1268
Blackbird's Fly Shop and Lodge, 1754 Highway 93, Victor, MT
1 800-210-8648
Bob Ward and Sons, 1120 North 1st Street, MT 59840 (406) 363-6204
Fishaus Tackle, 702 N 1, Hamilton, MT 59840 (406) 363-6158
Riverbend, 103 State Street, Hamilton, MT 59840 (406) 363-4197
Rvrbend@montananet.com

Hamilton Area Private Campgrounds:

Angler's Roost Campground and RV Park, 815 Hwy. 93 S., Hamilton, MT 59840 (406) 363-1268
Bitterroot Family Campground, 1744 Hwy. 93 S., Hamilton, MT 59840 (406) 363-2430
Riverside RV Repair and Park, 2101 N 1, Hamilton, MT 59840 (406) 363-3744
Sula Country Store & Campground, 7060 Hwy. 93 S., Sula, MT 59871 (406) 821-3364

Hamilton Area Lodges:

Alpine Meadows Ranch, 469 Bunkhouse Road, Darby, Montana
Fax: 1 619-755-4194 Email: omontana@pacbell.net
www.alpinemeadowsranch.com

Bear Creek Lodge, 1184 Bear Creek Trail, Victor, Montana 59875
(406) 642-3750 Fax: 406-642-6847 Email: info@bear-creek-lodge.com
www.bear-creek-lodge.com

Missoula Area Fly Shops and Sporting Goods:

Bob Ward and Sons, 3015 Paxson, Missoula, MT 59801 (406) 728-3221
Gart Sports, 2640 N. Reserve, Missoula, MT 59802 (406) 542-2112
Grizzly Hackle, 215 W. Front Street, Missoula, MT 59802 (406) 721-8996
The King Fisher, 926 East Broadway, Missoula, MT 59802 (406) 721-6141

Missoulian Angler, 420 N. Higgens, Missoula, MT 59802 (406) 728-7766
Sportsman Surplus, Tremper's Shopping Center, Brooks Street, Missoula, MT 59801 (406) 721-5500
Rock Creek Mercantile, 15995 Rock Creek Road, Rock Creek, MT 59825 406) 825-6440

Missoula Area Private Campgrounds :
Ekstrom Stage Station, Rock Creek, 1 mile south of I-90 at Exit 126
(406) 825-3183 Restaurant, playground, horses, fishing

Elkhorn RV Ranch, Rock Creek, 4 mile south of I-90 at Exit 126
(406) 825-3220 Private access to Rock Creek, cabins, trail rides

KOA El-Mar Kampground, 3450 Tina Avenue, Missoula, MT 59802
(406) 549-0881 Kabins, store, pool and seasonal food service

St. Regis Fly Shop: Clark Fork Trout and Tackle, P.O. Box 140, St. Regis, MT 59866 (406) 649-2538

Seeley Lake Sporting Goods: High Basin Sports, Box 1110, Seeley Lake, MT 59868 (406) 677-3605

Landing a Rock Creek rainbow.

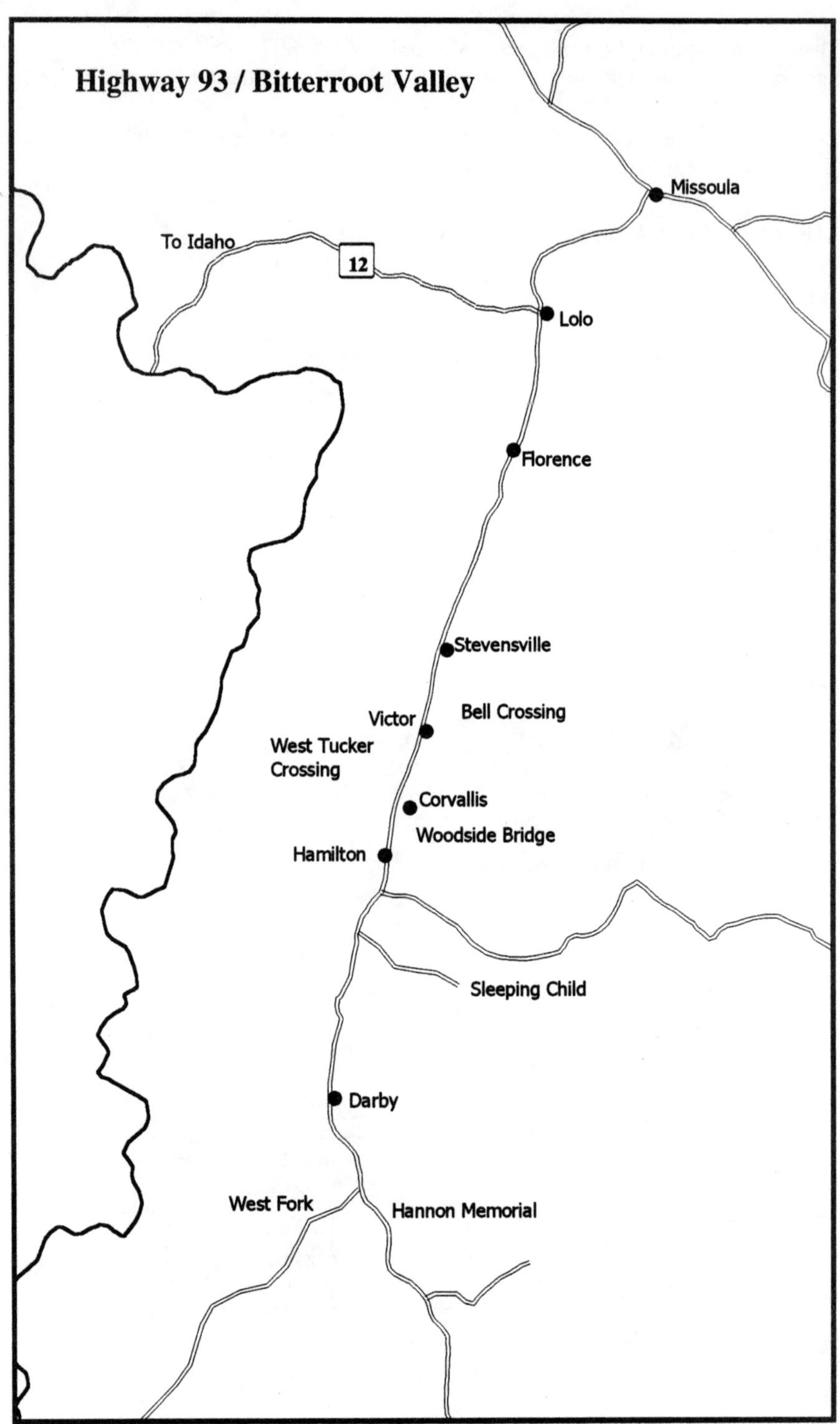
Highway 93 / Bitterroot Valley
Missoula
To Idaho
12
Lolo
Florence
Stevensville
Bell Crossing
Victor
West Tucker
Crossing
Corvallis
Woodside Bridge
Hamilton
Sleeping Child
Darby
West Fork
Hannon Memorial

Western Montana / Bitterroot Valley

Highway 93 from the Idaho Border to the Bitterroot Valley North to Missoula

The Bitterroot River: Crossing over from Idaho to Montana, Highway 93 plunges down the mountain to meet the east and west forks of the Bitterroot River and the beginning of the Bitterroot Valley. Bordered by the Sapphire Mountains to the east and the Bitterroots to the west, the river and highway stretch over 70 miles to join the Clark Fork River near Missoula. Popular with visitors and new arrivals, the Bitterroot Valley increasingly is losing its rural heritage. Losing prime bottomland and long slopes to developers, the suburban sprawl masks the marvel of the valley. In spite of increasing pressure, the Bitterroot River has few rivals for dry fly fishing and easy access. Its rugged west slope mountains cradle one of the nation's largest wilderness areas, the Selway-Bitterroot Wilderness. The freestone canyon feeder streams offer some of the best-concentrated crick fishing in Montana. Best of all, the Bitterroot River has maintained a clean bill of health against Whirling Disease.

Thanks to the support of local guides and outfitters and Trout Unlimited members, the state has implemented over 50 miles of catch-and-release zones and trophy management areas. Rainbows in the upper sections average 800-900 per mile along with an equal number of browns. With increased protective regulations, the cutthroat's population has exploded in numbers. I am always leery of fish counts in describing a river. Although I confess to be a romantic by nature, I truly do not have a disdain for science and statistics; after all I am an educator. I am merely puzzled by the results of electric fish counts. Often they do not seem reflective of the actual fishing action one has on a particular stretch of river.

Outfitter Dave Odell of Anglers Afloat, an outfitter I guided with for many seasons, rewards his clients who catch a 20+ inch trout. The "trophy" coffee cups use to be rewarded for an 18-inch trout. A number of years ago he was giving away so many custom made coffee cups, he upped the qualifications to 20 inches. He champions the Bitterroot River as a great fly fishing river. He now awards just as many cups for 20-inch catches! The Bitterroot River deserves high praise.

The upper stretch from Hannon Memorial (junction bridge with the West Fork Road just below Connor) to the Como Bridge is by far the most popular floating stretch, but fishermen must prepare to share the river with other floaters. In spite of the increased traffic, this section offers some of the highest fish counts, although there has been a small decline in the number of trophy trout (18 + inches). The upper stretch all the way down to Angler's Roost

Campground provides a mixed forest floor, gin clear water and lots of riffles and runs. This freestone stream slows down to runs and pools behind the city of Hamilton. Punctuated by an occasional riffle, the town section provides lush cover right down to the water's edge.

Below Hamilton the river loses its many braids and flattens out to receive the broad valley floor. For years this mid-section of the river historically suffered from de-watering and warmer temperatures. With the addition of habitat improvement for feeder stream spawning and increased regulations, along with guaranteed minimum stream flows, the mid river has experienced a rejuvenation. From Tucker Crossing, just south of Victor, to the Florence Bridge, catch-and-release regulations have steadfastly increased trout populations in both the numbers and size. Years ago I disliked having to guide on this section even though I lived within a mile. The trout populations were thinner than the upper sections, and the slow warm water in mid-summer created a crapshoot at best. Today this section is one of my favorite floating sections year around.

With the exception of those diehards who refuse to say "when," the season officially kicks off with the Skwala stonefly hatch in mid March and early April. Bill Bean of the Fishaus in Hamilton figures the hatch is good for a full six weeks if the weather cooperates. "One pattern to use for the Skwala is a bullet head fly tied with a black egg sack and dark body," he said. "The underwing is dark brown premo-deer hair. The fish seem to look for this hatch to begin their yearly feeding habits, and with the size of this stonefly, they can build bulk fast." Keep in mind, however, that weather patterns at this time of year are unpredictable. During my 15-year tenure as a guide, I would often be asked about the weather and the best time to book a trip.

The weather and words such as typical and normal are based on 30-year cycles. Since I began guiding in 1981, I have dropped those words from my vocabulary. During the drought years I would tell people the Bitterroot would be prime during the last week in June through July. September would see a return of water as irrigators cut back on their watering and the river would cool along with the nights. Correspondingly, the hatches return mid day and late afternoon. 1997 brought record snow accumulations and a very late run-off. Typically the canyon creeks warm up later and the insect hatches appear later as well.

I recommend waiting until mid or late July for fishing those creeks.
1998 was a year with half the normal snow pack so we eagerly anticipated the salmonfly hatch on the West Fork and East Fork. Mother Nature plays nasty tricks on Bitterrooters. June rainfall broke all the records, and all of the rivers in the area experienced high and muddy water throughout the entire month. So I would say, based on a typical year, to plan your fishing whenever you have the chance, "come hell or high water."

During April through June the river explodes with mayfly and caddis hatches on warm cloudy days. May and June typically see the Isoperla stonefly, Salmon Fly activity on the forks and the eagerly awaited green, gray and brown drakes. Mid summer settles into an early morning appearance of smaller mayflies which necessitates smaller tippets and size 14-18 Pale Morning Duns, Light Cahills and Parachute Adams. Chuck Stranahan of Riverbend Flyfishing in Hamilton recommends the Quigley Cripple during the drake hatches.

To borrow a wonderful phrase from Dave Whitlock, the heat of August brings forth "Hoppertunity Time". Terrestrials supplement the finicky appetite of Old Man Brown along with the tiny tricorythodes mayfly. Bring your raingear with you in August to arm yourself against the LATS. (Late Afternoon Thunder Showers) An effective hopper technique for cuts is to dress a Muddler and fish it both as a hopper pattern next to the bank as well as a sculpin pattern on the drift.

Bill Bean describes the summer fishing as "a continual opportunity for dry fly action. With the abundance of mayfly hatches, the expert as well as the novice fisherman can do well. If you are not capable of matching the hatch, a well-tied attractor pattern such as a Stimulator will usually do the trick. Opportunities abound for fishermen who prefer wading as well as those who prefer floating from a raft or a personal watercraft. Many access sites provide the wading fisherman ample stretches to spend a few hours or the entire day."

Falling cottonwood leaves and the orange splendor of mountainside tamarack correspondingly signal the arrival of the giant orange caddisfly along with progressively larger mayfly hatches such as the #10 rusty, green Emphermeralla Heccuba mayfly. With school back in session and many of the fly fisherman replacing their rods for bows, shotguns, rifles and chainsaws, the river offers up her finest fishing to the solitary fisher.

The Bitterroot Valley

Highway 93: Idaho Border (Mile-Marker 0) to Missoula

MM 12.7: Sula, Montana / East Fork of the Bitterroot River: Sula offers a gas station, private campground and country store. Just past this facility is the East Fork Road. After you cross the bridge, turn right (east) on the East Fork Road. From this starting point, the wilderness trailhead for the East Fork is 17 miles. The last four miles is dirt road. The East Fork is a beautiful "crick". Plan on hiking up the trail at least an hour to get to better fishing in the beaver ponds. In addition to the great scenery, the creek is loaded with small cutthroats in the 6-9 inch range with an occasional 12-14 "lunker." The East Fork along the highway is also fun fishing for smaller trout, although early in June some big fish are caught during the Salmon Fly hatch. From the highway **Jenny Creek Campground is** 10 miles and offers four camp units with toilet facilities. Fee area. **Martin Creek Campground** is 16 miles and offers seven camp units with water and toilet facilities. Fee area.

The East Fork of the Bitterroot River just above the Sula bridge on Highway 93.

MM 15.9: Spring Gulch Campground: 11 camping units. Water, garbage disposal, accessible toilet. Fee area.

MM 15.9: Warm Springs Campground: One mile to the west off of the highway. 14 camp units and picnic area. Water, toilet, and garbage facilities. Fee area. 50-55' level spots for large trailers.

MM 15.9: Crazy Creek Campground: Just past the Warm Springs Campground. Seven upper camp units for general camping; five lower units for campers with horses. Water and toilet facilities. Fee area.

MM 23: Connor Turn-off / Painted Rocks Reservoir / West Fork of the Bitterroot **Connor:** A few miles south of Hannon Memorial, you will see a sign to Connor. When you cross the bridge by the Connor store, you have just crossed the East Fork of the Bitterroot. You must enter the water from the bridge. I suggest wading downstream for some fun fishing in what is actually creek size water later in the summer. Wait until the summer has arrived so that you can stay in the water and easily move downstream. The East Fork braids in this area and becomes quite shallow, but there are some heavy 12-inchers in this section and some lunkers hiding.

MM 26: Hannon Memorial: 5 camping sites, picnicking, toilet facilities, and a raft launch on the other side of the bridge.

MM 26: Junction with Highway 473 – West Fork of the Bitterroot River

Side Trip: Highway 473 – West Fork of the Bitterroot River

About four miles south of Darby, Highway 93 crosses the Bitterroot River. Just after the bridge make a left turn on the West Fork Road. The West Fork both meanders and plummets down through the canyon from Painted Rock Reservoir. Above the reservoir the West Fork is a small brushy creek. The road mostly parallels the West Fork although most of the property is private. Nonetheless, sufficient access will keep a fisherman busy.

Although progressively smaller as you head towards Idaho, the West Fork is over forty miles long, and it is followed by a paved road to the dam and then a dirt road most of its length. Beautiful scenery and a clear running stream, combined with good catches of rainbows and cutthroats, make this a must visit if you are in the area. Surprisingly, the West Fork is lightly fished after the June Salmon Fly hatch.

MM 0: Junction with Highway 93

MM 3: Connor Cut-off to Highway 93: Connor has a country store.

MM 3.2: Access to the West Fork on private property. A popular take-out for canoes and rafts, this private property was posted a number of years ago. As of 1998 people are still using this site to exit the river with their rafts.

MM 6: Baker Lake access road: Road 363; trailhead 10 miles. Baker Lake is a popular local fishing spot less than two miles from the trailhead on an easy trail. Under 10 acres, it is good fishing for small 7-12" cutthroats.

MM 10.9: Easy to miss, this access has one tent campsite on the river.

MM 11.9: A primitive campsite only with access to the river for rafters and canoeists.

MM 13: State access point for launching rafts or canoes

MM 13.1 Boulder Creek / Sam Billings Campground (Road 5631) 1 mile: Boulder Creek is a brushy little creek with lots of small pocket water for small cuts. The campground has 11 camping units, toilet facilities and no water (creek).

MM 13.9: Ranger Station

MM 17.9: Rombo Campground: 15 camp units. Water, garbage, toilet facilities. Fee area. Excellent access to the river as well as beautiful campsites right along the river.

MM 21.5: Dam / Access to Bluejoint Creek: Bluejoint Creek is accessed by crossing the dam road and traveling to the north side of the lake. Bluejoint Creek has easy access. Fishing is good for 7-12 inch cuts.

MM 21.6: Little Boulder Bay Boating Site: Toilet facility and swimming area

MM 23.5: Slate Creek Campground: 4 campsites, toilet facilities, boat launch and beach area.

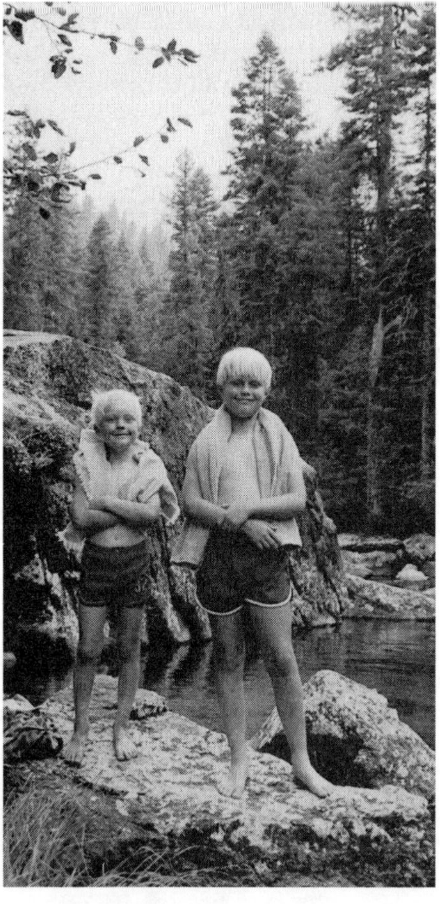

Brandon and Darin taking a break from fishing on the Selway River in Idaho. Take the Nez Perce Road just above Boulder Creek Campground.

 **MM 25.2 Painted Rocks State Campground:** Camping, picnicking, toilet facilities, boat launch and beach. Pack-in-pack-out policy with voluntary donations for maintenance.

MM 29.5: Alta Campground: 15 camping units. Water, garbage, toilet facilities. Fee area. Alta is a beautiful campground above the lake. At this point consider the West Fork a creek, a beautiful one at that!

MM 29.8: Hughs Creek: Hughs Creeks is a small, tumbling creek with easy access for small 6-9 inch cuts.

<u>**Return to Highway 93 Mile-Marker 27 Traveling North to Darby**</u>

Bitterroot River Access: Hannon Memorial and the West Fork of the Bitterroot River

As you cross the bridge, you will see a boat launch to the right and a small campground to the left. Here is an excellent area for foot fishing. Just upstream from the campground, some children of out-of-state property owners screamed at me about private property.

After I portaged around a log, I educated them on the rights of fishermen and nature's obstacles. Stay in the riverbed and below the high water mark, and the law is on your side. Montana floaters are ever-vigilant regarding stream access laws.

MM 29: Darby, Montana / Tin Cup Creek (Look for J&D Body Shop on the Left): From Highway 93 the road to the second trailhead is 4.5 miles. At 3.5 miles a sign will direct you left across a bridge where there is a trailhead. Continue straight another mile to the second trailhead which is through a piece of private property, a generous act of kindness these days.

The lower section of the creek that parallels the road is poor fishing for small trout. From the second trailhead to the first creek crossing is a 20-minute hike and another 20 minutes to the Wilderness Boundary. Tin Cup Creek looks better than it fishes.

I found the best fishing, naturally, in the wilderness area above and below the second creek crossing for 7-9 inch cutthroats. The trail is the easiest trail to hike of all the canyon creeks. The scenery is stunning, and the pools above the second creek crossing are beautiful and large, although the size of the fish varied little. Looking at the high water mark tells the story of a harsh environment during spring run-off.

Darby Bridge: Darby bridge has a small access on the south side of the bridge for floaters. Please do not block this access, and don't cross the bridge as it is private and posted. If you are going to wade fish, keep in mind that all of the surrounding banks are private property so stay in the streambed. From Highway 93 in downtown Darby, turn east on Tanner for two blocks. Turn right on Water Street for a half mile. Turn left on Darby Bridge Road.

United States Forest Service – Bitterroot National Forest Information Center, Darby, Montana: Warning 25 MPH!

MM 34.9: Como Lake Turn-Off

Como Lake (Rock Creek, Little Rock Creek and Little Rock Creek Lake): From Highway 93 to the boat launch is approximately four miles. Como Lake is a large lake, almost three miles long. Although it is popular with water skiers and jet skiers, it provides only fair fishing for smaller trout when they are so inclined. The lake is subject to extreme drawdowns during low-water years.

South Side: Boating area, large parking area, floating dock, boat ramp and dispersed picnic area with drinking water, toilet facilities and garbage service. Rock Creek Horse Camp: nine camping units; two accessible camping units; toilet facilities; no garbage service.

North Side: Lake Como Campground Area: 11 camping sites; one accessible site; one group camping site; electricity, drinking water, accessible toilet facilities and garbage services. Campground hosts. Fee area.

Upper Como Campground Area: 11 camping sites; drinking water, toilet facilities and garbage services. No electricity. Campground hosts. Fee area.

During the past couple of years campground facilities have been upgraded as was the boat launching site. The outlet is Rock Creek which is diverted into an irrigation ditch. The creek is almost completely dewatered as it enters the Bitterroot River. From the north side campground an eight mile trail loops around the lake. The trailhead to Rock Creek is 3.5 miles. Just above the lake are falls. The creek is excellent fishing for 7-10 inch cutthroats above the lake.

Little Rock Creek: Follow the signs past the Como Lake boat launch up a dirt road for another three miles. The dirt road traverses the mountain in a series of switchbacks over looking the lake for a breathtaking view. The road crosses over the ridge with an equally stunning view of El Capitan Peak. The road is bumpy and rough, but it is suitable for passenger vehicles with sufficient clearance. From the trailhead you will walk a short distance to an overlook of Como Lake, Rock Creek and its falls and Little Rock Creek canyon with El Capitan looming at the head of the canyon.

Saga: Little Rock Creek Lake Fishing Trip

The trail goes straight down to the bottom of the canyon to the beginning of the designated wilderness. I remember my first visit a few summers ago when I was lured up the trail. It was August when late afternoon thunderheads were swirling around the peaks, but I judged that they were breaking up. I had told my family I would be hiking up Tin Cup Creek, but I wanted to just check out the trailhead in the next drainage. Parked at the top of a mountain was one other vehicle from Minnesota. I thought to myself that I would just hike down to the creek, sample the fishing and head home before it rained.

I stepped down the trail at 1:45 knowing I would have to retrace my steps uphill on the way back, which seemed unusual. Shadow, my black Labrador, was eager. When I was a Boy Scout, I remember a father complaining about how difficult it was for him to walk down a steep trail. At ten years of age, I thought it was the most ridiculous notion I had ever heard. I reached the bottom at 2:18, and my knees were already swollen. The narrow, glaciated canyon walls bring early shade to the creek. Shadow and I stood over a small pool and watched 5-6 inch cutthroats cruise and feed right in front of us.

With my Polaroid sunglasses I searched the dark crevices and spotted a larger fish. I hurriedly tied on an Elk-hair Caddis and caught three nine inch trout in two little pools. I walked up the trail five minutes and repeated my catch. I looked at my watch and made the decision to head up to the lake, knowing I would have only an hour or so to fish before I would have to head back down the mountain and then up the mountain to my parked truck.

Little Rock Creek Lake: The lake is 4.5 miles from the trailhead. The trail is both steep and rough. In many places water spills down the trail, leaving many muddy bogs. Shadow eagerly ran up the trail. A few minutes later we met the Minnesota family heading out. No one in the party was a fisher, but they were detailed in their descriptions about all the leaping trout around the shoreline. What was their guess as to my hiking time? About two hours they replied. From the trailhead to the lake the hike took me three hours, and the return trip was only slightly shorter in duration. The trail gets thin in places, but I found the blaze marks on the trees and the piled rock cairns.

Although I had only an hour to fish, I was delighted with the numerous 9-10 inch cutthroats I caught in one hour's time. I caught all of these trout on the same caddis fly. I was letting it sink and twitching it. They would hit it on the slow retrieve or when I paused. They would follow the fly right into my shadow. Reluctantly, I headed down the trail. I had asked the Minnesota couple to leave a phone message on our phone recorder for the bed and breakfast so that Pauline would know where I was and that I would be getting back after dark. The next time that I return to Little Rock Creek Lake I will get an early start so that I can fish both the lake and the creek and still have time for a nap!

MM 35.3: Wally Crawford Fishing Access: Often referred to as the Como Bridge access, this is without a doubt the most popular stretch of water above and below the bridge for floaters. Although the fishery has withstood the increased pressure, as the summer flows decrease the larger fish head for cover. Plan on seeing up to ten other floaters on a hot summer weekend. Floaters from Wally Crawford to Angler's Roost must portage around Sleeping Child dam, which is easily done. Launching up river, the floaters have a choice of floating down from the town of Darby for a short run or putting in above Darby at Hannon Memorial Access where the highway crosses the river again south of Darby. All of these access points are good fishing areas for foot fishermen

MM 37.9: Lost Horse Creek and Twin Lakes: From the highway to the creek is approximately four miles. From the highway to the first lake is 20.5 miles. One-Horse Creek offers great picnic sites for the first five miles, but the fishing is poor as the creek is very small. If you plan on driving to twin lakes, be sure you have a truck, preferably 4X4. The road is rough for 16 miles, and you will average 10 miles an hour. The first lake is drawn down in the fall and is very shallow, which would account for the poor fishing. The upper lake is said to be fair fishing for small cutthroats. Plan your trip so that you return in the evening as moose, elk and deer are frequently seen along the road. **Schumaker Campground (Twin Lakes):** Five camping units, toilet facilities, no charge.

MM 38.2: River access

MM 43.2: Roaring Lion Creek / Sawtooth Creek: South of Hamilton on Highway 93, the highway crosses the Bitterroot River by Angler's Roost Campground. Look for Roaring Creek Road about 8/10 of a mile from the bridge. The trailhead, a popular trail with horse people and hikers, is approximately 3.5 miles on a bumpy road. The trailhead has no campground or picnic site. The creek is fished heavily and the majority of fish caught are in the 5-7 inch range. Roaring Lion Creek and Sawtooth Creek are located in two canyons side-by-side. However, access to Sawtooth Creek is from the Roaring Lion trailhead. "The distance from the trailhead to the first Sawtooth Creek crossing is approximately three miles. The first two miles of this section are in excellent shape. Between mile two and three, the trail generally is in good shape with several steep pitches. After the first creek crossing, the trail varies from fair to poor...." USFS

MM 43.4: Angler's Roost Campground: A few miles south of Hamilton, the highway crosses the Bitterroot River. This is also a popular section for foot fishermen. Angler's Roost owners have generously allowed floaters to launch their rafts from their campground. Be sure to sign their guest book and park in their designated parking spots. Show your appreciation by doing some business with them in their store.

MM 43.9: Sleeping Child Creek / Skalkaho Creek: Look for the Skalkaho Highway south of Hamilton on Highway 93. The highway actually turns south. Water diversion for irrigation and increasing development has impacted the fishing for the first 12 miles along Skalkaho Creek. Public fishing begins around mile 13 at Black Bear Camp ground. The best fishing is found in the upper reaches for 7-9 inchers between mile marker 15 and 19. After mile marker 19, the road climbs high above the creek. Look for pocket water as this is a very small crick. Look for Sleeping Child Road which continues south off of Skalkaho Road. Sleeping Child Creek is not worth fishing as it runs through so much private property. Hiking into the headwaters is also not worth the effort in my estimation given the proximity of other great fishing creeks in the area

MM 46: Hamilton, Montana

Bitterroot River Access: Hamilton: To the south of Hamilton the Bitterroot River is crossed at the Silver Bridge. In spite of the heavy fishing pressure as well as swimmers, fishing is good downstream from the bridge to Blodgett Park, a short distance downstream. The river braids through this section, and it provides excellent cover from downed cottonwoods.

Bitterroot River Access: Hamilton Sewage Treatment Plant: Don't let the facilities dissuade you. Some of the best fishing on the Bitterroot River runs behind the town of Hamilton. Turn west at the light at Adirondack Street from Highway 93. Two blocks up turn right on 7th and then immediately bear left. You may also reach the river by turning west on Main Street and driving a short distance to the Main Street Bridge.

MM 47: Main Street / Canyon Creek / Blodgett Creek: Follow the directions to Blodgett Canyon as Canyon Creek is the first canyon south of Blodgett. Look for the Forest Service sign (road number 735). Canyon Creek is a small, brushy creek that supports 6-8 inch cutthroats, but the creek is tough to access and even tougher to fish. The trail is steep. I would not recommend the trail for small children. However, from the Canyon Creek Trailhead, take the Blodgett Overlook Trail for a spectacular view.

"The Blodgett Overlook trail is open to hiking and mountain biking, but no motorized use is allowed. The trail winds around Romney Ridge and provides hikers with a scenic view of Hamilton, Blodgett Canyon, Canyon Creek and Canyon Creek Falls. This gradual 1.5-mile trail winds along the southeast facing hillside of ponderosa pine, arrowhead balsamroot and exposed bedrock covered with ground moss and lichen. There are numerous benches along the way to rest on and enjoy the view. The trail ends at the steep cliffs of Blodgett Canyon Overlook." USFS

Darin's hefty rainbow.

Blodgett Canyon (Creek): Traveling on Highway 93 through Hamilton, turn west on Main Street. After you cross the Bitterroot River, Main Street changes to West Bridge Road and then to Canyon Creek Road. From the intersection of Main Street and Highway 93, the distance to the campground and creek is 5.7 miles. The road out of town meanders until it intersects Blodgett Camp Road. Turn left on Blodgett Camp Road, which is designated as road 736. The last two miles to the campground is a dirt road.

Blodgett Canyon Campground: Six camping or picnic units, toilet facilities, and no charge. The campground has an excellent picnic site for those hot days in August as it is shaded. Blodgett Canyon is noted for its spectacular rock formations. The creek is excellent fishing for small trout in the 6-10 inch range.

Brandon at age 5 with his first big fish caught all by himself. "No! I am not going to release him." (Silver Bridge, Hamilton, Montana)

MM 48: Headquarters for Bitterroot National Forest

MM 50.2: Silver Bridge Fishing Access

MM 50.4: Blodgett Park: Fishing access, day use only.

MM 52: (Turn right) Woodside Road to Corvallis Bridge Fishing Access

MM 52: (Turn left) Dutch Hill Road / Mill Creek: Turn west on Dutch Hill Road and drive 2.5 miles until you arrive at Bowman Road. Turn left on Bowman Road. Drive 3/10 of a mile and turn right at the Mill Creek Trailhead. The trailhead is one mile. Mill Creek is a small creek tumbling down a steep canyon. For the first mile the creek is right along the trail and offers lots of pocket water for small trout.

Mill Creek fishes almost the same as its neighboring creeks, although I believe it gets a little more pressure. The first half mile the creek parallels the trail through a steep section of the canyon. Boulders the size of bean bags to bunk beds slow the water tumbling down the canyon, forming little pockets and pools. All along the trail are scuffmarks and slides left behind by eager fishermen. Looking down the 15 to 20 foot slides, I decided to wait. When the trail was only four or five feet above the creek, I scrambled down the trail and caught my first nine inch cutthroat on a small hopper.

After I had released the fish, I thought of the question posed to me by a guest staying in my bed and breakfast. An accomplished fisherman from back East, he asked me in all seriousness what I considered a pan fryer. I glibly mumbled, "I don't know. Anything that fits in a frying pan." No response was forthcoming. It was, after all, not a question to be expounded upon. Later I discovered I did indeed have an exact definition of a pan fryer. A pan fryer is an 8 to 9 inch trout with its head and tail cut off to fit perfectly at the bottom of a 5 1/2-inch, official Boy Scout mess kit.

MM 56: (Turn right) Tucker Crossing Fishing Access: Look for Blackbird's Fly Shop and Lodge just in front of the access road on the east side of the highway. You will see an old, rusting teepee burner. In typical years I would not recommend floating downstream as the channel often splits and braids which can make for some tough floating. This is also a popular site for walk-in fishing in both directions. If you turn to the left, you will be on Bear Creek Road, which will take you to both the Bear Creek trailhead and the Fred Burr Creek trailhead.

MM 56: (Turn West) Bear Creek / Fred Burr Reservoir: Bear Creek has been recorded in my endless favorite creek list. The first quarter of a mile of the trail, the trail winds above the creek through a talus slide. Looking across the canyon and listening to the beckoning call of the creek softly extolling its piscatorial praise of native cutthroats, I broke a vow I made to myself sometime around my 50th birthday -- stay on the trail!

For years I have held the belief that 80% of the fishermen are too impatient to walk up the trail more than a half of a mile. I also harbor the belief that 90% of serious fishermen under the age of 50 look for areas that they are convinced no one else would bother hacking their way through the brush to reach. My third belief is that 75% of the proficient fly fishermen will pass up fishing a hole within the first half mile convinced that the local bait bugaboo has decimated the pool. A hodge-podge of contradictory beliefs? Of course! Acted on? Absolutely!

So there I was poised high on the canyon trail overlooking a canopy of treetops and gnarly brush. "Don't do it," the 53-year-old in me warned. "Don't listen to that old curmudgeon," the kid in me responded. "You are only as old as you DO. Think of all those untouched pools. No one is going to bail off this trail after just leaving the parking lot. Even the impatient ones are going to go further on. And the serious guys are going to pass it up figuring the campers will have hit it pretty hard." Good point, I thought to myself. This could be worth the effort.

Off the trail I plunged into the Heart of Darkness. Bruised and scratched, only 30 yards off the trail, I was down on my knees thrusting my rod through any patch of light I could find. The horror! Even Shadow, my faithful lab companion, was disgusted with me. When I finally broke out onto the creek, it was no more than a series of thin braids with little holding water. I finally worked my way up to the point where the creek was one, and after catching a number of fat 8-10 inch cutthroats, I was one with the creek and the canyon, and the cascading brook. At one juncture I caught a small bull trout and a nice 10-inch cut in a pool right below the trail. A familiar worn path led from the trail to the pool. Unlike my youth during the fifties and early sixties, I am glad we live in a time of catch and release. I have no idea as to the fishing further up the trail. I only covered the first mile!

Fred Burr Reservoir: (Victor) Follow Bear Creek Road west towards the mountains until the road intersects with Red Crow Road. Turn west on Red Crow Road. The road will veer to the left (south), but keep straight ahead on Fred Burr Road for 1.5 miles to the trailhead.

Private landowners restricted access to the National Forest in Fred Burr canyon until 1995. Fred Burr Creek is heavily traveled by hikers, bikers and riders. Most of the trail is actually a jeep trail that leads to Fred Burr Reservoir, which is approximately five miles from the trailhead. Fishing along the creek is excellent for small 6-9 inch cutthroats. I spoke to a number of horseback riders coming down the trail, and all of them seemed pleased with the fishing in the reservoir. Huckleberry hounds, watch for those tiny, purple treats along the trail late in July for an extra bonus.

I fished the creek in July with Tony Swallow, a long-time volunteer and board member for the local public television station. We only covered the first mile. Tony was one of those rare anomalies who had reached middle age without ever fly-fishing. I assured him he could be successful on his very first outing with me as his instructor. Over confidence on my part? A touch of braggadocio after fifteen years of being a fly-fishing guide? None of the above. Summer fishing on any of the Bitterroot's canyon creeks should be considered one of those basic laws of nature -- you will catch fish.

Keep in mind, however, that you must adhere to four principals: 1. Keep your fly high and dry; 2. Be sure your fly floats naturally without any line drag; 3. Allow your fly to land gently; 4. Get in the middle of the creek and cast upstream. Tony, hoping to catch at least a couple of fish, followed all of the above rules and lost count after catching 10.

MM 59: Victor Crossing: The bridge at Victor Crossing washed out in 1997. Although this is an excellent access to river fishing, be forewarned that the road comes to a barrier, and there is little room to turn around. Construction of the new bridge is set for the summer of 1999.

MM 59: Victor, Montana: (Victor has a great steakhouse and a great Mexican restaurant and the Hamilton House Bar serves a great fish dinner!) **Sweathouse Creek:** Sweathouse Creek is a small creek right above the town of Victor. A narrow canyon with fast, tumbling water, fishing is good for 6-9 inchers. From the town of Victor, turn onto Main Street and then right on Chief Victor's Camp Road and then left on Sweathouse Creek Road to the trailhead.

MM 61: (Turn east) Bell Crossing Fishing Access: Opposite the turn off to Big Creek Lake, Bell Crossing is a state access point to the river for floaters floating down to Stevensville. Wade fishers will have to hike both upstream and downstream for selective fishing.

MM 61: (Turn west) Big Creek: The turn-off for Big Creek is between Victor and Stevensville on Highway 93. Look for the dirt road directly across from Bell Crossing Road. You will see an electric company's fenced substation across from the access road to the east. The headwater trailhead is approximately four-to-five miles from the highway. The road makes a few turns, but it is clearly marked with Forest Service signs and arrows. Big Creek is probably the most popular creek in the area as it carries the most water and offers a more graduated drainage. It was not uncommon ten years ago to land rainbows and a few browns in the 12 inch range. Now the creek is over-populated with 3-5 inch cutthroats in the canyon below the trailhead.

A short walk up the trail, however, will keep a fisher busy with 6-10 inch cutthroats. The trail to the lakes is approximately 12 miles and offers wonderful fishing all the way. Having once decided I would cut and hack my way through the brush to reach seldom-if-ever-fished sections of the creek away from the trail, I will assure you that the fishing isn't much better than what is easily available to you from the trail.

Big Creek Lakes is really a misnomer as it is really just one large 240-acre lake that splits into two lakes on low water years and during the fall. My son and I fished this lake in late August 1996, and it lived up to its reputation. The lake is loaded with 12 inch rainbows, and although I had heard that it was not uncommon to catch trout in the 16" range, we couldn't find them as the 12 inchers were harassing us on every cast. What fun. We caught fish on drys, nymphs and streamers. The scenery is breathtaking as the shore is edged with conifers in a large glacial canyon. For those individuals, who are somewhat reluctant to meet the challenge of a 12 mile backpacking hike, I would recommend backpacking seven to eight miles and camping on the creek; then hike up to the lake the next day with just a lunch and fishing gear. This is the best of both wilderness experiences, and it is just a few miles above the populated Bitterroot Valley!

MM 66.8: Stevensville, Montana : Junction to Highway 269
Bitterroot River Access: Stevensville Bridge and Burnt Fork Creek

The Stevensville Bridge is a popular put-in and take-out for float fishers either floating downstream to Florence or floating from Bell Crossing Bridge. This is a good access point for foot fishermen upstream or downstream. The entire area is a managed trophy trout section and, as such, is catch and release. During the last few years, the stretch from Stevensville to Florence has seen an increase in the number of boats plying the river on any given day of the season.

This section of the river can be fickle and torment floaters all day, or it can reward you with a most memorable day of fishing. I will confess to fishing a number of seasons without catching a trophy trout on the Bitterroot River (20 + inches). September 1997, I slipped my Little Dipper drift boat into the water at the Stevensville Bridge and within the first two miles I had caught a 23" brown, an 18" rainbow and a 17" rainbow.

I celebrated all day long as I floated down the river. The moon and planets and stars were surely all aligned.

Burnt Fork Creek / Gold Creek Campground: Four camping units, toilet facilities, no water, no charge. Not advised for RV or large camp trailers. I recently returned to Burnt Fork Creek after at least a ten-year hiatus. When my two sons were young, we would travel up the Burnt Fork for our first spring outing of catching little cutthroats and roasting hot-dogs to celebrate the coming of summer. For solitude and fun fishing for small fry, the Burnt Fork is unsurpassed. From Stevensville's Main Street, drive one mile south to the Burnt Fork Road. Turn east and travel 10.1 miles to where the paved road curves to the right. At this point the road changes to Burnt Fork School Road. Exit from the paved road straight ahead on Mid Burnt Fork Road. Follow this dirt road approximately six miles to the Gold Creek Campground. From the Gold Creek Campground, you can continue on the same road for 2.4 miles until you come to the end of the road for the trailhead. The road is bumpy and narrow at this point, but it is still suitable for passenger vehicles with sufficient clearance.

Covered with a canopy of alder and mountain mahogany, the creek is shrouded in shade, which produces brilliantly colored cutthroats. Unlike their cousins in the Bitterroot River who are drenched with sun all summer, the Burnt Fork cutthroats have a swath of bright orange from their jaw all along their underbelly. Their dark back and shaded penciled sides provide distinct markings, and best of all every pocket of water holds two or three 7 to 9 inch fish.

Like the creek I grew up on, this is not a place for purists and dry fly fishermen. The creek demands stealth and swing casts. A short, stout 3X leader provides all the necessary tensile strength when you miss a strike and find your fly snagged on a branch overhead. I recommend the bow shot for those hard-to-reach pockets where you can't even swing your fly. Get down on your knees, grab your fly between your fingers with the hook facing up, bow your rod, aim and let fire!

I recommend using a size 10 Girdle bug or Yuk Bug. Fish them just like a dry fly. Naturally they will sink, but their white, rubber legs in the dark, moss-lined pools provides a lure which is easy to follow. When you see a trout flash, set the hook just as you would a dry fly. Here is a very small creek for the entire family to have fun.

MM 67.8: Kootenai Creek Trailhead: The trailhead is two miles from the highway. Kootenai Creek is a fast, tumbling creek heavily used by rock climbers, backpackers and local fishermen. It is a great place to wet a line during the heat of the summer. Shaded most of the day, the creek offers an abundance of 6-8 inch cutthroats. This is pocket water fishing, and as such it requires scrambling up and over boulders and staying right in the water. Don't come too early, however, as the creek rages down the mountainside long after the Bitterroot has settled into its summer flows.

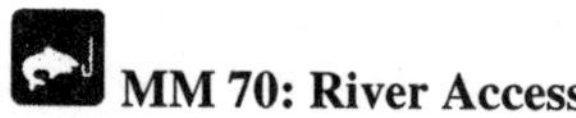
MM 70: River Access

MM 70.2: Bass Creek / Charles Water Campground: 20 camping units, 4 picnic spots, water, garbage and toilet facilities. Fee area. The trail head is 2.5 miles from Highway 93. The campground is designed for trailers and RV's and is very nice. The creek is a brushy tumbling creek with difficult access. Nonetheless, there is fair fishing for small trout wherever you can climb down off the trail to a pocket. It is a moderate hike to the picnic spot. The area just above the shallow ponds is good fishing for small cutthroats.

Bass Creek Saga

When two four legged animals come face-to-face on a precipitous trail at a blind spot, you have the makings of a high, country rodeo. Shadow, my black lab, let out an alarmed woof. The mounted rider in the rear yelled, "Bear!" The horse reared, the rider grabbed the pommel with both hands, and I flashed forward to a courtroom where the first question asked of me was, "Did you have your dog on a leash and under control?"

"But your honor, not all the blame should rest solely on my shoulders. Shouldn't there be some shared responsibility with the wife who mistook my Labrador retriever who weighs 80 pounds for a premature grizzly release? And what about the husband? What's a pampered, citified, horse doing on Bass Creek Trail? And what about Shadow. Doesn't she have the right to let out a choked snort when she is confronted by an alien sighting? Why, the man had on a huge white Stetson, a scarf and a John Wayne shirt with a string of buttons in a figure seven configuration!"

I wish I could say I made it all up, but it happened. I was horrified as I watched the horse spin on the up side of the trail with the rider holding on for dear life. I walked to higher ground where the horse could see us and talked to the two riders, but the horses were in a panic and would not come up the trail. I quickly leashed Shadow and walked down the trail, and all was well. The husband was apologetic for his horse, saying the horse had been trained around dogs and shouldn't have reacted. I was feeling much relieved when he openly confessed to his share of the responsibility. It seems that he had just looked down the cliff and thought to himself, "Oh, please, God, don't let me run into anyone on this spot. Suddenly Shadow appeared, his wife yelled "Bear" and he spooked an already panicked horse that was suffering from altitude sickness.

Bass Creek Lake trail winds up the canyon for eight miles to the lake at an altitude rise of over 3,000 feet, according to another middle-aged hiker I met. I planned a one-night stay-over, and in retrospect I made the right decision. The lake was not at all as accommodating as Big Creek Lakes, my previous summer trek. I was too exhausted to hike to the back of the lake in search of a relatively flat 6x6 spot to pitch camp, so I joined the other two hikers and set up my camp on the level top of the earthen dam.

On the way back down I fished the creek in a beautiful park setting, but between the flies and the mosquitoes, we were punished severely for my off-trail fishing adventure. Sitting on a log in the middle of the tiny creek, I caught five small cutthroats, about the same size and the same number I had caught on the lake the previous evening. What Bass Creek lacks in fishing prospects, compared to the other creeks in the area like Kootenai Creek, it makes up for in scenery. One hour up the trail is a great picnic spot where the creek flattens out above an old timbered dam. The water is shallow, and it makes for a great day's outing for children. If you have never taken an evening stroll on one of these creeks, do so and discover the Bitterroot wilderness' front yard.

MM 71.6: Poker Joe River Access: During the heat of the summer, fish a nymph on the bottom, or fish a hopper with a dropper down past the riprap car bodies above the railway bridge. This area is good foot fishing in the fall. Prior to the run-off in 1998, I floated through this section during an incredible drake hatch. I couldn't believe the number of 12 to 14 inch rainbows. Regardless of how poorly this section fishes during the heat of the summer, I can assure you that you are dragging your lure over more trout than I could imagine until I saw them all boiling on the surface. Yes, I caught a lot of fat fish, but I must confess that it wasn't easy. Everywhere I cast, my fly was surrounded by a regatta of brown drakes. One other shore fisherman was on the stretch above me. After a while I walked up to him eager to share my experience. "Can you believe it?" I said. He replied, "Unbelievable, but you should have been here yesterday!"

MM 74: Florence, Montana: Florence offers gas, food, bars and Rhino's sporting goods store where you can buy a fishing license.

MM 74: Bitterroot River Access: Florence Bridge

As you enter Florence, watch for the Conoco Gas Station on the left and move into the right lane. Turn onto the East-Side Highway and drive one-mile to the bridge. The Florence Bridge is a popular exit point for floaters entering the river at Stevensville. This section of the river can be very productive fishing or VERY slow fishing. It is especially good fishing during the Skwala hatch during the spring and later when the autumn nights cool the river.

MM 76.8: Chief Looking Glass Campground

Chief Looking Glass is a beautiful campground and local swimming hole. Watch for the sign between Lolo and Florence. This section of the river is poor fishing during the summer as the water is slow and warm. Comparatively speaking, this section has a low fish count, but I would recommend fishing this area in mid September during the Ephemerella Hecuba mayfly hatch. The pattern is a size #10 rusty, green.

MM 83.3: Lolo Creek: (Exit Highway 93 to Highway 12 West) Just a few miles south of Missoula, Lolo community rests at the junction of Highway 12, which leads to Idaho and the Lochsa River. A resting place for the Lewis and Clark Expedition, Lolo Creek parallels the highway for over 30 miles. Hosting a variety of species of trout, the creek, however, proffers smaller 7- 9 inch trout with the occasional spawning laggard. Years of logging and drought cycles have taken their toll on this pristine little "crick." This little creek gets pounded late spring and early summer. Some of the ranchers are becoming quite irritated over liberal interpretations of the high water mark. For a little seclusion, look for National Forest land where the creek falls away from the highway. Spring runoff turns this gentle canyon creek into an angry avalanche of water.

Lewis and Clark Campground: 15 miles west of Lolo. 17 campsites. Drinking water. U.S. Fee Area. **Lee Creek Campground:** 26 miles west of Lolo. 22 campsites. Drinking water.

MM 83.5: Lolo, Montana

South Fork Lolo Creek: For years I had disdained fishing Lolo Creek, knowing it was heavily fished and heavily dewatered. But then I learned of the South Fork of Lolo Creek. It is a beautiful creek and loaded with 7-12 inch trout after you hike up the trail a few miles. If you would like to visit the South Fork of Lolo Creek, turn west on Highway 12 in Lolo and travel 10.2 miles until you see the sign for Elk Meadow Road on the left. Follow Elk Meadow Road 2.4 miles until it forks.

Follow the signs to the South Fork Lolo Creek Trailhead, which is two miles to the left. When you cross the bridge, you are at the trailhead, but 1/10 of a mile down the creek is a parking and unloading zone. This spot is a picnicker's dream. Walk down the closed road a hundred yards to a field of daisy's and bluebells. I fell in love with this spot on the creek. When I was there July 19 the yarrow was in bloom as well as a number of other wild flowers. This beautiful creek is only 14.5 miles from Lolo, and it is perfect for children.

South Fork Fishing Saga

After huffing and puffing up through a series of switchbacks and then hacking my way down a steep canyon with downfall (an apt description), I was poised for my first cast at what looked like my only opportunity after such an arduous descent. The creek was raging, and I could see that it was still too early to wade up the creek and avoid the brush and downed lodge pole. Stepping into the creek, I made my first cast, and my faithful Labrador mistook the move for a crossing. Later I recalled reading about Jack London's dog Buck in Call of the Wild. In a demonstration of obedience, Buck almost plunges over a cliff.

Shadow is not nearly so dutiful; she is more on the impetuous side. And in she plunged at the worst place. Shocked, I stood powerless to help as she tumbled and glided through a series of falls and chutes. Swinging to the far side about 20 yards down the creek, she reminded me of an Olympian kayaker. She didn't whine, but her forlorn look and those droopy wet ears clearly communicated that we were separated, and she wanted me on her side of the "Creek of No-Return."

The far side provided three or four separate pockets to fish. In a space of forty yards I caught six fish, the largest a 12 inch German brown. I also landed a 10 rainbow and four very small cutthroats. Satisfied, I looked for a crossing, knowing I would be back later in the month when I could stay in the creek and have more freedom of movement. Shadow refused to cross at the spot I selected and subsequently lost considerable ground. Although it was less harrowing than her first crossing, I was still concerned for her. She appeared to shake both the water and the experience off as she lunged up the mountain with her faithful master huffing and puffing behind her. Up the mountain she would run and then back down to stop in front of me with tilted head. I couldn't tell if she was giving me a look of kindness or pity as I groped for every lodge pole in my reach.

Return to Highway 93

MM 83.9: Lolo Sewage Treatment Plant – River Access
Turn east on Glacier Road. A few blocks down Glacier Road, you will come to a T intersection in a residential neighborhood. Turn left and follow the road to the sewage plant where there is a day use park on the river. This is the logical exit point if you are floating down from the Florence Bridge or Chief Looking Glass Campground, but you have to drag or carry your raft or canoe up to the parking lot.

MM 87.1: River Access (Walk upstream)

MM 88.9: Blue Mountain Road: Blue Mountain Road follows the Bitterroot River until it intersects with the Clark Fork River. The first fishing access is Maclay Flat. Blue Mountain Road turns to the Southside Road that goes all the way to Petty Creek, which is an exit on Interstate 90. The road winds around the hillsides for miles. Sometimes it follows the Clark Fork River; at other times it follows the ridges far above the river. If you plan on wade fishing the lower Clark Fork, this is the road for you. It may also be accessed from Interstate 90 onto Reserve Street. Follow Reserve Street until you come to Mullan Road. (Perkin's Restaurant) Turn right on Mullan Road. Follow

Mullan Road until you come to Kona Bridge Road. Turn left on Kona Bridge Road until it intersects with Southside Road. Follow the signs to Deep Creek Shooting Range, and you will know you are on the right road. Past the turn off for Deep Creek is the Old Harper's Bridge, which is a take out point for floaters launching from Spurgin Road.

This area of the lower Clark Fork is a challenge for beginning fly fishermen as it has long stretches of flat water. The Clark Fork does not have high trout counts. What counts is knowing where they are. When you find one trout, you usually find a pod. I do not recommend this stretch for wade fishermen during the heat of August unless you are on the search for sippers. If it is an overcast day in August or September with the promise of some light showers, do not pass up the opportunity to fish the Clark Fork.

Highway 93 (Reserve Street to I 90 on ramp)
As you travel north on Reserve Street, you will cross South Avenue and then come to Spurgin Road. Spurgin Road Fishing Access is tucked behind a very affluent neighborhood. In fact, you drive right between two fenced homes to get to the day use fishing access. When you reach a T intersection, just turn right and then left again as Spurgin Road takes a jog. The access has a boat launch, but during dry years you will have to pull your boat down to the Bitterroot River where it joins the Clark Fork River.

Highway 93 from Missoula to Kalispell Continues on Page 37

Popular Float Trips on the Bitterroot River

Float Trip 1: West Fork of the Bitterroot: During the spring and early summer, this section can be dangerous. Check with one of the shops for the latest information.

Float Trip 2: Hannon Access (the bridge just south of the West Fork Road) to Wally Crawford (Como Bridge). By far this is the most heavily floated section, and yet the fishing is excellent. Plan a full day float or a short float to Darby Bridge.

Float Trip 3: Wally Crawford to Angler's Roost Campground. Be sure to register at Angler's Roost. Plan for a full day float, and be prepared to portage at Sleeping Child Dam.

Float Trip 4: Angler's Roost to Woodside (Corvallis Bridge). Be prepared for a sharp turn and a huge rock just above Hamilton's Main Street Bridge. Below the bridge you will have to portage around a diversion dam. If you go over it, unload your passengers on the right bank above the dam. After you float under the silver bridge south of town, the river forks to the left past Blodgett Park (an exit site) or to the right. The right channel gets very low late in the summer, and the left channel can be snaggy and dangerous during high water.

Float Trip 5: Corvallis Bridge to Tucker West. Stay in the left or west channel. This mid section of the river from Tucker West to Bell Crossing loses a great deal of water from late July on, which makes for slow floating and on low water years some boat dragging.

Float Trip 6: Bell Crossing to Stevensville, a full day float.

Float Trip 7: Stevensville to Florence. This is a very full day float if you fish hard. Plan on taking out after the cocktail hour.

Float Trip 8: Florence Bridge to Lolo Sewage Treatment Plant: This too is a very long float both in mileage and slow water. You may shave off a couple of miles by launching at Chief Looking Glass Campground. Keep in mind that you will have to portage your boat about 40 yards up a bank to the parking lot. Due to the warm summer water conditions, the fishing is generally poor until fall.

Bitterroot River Mileage Chart

The following mileage between access points is approximate calculations starting from Missoula and moving to Hannon Memorial south of Darby.

1. Maclay Bridge (Missoula - North Avenue) to Buckhouse Bridge (Missoula - Highway 93 **5.8 miles**
2. Buckhouse Bridge to Lolo Treatment plant **10.5 miles**
3. Lolo treatment plant to Chief Looking Glass **12.7 miles**
4. Chief Looking Glass to Florence Bridge **2.2 miles**
5. Florence Bridge to Stevensville Bridge **10.1 miles**
6. Stevensville Bridge to Bell Crossing Bridge **9.5 miles**

7. Bell Crossing to Victor Crossing
2.7 miles
8. Victor Crossing to Tucker Crossing
4.2 miles
9. Tucker Crossing to Woodside (Corvallis bridge)
4.8 miles
10. Woodside to Silver Bridge (Hamilton city limits)
3.1 miles
11. Silver bridge to Main Street Bridge
2.0 miles
12. Main Street Bridge to Angler's Roost
4.5 miles
(Ask for permission at Angler's Roost campground.)
13. Angler's Roost to Como Bridge
9.8 miles
14. Como Bridge to Old Darby Bridge (private)
6.3 miles
15. Old Darby Bridge to Hannon Memorial **3. 8 miles**

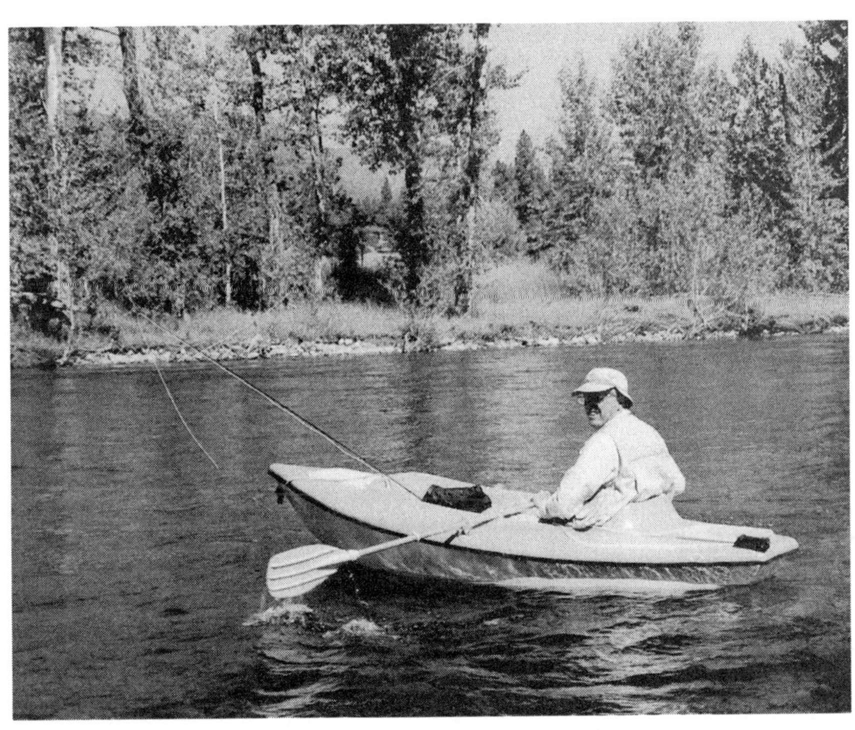

The author launching on the Bitterroot River at Angler's Roost.

Major Insect Hatches on the Bitterroot River

By Dave Odell

Spring Insects
March - April (progressive hatches)
#18-#22 gray, olive; chironomidae midge*
#18 black; Capnia stonefly
#14 gray; Nemoura stonefly
#10 golden gray; Skwala mayfly
#16-#20 blue-wing olive; Baetis mayfly*
#12 olive-brown; Ameletus mayfly * also hatches in the fall
April - May
#14-16 gray, brown; Brachycentrus caddisfly

Summer Insects
May - June
#14 yellow; Isoperla stonefly (mid May through mid July)
#4- #6 orange; Pteronarcys Salmon Fly
June - July
#6 big golden; Perlidae stonefly
#10-12 golden; Pteronarcella stonefly
#12 green, gray; Ephemerella mayfly
#12- #18 gray, brown; Hydropsychidae caddisfly
July - August
#14 sulfer cream; Ephemererlla mayfly
#12-#16 light cahill; Heptagenia mayfly
#14-#16 orange-butt yellow; Isoperla stonefly
August - September
#12 golden tan; spruce moth
#4-#16 many colors -- hoppers, crickets, ants
Fall Insects
#18-#20 white wing black; Tricorythodes mayfly
#10 rusty green; Emphemerella Hecuba mayfly
#12-#14 brown; Rhithrogena mayfly
#10 gray; Isonychia mayfly
#8 orange; Limnephilidae caddisfly
#12 chocolate brown; Paraleptophlebia mayfly
#4 blue; Anisoptera dragonfly

Hatch chart compiled by Dave Odell 1984

Dave Odell is a fly fishing outfitter and fisheries consultant who may be reached at home at 2742 Alpenglow Road, Stevensville, Montana 59870
Phone (406) 777-3421 Toll Free 1-800-484-9539-8884

Saga: Biking for Beatitudes and Beauties

August 13,1997, I replaced a flat tire on my mountain bike and cleaned out the saddlebags of old candy wrappers from a previous trek taken a number of years ago when I bought the bike as a way to keep in shape. I waited all morning gauging the rain clouds over the Bitterroot Range. Finally, after pumping up the tire and my confidence, I decided it was now or never. I started up the Fred Burr Reservoir Trail at 11:40. At 11:42 I was walking. The entire trip, with intermittent riding, took an hour and forty minutes.

I had only gone a short distance when my seat dropped, my knees pushed up to my chin, and I was soaked. My raincoat was tucked in my saddlebags, and I was hot and panting. Shadow's tongue was still concealed as she kept turning back waiting for me. Reluctantly, I put on the raincoat that I have been trying to wear out for seventeen years so I can buy a Gore-Tex model. The coat was bought at a ranch supply store in Bozeman. Made from rubberized canvas, it is destined to be a real Montana heirloom.

Huffing and puffing, my resolve weakened and I thought of locking the bike to a tree using my combination lock chain that I could not recall ever using. Did I use my birthday numbers, my social security numbers or part of my telephone number? I gave up trying to remember. My mantra became, "Rolling, rolling, rolling down a river." Finally I arrived. It was pouring, and I huddled under a tree that a group of men and boys vacated just as I arrived. They too were soaked. They informed me the fishing was lousy and headed on down the trail. Shadow and I shared a ham sandwich, and then I hiked to the back of the lake up the trail to fish the upper portion of the creek. In spite of the rain and fogged up glasses, I caught a number of colorful cutthroats from 8-10 inches. I made a few sloppy casts on the lake on my way back, and then I headed back down the trail, pleased with the beauty of the lake and the fun fishing I experienced.

Grasping the handle bars of my mountain bike, I prepared myself for the ride down the trail. I turned my thoughts to Kiddo, a childhood friend who I had thought of for the first time in probably thirty-five years on my way up the trail. As I pushed my bike up the trail earlier, my sweating brow and the long haul reminded me of Turnbow Canyon Road and a summer day in 1957. After visiting half a dozen second hand stores, I found my treasure, a twenty-year-old beat-up baby buggy. I had promised Kiddo the adventure of his life, a soap-box ride from the top of Three Palms down to the valley floor.

Dismantling the buggy, I had the best ball bearing wheels and axles that money could buy, short of buying the official SoapBox Derby wheels which only rich families could afford. We built the racer with the axle cut and mounted on a wide two-by-four with a large bolt in the center. The back axle was only about two feet wide. Our steering was a hemp rope nailed to the front two-by-four with a couple of old, rusty nails. We pulled the racer up through the canyon for over six hours, stopping only to eat our lunches.

Reaching the top of the canyon divide, we could see the three palms above us gently swaying from the afternoon Santa Anna breeze. Off into the distance, we could see square miles of carefully laid out orange groves. Kiddo was a new friend. After his father died and his older brother was jailed, his mother packed up her family and moved to the country. Kiddo looked tough for a fifth grader. He wore a ducktail haircut that I admired greatly. He wore peggers, all of which my mother disapproved. But my mother encouraged the friendship as she saw a very gentle and kind young man hidden behind the gang look of the fifties. Kiddo rarely laughed.

When we shoved off and began to pick up speed down the canyon, Kiddo laughed with gusto. We both began shrieking and whooping with reckless abandon, and reckless it was. Our makeshift brake broke on one of the first turns. We had passed the point of stopping, reaching speeds that I would have to guess was in excess of 40 miles per hour. Our laughter quickly subsided, replaced by white knuckles and quick maneuvering on hairpin turns. Suddenly, coming around a bend, we were faced with a sedan right in front of us traveling down hill. I had a quick decision to make -- shoot off the cliff like a Stinger missile, be decapitated by a 1948 Packer or pass on a blind curve.

I attribute that reckless moment as part of my rite of passage. In the split second that I jammed my right leg forward to turn the axle, I knew the fear that all parents harbor for their sons. After I shot through the blind corner, Kiddo and I laughed hysterically. Kiddo's laughter was from turning to look at the old lady's expression; mine was initiated from a vision of death as the tears streaked from the corner of my eyes. Three miles down Turnbow Canyon Road, we lost a wheel. Kiddo shifted and two blocks later we crashed into a curb and were thrown into an orange grove. Bruised and dirty, we looked at each other and began laughing again. It was cool under the shade of that orange tree, and we lay on our backs for a long time just laughing.

Kiddo's mother, after losing her next eldest son to insanity, packed up her fragile family and moved to her rural hometown in Kansas. Two years later I received a report of Kiddo's death when he was thrown from the back of a pick-up truck on a Kansas farm road.

I pushed off on my mountain bike and thought, I still remember you, Kiddo. The return trip took 50 minutes.

Missoula Area Fishing

Highway 93 runs south to north and intersects in Missoula with Interstate 90 which runs east to west. Before I continue with the fishing and camping prospects on Highway 93 north of Missoula, let me guide you through the Missoula area and all of its wonderful fishing opportunities on the Clark Fork, Rock Creek, the Blackfoot drainage and the Seeley-Swan area. Highway 93 north of Missoula continues on page 38.

The Clark Fork River above and below Missoula:

Interstate 90 From St. Regis to Butte

Like the famous Muhammad Ali match with George Foreman, the Clark Fork of the Columbia has been up against the ropes, pummeled and battered by powerful forces, for over a hundred years. Designated as one of the largest Super Fund clean-up sites in the nation, the Clark Fork vies for the title of the comeback kid with the likes of Ali and Rocky Balboa. After a hundred years of mine waste discharge and heavy metal accumulation at the Milltown Dam, the river has yet to be declared champ, but the restoration and rejuvenation of the Upper Clark Fork has been stupendous. With fish counts at zero in the late '60s in the Warm Springs area and reaching over a 1,000 per mile 10 years later and almost doubling again, the brown trout population has attracted a great deal of angling pressure. From Warm Springs to Rock Creek the river varies considerably in the number of trout per mile due in part to thermal seepage, irrigation, years of drought, algae blooms and the insidious presence of Whirling Disease.

But the good news is that the river from Missoula's Kelly Island to the confluence of the Flathead River continually improves. Fish, Wildlife and Parks Biologist Rod Berg estimates on average about 600 rainbows per mile with the larger 18-20" fish in the Superior and St.Regis area. Beware of the Alberton Gorge just below the town of Alberton and extending for approximately 18 miles to Forest Grove.

Lewis and Clark were warned, and if you haven't already heard of this section, consider it the playground of experienced whitewater rafters and kayakers. During my first year of guiding in 1981 for Grove Hull, he came back jubilant from a fishing adventure in the gorge with an experienced whitewater oarsman. Constantly trying to balance himself and cast without being thrown out, he had one of those great bragging days on the river. When he suggested I join him, I quickly responded, "Your boat!" No deal he said. To this day I have never wanted to risk my raft or my life fishing the canyon. Those big rainbows would just be too distracting.

Popular Clark Fork River Float Trips

Float Trip 1 & 2: Beavertail State Park to Clinton and Clinton to Turah

Fishing the Clark Fork from Beavertail State Park past Rock Creek and finishing at the Schwartz Creek Bridge outside of Clinton has declined in the last number of years; however, given the right conditions this section can be outstanding during the Salmon Fly hatch as the hatch moves up Rock Creek. It is a long float trip, and it offers great scenery, albeit fair fishing. The section from Clinton to Turah is similar. The Turah takeout is a state campground, and right across the street from this campground is the Turah store and campground. Do not float past Turah, as there is no take-out from that point down to the Milltown Dam. Wade fishermen will find the Schwartz Creek access a better access point for hiking up and down the river.

Float Trip 3: Spurgin Road to Old Harper's Bridge

Missoula's first launching place is at the access on Spurgin Road. Don't be surprised when you drive through a very wealthy neighborhood and drive right between two houses. Fortunately, the access was in place before the developers plotted out the neighborhood. Take Reserve Street and turn west on South Avenue. Turn right on Clements Lane, and then turn immediately left again on Spurgin Road. Late summer during drought years, the small side channel drops really low, and quite often you must drag your raft through the shallows a short distance to the Bitterroot River. A hundred yards downstream the Clarkfork meets the Bitterroot. The takeout point for smaller craft such as canoes can be the Kona Bridge. Typically, however, floaters take out on the left side of the old Harper's Bridge.

Float Trip 4: Harper's Bridge to Huson (Interstate 90, Exit 85 is approximately 16 miles from the Reserve Street on-ramp.

Float Trip 5: Huson (Interstate 90 exit) To Petty Creek

Leave Interstate 90 at Exit 85. Take the service road that runs west along side the interstate. This is an excellent walk-in area, especially in the fall. It is also a rough take-out for floaters floating downstream from the old Harper's Bridge. Floaters may also launch from this spot and float down to Petty Creek.

Petty Creek (Exit 77 -- 24 miles from the Reserve Street on-ramp). Petty Creek is a very small creek with very small fish. However, wade fishing is excellent on the Clark Fork above Petty Creek.

Interstate 90 from Idaho Border to Rock Creek

MM 0: Idaho Border

Exit 22: Cabin City Campground: Exit 22 at Henderson. Travel east 2.5 miles on Camel's Hump Road 22148. Turn left (west) at the Cabin City Campground sign on Twelve Mile Creek Road 353 for 0.2 miles.

Exit 26: Ward Creek Road: Follow Ward Creek Road (Road 889). The road is a single lane road with very few turnouts. The creek is very small and almost impenetrable, although it does hold small brookies. From the I-90 exit to the **Hazel Lake** trailhead is 6.6 miles, and the trail to Hazel Lake is 3.2 miles for small cutthroats.

Exit 30: Two Mile Road Fishing Access

Exit 33: St. Regis, Montana / The Lower Clark Fork River

When you exit the Interstate 90, *Clark Fork Trout & Tackle* is right in front of you. Operated by a young couple, Brooks and Jackie Sanford, the store offers guided float trips, shuttle service, fishing tackle and daily fishing reports. During my tenure as a guide in western Montana, the furthest I had ever floated and fished the Clark Fork was from Forest Grove down to Superior, and those trips were few and far between. I found Brooks and Jackie to be both knowledgeable and enthusiastic about the fishing in their area. Brooks said, "The lower Clark Fork has excellent pre-season fishing in March and April, but in typical years the fishing doesn't get good again until mid July."

Brooks recommended using Woolly Buggers and Bitch Creeks in the spring along the lower St. Regis River as the browns follow the spring spawners to feed on the egg deposits. The opening day for the St. Regis River is the third Saturday in May. When I asked about the St. Regis River in general, Brooks said, "The river gets scoured every year. The best fishing is in the first two miles, and I wouldn't fish any further up than four miles except during spring and fall spawning runs up to about 12-Mile Creek." Pre-season flies include Skwala stonefly March 15- May 15; Gray Drakes (Amoletus) April 1-June 15; Blue winged olives April 1 –June 1; Nemoura Stonefly March 1 – April 30 and March Brown March 25-April 30.

Most of the locals are spin fishermen and favor black Panther Martin's and black Mepps. During mid summer Brooks and Jackie prefer floating from St. Regis as far down as the 14-Mile Bridge. Brooks recommends a caddis pattern in the evening until mid August as well as a Parachute Hopper right into September. September through October they recommend a Blue Wing Olive and the October Caddis. Brooks said the local guide's favorites are the Royal Wulff and the Madam X. As the water drops later in the summer to around 9,000 CFS, the fish in the Superior to St. Regis area tend to pod together as the water drops, providing an opportunity for some great fishing. In the late summer and fall, Brook and Jackie also recommend hoppers Slate-Wing Olives and Mahogany Duns. When I pressed Jackie for her favorite local lakes that could be reached by driving or a short hike, she said that there were a lot to choose from, but her favorites were Moore Lake, Diamond Lake and Cliff Lake.

Moore Lake / Little Joe Creek: Follow the main street in St. Regis .05 miles west. Turn left when you see the sign South Fork Little Joe Creek and Moore Lake. The mileage to Moor Lake is 14 miles, and this is the only sign to Moore Lake you will see again until you are zig-zagging up Road 221. (If you miss Road 221 you will wander like I did to the top of the pass and the Idaho State Line.) Turning at the sign just outside of St. Regis, the road will cross over the Interstate and St. Regis River. The road turns to gravel, but it is well maintained. At 3.3 miles there is a camping spot and an access to Road 221. Turn left on Road 221. The road follows the creek and is one lane and bumpy at times, although you don't need a 4x4. Follow this road 6.9 miles until the road makes a turn to the right. (The second Moore Lake sign). The lake is 3.4 miles from the sign. Moore Lake has a turn around and an outhouse. The lake is 200 yards from the parking area and does not have any campsites. Nestled in a tight bowl, this 13-acre sub-alpine lake offers good fishing for 8-12 inch brook trout.

Little Joe Creek is a very small creek, but up in the canyon on the way to Moore Lake the creeks is backed up by many downfalls, providing little pools for small brook trout and cutthroats.

Exit 43: Diamond Lake / Cliff Lake: Heading eastbound take Exit 43 off Interstate 90. Turn right at the stop sign, and proceed over the railroad tracks. Continue .07 of a mile and turn right on Road 342. The lake is 13 miles. Four miles from the lake, you will make a left turn at a T intersection. Diamond Lake Campground is suitable only for tent camping. The road is a one lane, steep climb suitable for cars. Diamond Lake is a popular spot, as it is one of only a few lakes reached by road in the area. It is a 17-acre, deep lake in heavily timbered country, and it is full of small brookies. To define small, I fished the lake with a father and son from Maine. We dragged and carried three of my one-man boats about 200 yards before we could launch them. (The campsite end of the lake is jammed with logs so if you plan on launching a canoe, plan on a portage.) In the space of two hours, Tom and Lincoln and myself managed to catch only 15 fish between us. Not one measured over nine inches. Much larger than Diamond Lake, Cliff Lake is reached 1.5 miles up the trail from Diamond Lake. The lake reportedly has 14 inch cutthroats. I spoke to two fishermen coming down the trail, and they said they couldn't even cast from the shore because of the cliffs and the debris and half-sunken logs surrounding the lake. Eager to float the Clark Fork that same day, we passed up the hike.

Exit 43: Dry Creek Road (Camping and Fishing Access) After you exit the Interstate, you will come to a T intersection. Turn right for the boat launch and turn left 3.2 miles for **Slowey Campground**. The campground is right on the water with numerous campsites adjacent to the river. This would make a nice destination for a short evening fishing trip from Superior. Slowey offers 16 campsites plus 10 trailer pull-through sites as well as horse camp facilities, cold drinking water, and a canoe or raft launch. (See information on Diamond Lake and Cliff Lake above.)

Exit 47: Superior, Montana / Fishing Access: Cross the bridge and make a right turn. Head east one mile to the Big Eddy Fishing Access. **Trout Creek Campground:** 7 miles southwest of Superior on Trout Creek Road #257. 12 campsites. Drinking water. No garbage facilities.

Exit 55: Floaters wishing to float down to Superior will find access points along the access road, but most of them require sliding your raft down an embankment.

Exit 58: Quartz Creek Campground: (USFS) Quartz Creek Campground is divided by the Interstate although there is a tunnel joining the two loops. Popular with travelers and white water rafters, loop C has access to the river. 52 campsites. Cold drinking water. Flush toilets. Waste disposal site. U.S. Fee Area.

Exit 61: Tarkio Fishing Access: The fishing access is a popular whitewater boat launch one mile from the Interstate 90 exit. The access provides toilet facilities and long stretches above and below the access for wade fishermen.

Exit 66: Fish Creek: Fish Creek empties into the Clark Fork. From the Reserve Street on-ramp, Fish Creek is 35 miles due west. Take Exit 66 off of Interstate 90. Take a right turn to Rivulet if you want to fish the creek from the confluence up stream. Spin fishers and fly fishers heavily fish this section. Deep pools and heavy pressure keep the trout very wary and shy. Nonetheless, what it lacks in numbers, it can make up for in the size of the fish. In the first half mile of the creek, I caught only three fish on a hot August day, but one of the fish measured 16 inches and jumped eye-level to me three times.

Further up the creek the water is flat and shallow and heavily fished as the road parallels the creek. Years ago I used to take my sons to Fish Creek early in the summer for good catches of 8-10 inch trout, and having talked to three high school students from Huson, not much has changed with the exception of some crafty bull trout which makes Fish Creek very fishy!

If you fish the lower section, you might as well make a day of it and fish the Clark Fork as well. Continue the four miles to Rivulet, which is a railroad spur with two houses. Just above the two houses the river offers a half a mile of riffles with large side pools. You will have to slide on your butt down to the river through a lot of brush. Take a lunch and keep an eye on the pools.

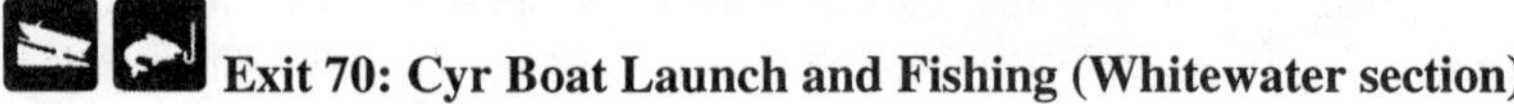

Exit 70: Cyr Boat Launch and Fishing (Whitewater section)

Exit 72: Fishing access (east bound only)

Exit 75: Alberton, Montana (Fishing access)

Exit 77: Petty Creek: Petty Creek is really not worth fishing, although there is some great fishing access to the Clark Fork River above the creek.

Exit 82: Nine Mile Road: The upper stretches of Nine Mile Creek offer some nice camping sites, but the creek is not worth fishing, and the lower stretches of the creek pass through private property.

Exit 85: Huson, Montana (Fishing access / boat "launch")

Exit 89: Frenchtown, Montana

Exit 96: Highway 93 North to Flathead Lake
Exit 99: Missoula Airport
Exit 102: Reserve Street Exit – Missoula, Montana

Exit 104: Orange Street Exit - Missoula

Exit 105: Van Buren Street / Rattlesnake Creek: Here is a great creek right outside of the city limits, but you need to be prepared to walk about six miles before you can wet a line in the catch and release section. The creek is closed to fishing from the city water supply dam of Mountain Water Company up the creek to the mouth of Beeskove Creek, which is a distance of about six miles from the parking lot to Beeskove Creek. But what a spectacular hike! The trail is a popular trail for both hikers and mountain bikers entering the Rattlesnake Wilderness. Wait until at least mid July if you plan on fishing for pure strain Western cutthroat. From Beeskove Creek all the way up to the headwaters is catch and release fishing. If you have a bike, go all the way to the footbridge and fish above and below the bridge for 7-12 inch beauties. Van Buren changes to Rattlesnake Drive. Follow the Rattlesnake Wilderness signs.

(The lower section of Rattlesnake Creek below the city water supply site to the mouth is open to fishing. Be sure to check the regulations.)

Exit 107: East Missoula, Montana

Exit 110: Junction Highway 200 / Blackfoot River (Read about the Blackfoot River drainage on page 111.)

Exit 113: Turrah, Montana: Fishing Access / Boat exit

Exit 121: Clinton, Montana: Fishing Access / Boat launch

Exit 126: Rock Creek: Rock Creek is probably the most famous creek in western Montana. It is a 20-minute drive from Missoula traveling east on Interstate 90. **Norton Campground:** Follow Rock Creek Road eleven miles south of I-90 on Rock Creek Road. 10 campsites. Drinking water from hand pump, toilet facilities. **Dalles Campground:** 14.5 miles from I-90. 10 campsites. Drinking water from hand pump. **Harry's Flat Campground:** 17 miles south from I-90. 18 campsites. Drinking water from hand pump. **Bitterroot Flat Campground:** 23 miles from I-90. 15 campsites. Drinking water from hand pump. **Sira Campground:** 28 miles from I-90. Four campsites. No drinking water.

Nymphing on Rock Creek for Bigger and Better Returns

By Doug Persico

Western Montana fly fishers overwhelmingly rate Rock Creek as their favorite dry fly stream. Generating legendary hatches, this quintessential stream offers riffles, pools, long runs and deep holes. Best of all, it is the perfect size to wade and cast, especially to rising fish. Except for a fairly brief period in the spring during the spring runoff, the stream can be waded almost anywhere along its 50 odd miles, and it is almost never crowded compared to the more fabled waters of the Yellowstone Park area.

However, if a fisherman were to consider Rock Creek as only a dry fly stream, he or she would be missing the best fishing opportunity Rock Creek has to offer. Rock Creek nymph fishing exceeds its reputation as a classic dry fly fishery. Nymphing produces consistently bigger fish and greater numbers of fish. Best of all, nymph-fishing produces during those times when there is no dry fly-fishing.

Techniques:

Dead drifting a nymph on the bottom and fishing a nymph on or near the surface, either by itself or in tandem with another fly, are the two most productive methods of nymph fishing. Dead drifting simply means figuring out where the fish are holding on the bottom, weighting either the fly or the leader enough to get the fly down to where the fish are, and drifting the fly through the holding water until a fish takes it. Recognizing the take and setting the hook follow. Sounds simple, right? It is until you consider such questions as how do you know if you are deep enough, and how do you recognize the take.

The answer to the first question is easy. If you are getting hung up on the bottom and losing an occasional fly, you're deep enough. To answer the second question opens up one of the big debates currently in fly fishing -- are strike indicators nothing more than bobbers and an open acknowledgment that the fly fisher hasn't mastered his craft?

Most of my customers use strike indicators to recognize takes when dead drifting a nymph. Strike indicators are simply something the angler can see under any condition. They are attached to the leader far enough away from the fly so that they can be seen on the surface as the fly drifts on or near the bottom. The strike indicator telegraphs to the fisherman the fact that the nymph is no longer drifting. The angler must then quickly set the hook before the fish spits the fly out. Strike indicators are a valuable aid to increase productivity. As a fly shop owner, I make and sell indicators, and I consider them a valuable source of revenue for the shop.

The other method of nymphing used most often on Rock Creek is fishing a nymph unweighted either as a wet fly on the swing or as a trailer to a dry fly. To fish a nymph on the swing, simply cast across the current and start stripping line slowly in as the fly starts swinging below you. In most cases the fish will hook itself.

A technique that is becoming increasingly popular is to fish an emerger imitation in tandem with a dry fly during the hatches. A section of tippet is attached to the bend of a dry fly hook. The tippet section is from 16 - 18 inches long, and an emerger nymph is attached. The dry is drifted and catches fish in its own right as well as acting as a strike indicator for the trailing nymph. This method is proving itself deadly and increases in popularity every year.

Fly Patterns:

Just as there are a number of techniques that work on Rock Creek, there are a number of patterns that seem to work well. Some patterns work well all the time, and some work best during a particular time of year. If I were limited to just one pattern and size of nymph to use on Rock Creek all year long, that pattern would be a size 10 Prince, with or without a bead head. For some reason known only to the trout, this pattern works any time of year. Other patterns will work better than a Prince at various times, but day in and day out during the entire year, a size 10 Prince will always produce fish.

During the winter the fish are not very active, but when the weather is warm and sunny enough, and there is no slush ice floating down the creek, a dark stonefly dead drifted through the deep holes can produce some big browns. I sell more Kauffman and Brookes' stoneflies in sizes 4 and 6 than all other patterns combined.

During the latter part of March, Skwala stoneflies and Western March Browns start to hatch. This is the time to dead drift smaller stone fly patterns for the Skwala and size 14 Pheasant Tails for the March Browns. It is also the time to trail a crippled March Brown emerger behind a dry fly. We have particularly good results sinking a Quigley Cripple in the surface film behind a size 14 Parachute Adams or even a size 10 Skwala Stimulator. For a lot of locals, this time of the year is their favorite. I know that this is my favorite time of year to fish dries on Rock Creek, as long as I can trail the emerging nymph behind them.

Once the Skwala and March Brown hatches are over, we begin the countdown to the Salmon Fly. This hatch is easily the best known in the state, since it occurs in a lot of our major streams. I consider Rock Creek's hatch to be at least as good as any in the state. However, to a dedicated nympher, the hatch itself is less important than the weeks preceding it. During this time there are Caddis emerging. Dry attractor patterns are fooling some good trout, but the nymph fisherman knows that the major story is being told on the stream bottom where both the Salmon Fly and Golden Stone nymphs are preparing for their destiny.

Both of these stonefly species hatch on land. When the time is right, the nymphs wiggle out of the water, split their cases, and the adults emerge from the cases and climb onto bushes near the stream banks, which is where they will spend the major part of their adult lives. Prior to this momentous event, the stonefly larva have been moving around the stream bottom. The trout, of course, are not indifferent to this movement since the larva of the various stoneflies is a major part of their diet. As the date for their hatching gets closer, the larva migrate closer to the stream bank. Finally, on the appointed day, out they come.

Not all stoneflies hatch on the same day. The hatch is progressive. It starts near the mouth of the creek and progresses several miles upstream from where the insects are actually hatching. I dead drift a big black nymph as close to the bank as I can get it. Anyway, I used to fish like that. Since opening a fly shop, my outings during the stonefly season have been few and far between. I have sold a lot of large black nymphs, however.

After the stoneflies are done, Rock Creek settles into its summer pattern. The primary hatches are caddis and Pale Morning Duns. This is the premier time to fish emerging nymphs just under the surface, trailing behind a high floating dry. Sparkle Duns and Quigleys work extremely well for PMDs and Sparkle Pupas are devastating in the evenings as caddis imitations. For those anglers who like the bottom, Gold Ribbed Hares Ears, Pheasant Tails and the ever-present Prince, either with or without bead heads, will almost always take fish.

As the season starts to wind down, the hatches change. Late August brings the Blue Winged Olive and the beginning of the Giant Orange Caddis. Fishing the olives is pretty much like fishing the PMDs. Small Pheasant Tails do a good job on the bottom, and olive Sparkle Duns in the surface film can be killers.

But the real star of the fall on Rock Creek is the big orange caddis. This guy is big with a body almost two inches long. If you want to see the adult, they will be on the water in the evening although not in large numbers. My personal experience with this insect, at least as a dry, has been frustrating. I can count on one hand the number of fish I have taken on dry imitations of this caddis.

A couple of years ago I began experimenting with different nymph patterns to try and imitate the insect. After a lot of false starts, I came up with a size 8 Serendipity. This is perhaps the simplest caddis nymph there is, but it has proved to be absolute dynamite on Rock Creek in the fall. It can be dead drifted on the bottom for big browns or fished as a wet fly to imitate an ovipositing caddis. In either case, we've had a lot of success with the pattern.

The orange caddis stays with us until the snow starts to fly. As soon as the ice and snow start to build up on the banks, both the trout and the anglers seem to go into hibernation. The cycle has been completed, and we are back into the stone fly larva on the bottom we started with. If you're planning to fish Rock Creek at any time during the year, the techniques and patterns discussed here should help to make your experience more enjoyable. Even if you're a dryfly bigot, remember that there will be times when there is no dry fly fishing. And if you're going to fish and want to catch something other than a cold, you're going to have to go under the surface. And when you do, you will be surprised both by how challenging it is and by how rewarding it is.

About the author: Doug Persico is the owner of Rock Creek Fisherman's Mercantile located at 15995 Rock Creek Road, Clinton, MT 59825
Phone: (406) 825-6440 Exit Interstate 90 at Exit 126.

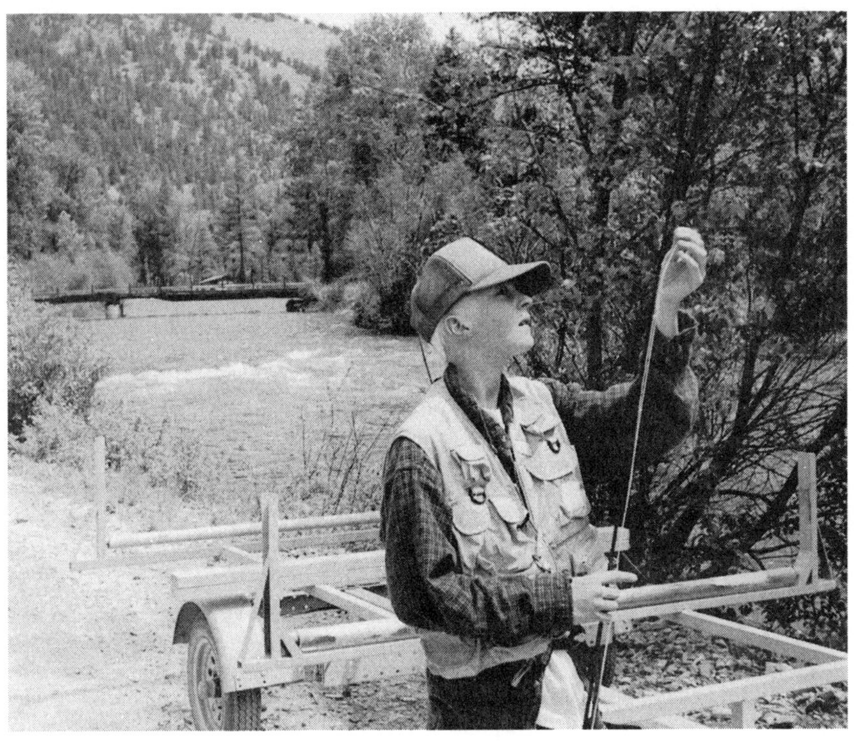

Rock Creek, 20-miles up and the Salmon Flies are on the water.

The Blackfoot River

Highway 200 from the intersection with Interstate 90 at Bonnor past the town of Ovando

During the early '80s I got a call from one of the longest tenured guides in western Montana. He asked me if I had guided much on the Blackfoot River. I was honest in telling him I had never floated the Big Blackfoot. "It doesn't matter," he countered. "I need three boats for a scenic float trip. Only one member of the group will fish, and he will be in my boat. You get the women and kids." The next morning I backed up my trailer close to the ramp and waited my turn. Looking down the 30-foot ramp to the beach and the boulder-strewn river, I took a deep breath.

Fred had confidence in me as a rower and guide because we had worked together on the Bitterroot River and Rock Creek, and he knew of my guiding experience in Wyoming. Sauntering up to me as I gazed down the river, he slapped me on the back and said, "Don't screw up. The river is more dangerous now than it was a few weeks ago. Now you have to do a whole lot of dodging and fancy oar work. You're going to earn your pay today."

We had talked about the rock garden on the Green River in Wyoming, which we had both floated through, but I was not prepared for the Big Blackfoot's Rock Garden. Inexperienced rafters should shun the stretch from Roundup to River Bend Campground and from Russell Gates Campground down to Roundup. After the spring run-off is over, the Rock Garden will challenge any oarsman, but particularly the oarsman who must both navigate the river safely as well as aligning the boat for those passengers who want to cast. The rocks come at you so fast that you can scarcely decide which way to turn, and once you make the decision of which way to turn, you immediately have to start another maneuver. As each season passed I prided myself inwardly about never touching a rock, but on every one of those days I was bone-shoulder weary at the end of the day as I approached 50.

The Blackfoot River has steadily improved as a fishery during the last decade thanks to the concerted efforts of environmentalists, ranchers and local members of Trout Unlimited. Popularized by Norman McLean's novel, *A River Runs Through It,* the Blackfoot's real legacy is that it is host to two of Montana's native salmonids, the westslope cutthroat and the bull trout. Although restrictions exist for purposely fishing for bulls, the river is rich in trophy size browns and hefty rainbows and cutthroats in the 14 to 17 inch range. Although the river is approximately 130 miles long, the best fishing stretches start at Ovando down to the confluence with the Clark Fork River at Bonnor.

Cottonwood Creek -- Mileage Marker 37.9

Spanning 26 miles, the Blackfoot River Recreation Corridor provides both picnicking and camping at 13 locations. Both improved and unimproved camping spots exist all up and down the Blackfoot River. For the camper who wants to fish with younger children, I would recommend the unimproved campground at River Junction on the North Fork of the Blackfoot. Regardless of which campground you select, the beauty of the Blackfoot River overwhelms the first time visitor. Carving its way through the canyon, the river floats by 100-foot cliffs. Ocher in color the tinted shades and moss-lined shadows make the Blackfoot one of the most scenic rivers in Montana, as well as offering great fishing.

Blackfoot River

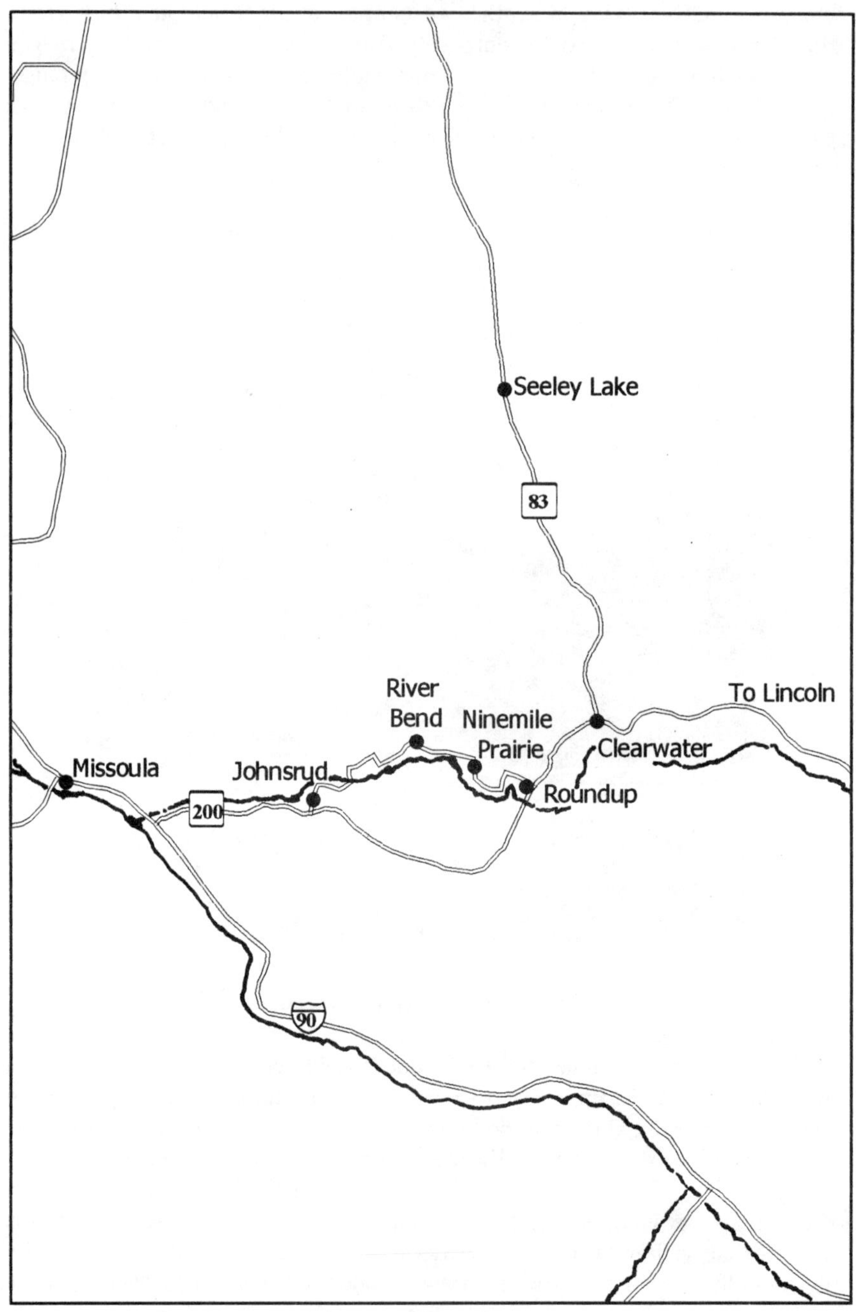

The Blackfoot River – Mileage Markers

Highway 200 from the intersection with Interstate 90 at Bonnor to the town of Ovando

Mileage Marker 0: Exxon Travel Plaza (Mill Town) – Exit from Interstate 90 onto Highway 200

MM 1: Access: dirt pull-out

MM 2: Marco Flats: Marco Flats is easy to miss as it takes a sharp turn backwards and drops to the river.

MM 6: Angelvine Park – A nice rest stop if you are pulling a trailer.

MM 8 - A narrow gravel pull out with no turn around area for trailers or large rigs, short trail to river; MM 8+ pull-over with a drop off to the river.

MM 9: Gold Creek: Follow Gold Creek Road seven miles up the mountain to the first unimproved campsite. I do not recommend this road or the campsite for trailers as the actual camping spots are off the main road, and they are rough and rutted. Surrounded by grassy meadows, the creek is ideal for children and families who want to rough it. Keep in mind that this is a "Pack it in – pack it out!" area. The area is owned by Plum Creek, and it is sad to see how slovenly some campers are. If you wish to access the creek lower down, make a right turn just short of the 2-mile marker. Follow the road 2.8 miles until you reach a small bridge. Park by the bridge as the road that angles up along the creek is blocked a mile up the canyon and there is no turning around. The canyon is excellent fishing for small cutthroats.

MM 10: Blackfoot Recreation Corridor: Thanks to the cooperative efforts of land owners and the Department of Fish, Wildlife and Parks, a 26-mile corridor has been made available to recreationists. Johnsrud Park offers camping, picnicking, swimming and an excellent take-out for floaters who launched at Roundup at the Nine-Mile Prairie Road exit. **Floaters Warning:** The section from Johnsrud Park all the way up to Roundup is interspersed with dangerous rapids. You may follow the Blackfoot River on an 18.2-mile dirt road that will swing around and rejoin Highway 200 at Roundup, which is the next highway crossing of the Blackfoot River. The road is narrow at times and very bumpy, and as such it is not safe traveling for a camping trailer. Throughout the course of this road there are numerous day-use access points. The two campgrounds, Ninemile Prairie and River Bend, are best reached just short of mileage marker

27 as you cross the bridge at Roundup. Launching a raft or drift boat at Roundup requires use of a 30-foot ramp down to the water's edge.

MM 22: Garnet Ghost Town: The last remnants of this bustling ghost town have been preserved in its original state of natural decay. From the highway, take the Garnet Road 11 miles. For more information call (406) 329-3914.

MM 26.5: Roundup: Just as you cross the bridge, you will note a 30-foot ramp for launching rafts on this popular stretch of the Blackfoot. Most rafters take out at River Bend campground or Whitaker Bridge, which is about 9.5 miles.

MM 31:Clearwater River: The Clearwater River access is a park like setting and offers good access for fishermen. Fishing is excellent in the spring as the river is clear. From this crossing the Clearwater offers a short float trip or canoe trip to the Blackfoot. Floaters will drift under safety fence partitions. This is a popular run for summer tubers.

Clearwater Junction: Highway 200 intersects with Highway 83 to Seeley Lake.

MM 35: Russell Gates Campground: The campground is right off the highway on the river's edge, and it is a popular floating take-out.

MM 37.9: Upsata Lake & Cottonwood Creek: Exit on Woodsworth Road. 1.4 miles from the highway turn left at the Blackfoot Clearwater Game Range. Drive one mile to the bridge on Cottonwood Creek by the fish and game house and barn. Fish upstream or down, but be prepared to navigate through heavy brush. The creek hosts small cuts and surprisingly hefty browns in those tough-to-fish willow over-hangs. A couple of miles up from the Cottonwood Creek access, Woodworth Road leads you to Upsata Lake. Upsata is a small, shallow lake bordered mostly by private property in pothole country. Periodically stocked, the lake produces fair fishing for smaller rainbows. If you have a canoe strapped on top of your rig, this would be a good choice for some evening casting and paddling. Woodsworth Road turns to the left towards Kozy Corner and then continues to Highway 83 by Salmon Lake.

MM 39: River Junction Campground & Scotty Brown Bridge: Follow the access road a short distance to the Scotty Brown Bridge. The landowner forbids any launching of watercraft from his property; however, he has provided four parking spaces for wade fishermen. Be sure to respect the rights of property owners and stay below the high water mark. River Junction

Campground is one of the most beautiful, unimproved campgrounds in the area and provides an opportunity to fish both the main stem of the Blackfoot River and the North Fork. The road to the campground is approximately nine miles, and it is not recommended for trailers.

MM 40: Monture Creek Campground: Monture Creek Campground is a small campground at the bottom of a ravine just off of the highway. The campground is mowed and the campsites sit on the waters edged surrounded by trees and wild roses. Monture Creek is usually fast and clear in the early summer and provides fair fishing down to the mouth of the Blackfoot River for spawning stragglers. By mid summer the creek warms up and the trout look for small pools to hide in. Look for the access road further down the highway for the 12-mile drive to the headwaters. Although the creek fishes well for small fry, be prepared to scramble and climb through brush and downed timber in its upper reaches.

Ovando: A short distance up the highway from Monture Creek Campground, the small town of Ovando rests on the hillside overlooking the highway. A cluster of homes, Ovando offers a small store, an inn, a trading post, a brand museum and a post office. (On a knoll just off the highway above Ovando, stop in at Trixie's Bar and Grill for a great hamburger.) From Ovando follow the road 3.5 miles to the **Harry Morgan Campground**, which is a popular launching place for floaters. The campground offers only a few sites, but when the river clears you will be hard pressed to find a parking spot amongst the outfitter's rigs. Harry Morgan access is a great wading access for fishing the North Fork of the Blackfoot. Traveling another 5.5 miles up the road will take you to **Brown's Lake,** which is a good fishing lake, but don't expect a lot of shade in summer. Popular with boat fishermen and belly-boaters, Brown's Lake is stocked with some whopper brood stock. Stocked trout grow fast and fat in this lake. Another 1.5 miles down the road will take you to the last floating access point, **Cedar Meadows.**

MM 51.1: North Fork of the Blackfoot Trailhead & Cooper's Lake: Exit onto Kleinschmidt Road and follow the signs 11 miles to the trailhead. The North Fork of the Blackfoot is a popular trailhead for back-country horsemen and fly fishermen. For years I had never found the time to actually hike back into the wilderness and fish the North Fork. July 5, 1998, I finally hiked the trail. Following the wettest June on record, I looked down the canyon at the turquoise, silted river and inwardly prejudged the fishing I would have. Much to my surprise, in a 200-yard section in a steep canyon, I picked up six cutthroats, one of which was a fat 16 incher. Elderly fisherman may want to pass up the North Fork, as it is a tough hike down the narrow canyon to the water. During high water, you have to scramble up the canyon wall to a bench every 100 yards when it becomes impassable. At age 53 I was huffing and puffing, and I was damn glad that I could still huff and puff for fat westslope cutthroats. The mountainsides look like the back of a porcupine. Gray, burnt-out lodgepole trees blanket the entire area from the 1988 Canyon Creek Fire that destroyed 247,600 acres before it was contained. **Cooper's Lake:** Cooper's Lake is a short distance from the trailhead. Follow Whitetail Ranch Road to the lake. The lake is a fairly large lake surrounded by cottages. Public access is limited to a few tent sites and a boat launch. Fishing is only fair.

North Fork of the Blackfoot River

Highway 200 from Ovando to Lincoln: Slow winding water and lots of mud, brush and sediment characterize this section of the river. Although it can produce some hefty browns, it generally does not produce good habitat for rainbows and cutthroats.

Popular Float Trips on the Blackfoot River

Float Trip #1: Harry Morgan to Russell Gates

Harry Morgan Campground is a couple of miles outside of the little town of Ovando just off of Highway 200. From here floaters generally float down to the Russell Gates Campground (County Line), which is easily seen from the highway. One may float further down to the confluence with the Clearwater River. Floaters will have to carry their rafts about 20 yards up a gradual bank to the parking area. The section from Russell Gates to the Clearwater Bridge has numerous rapids. The canyon drops quickly in this section, and casters have to work the pockets and rocks diligently. From the Clearwater Bridge to Roundup is extremely dangerous and should be avoided by all floaters, in my opinion.

Float Trip #2: Roundup to River Bend Campground or Whitaker's Bridge

Only expert rowers should float this section as it is extremely dangerous with all the boulder-strewn rapids. A short float would be to River Bend Campground, and a full day's float would be Whitaker's Bridge.

Float Trip #3: River Bend Campground or Whitaker's Bridge to Johnsrud Park

It only takes one nasty drop-off and a sluice of water with huge rocks to make for an unpleasant day, or to take your life. Standing on the water's edge, Thibodeau Rapid doesn't look all that impressive, especially during high water when half of the boulders are submerged and out of sight in the murky water. When the water drops, however, make no mistake. I always have my passengers exit from my boat just upstream on the right side. They can take a well-worn path just below the bottleneck.

Throughout my years of guiding in my raft, I enjoyed this small challenge. During my last year of guiding, I had to maneuver through Thibodeau in a pram I had designed and built. Without the cushion of air and the forgiveness of a raft, compared to a drift boat, I was scared. When my last client stepped out of the pram, he turned to me and said, "I'd really like to show off in front of my wife and run it with you."

I replied, "No, I am being very safe and prudent by allowing no passengers."

What I didn't say was that I had a knot in my stomach, and I wasn't sure how my pram would handle in the fast water chute. As it turned out, the boat handled well, but I had to do some artful dodging in that short drop-off. Turning around, I marveled at how simple it looked, but I know tales and true stories of river carnage.

Seeley-Swan: Highway 83

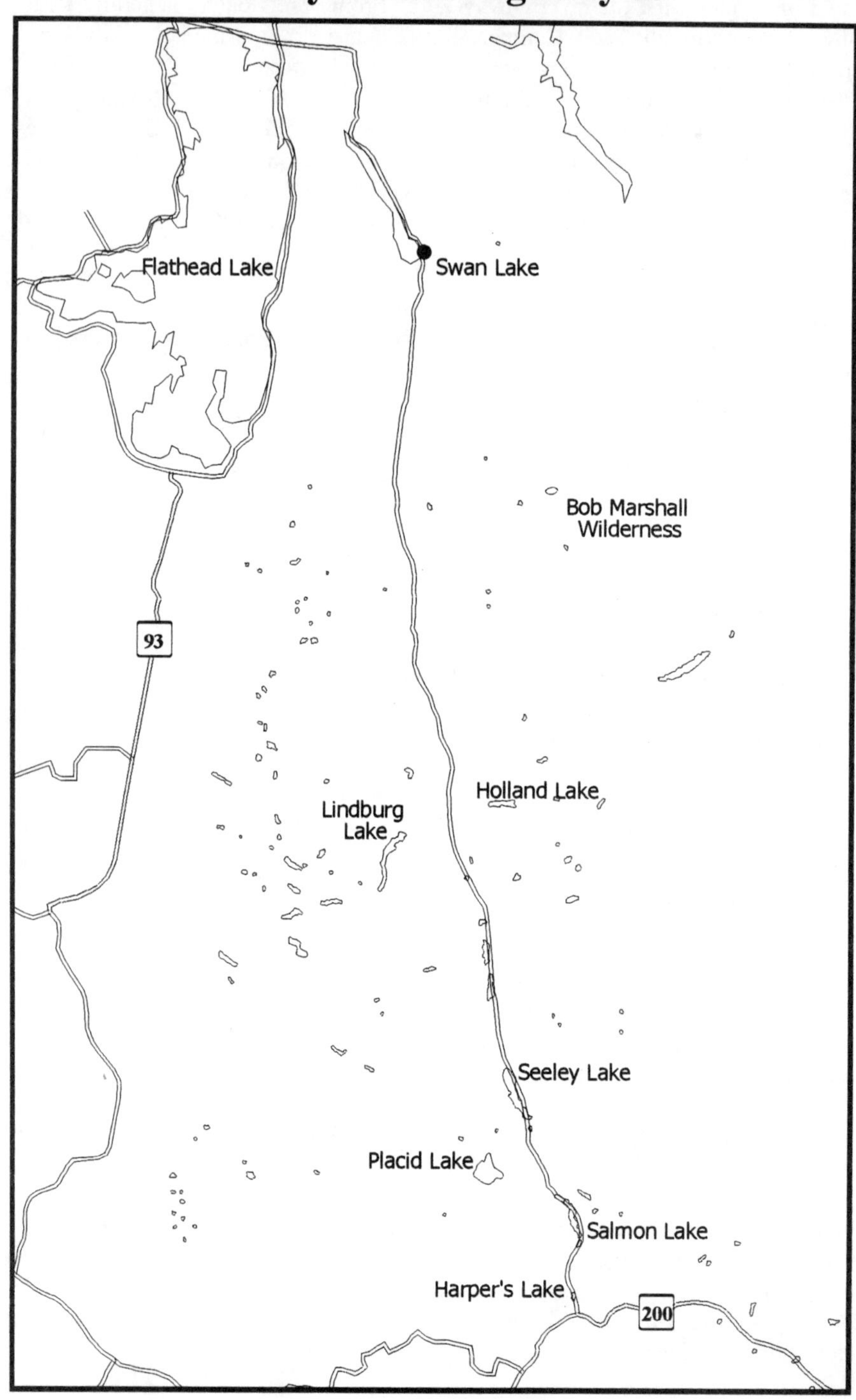

Junction: Highway 200 with Highway 83: Seeley-Swan Valleys

From Mile Marker 0 at Clearwater Junction with Highway 200
To the Town of Bigfork

Seeley-Swan Fishing

Some fishermen travel in packs and grudgingly compromise on their fishing itinerary; others travel with loved ones and, to the chagrin of family members, plan their family vacations not by destination resorts but by river tributaries. For the fly fisher who cajoles and pleads and promises the moon to his family in order to just wet a line on another river, the Seeley-Swan promises something for everyone in the family. Nestled between the Mission Mountains Wilderness and the Bob Marshall Wilderness, the Seeley Lake recreation area and the Swan River basin offer summer recreation at its best.

Golfing, swimming, canoeing, jet skiing, water skiing, trail riding and wilderness excursions provide just some of the many activities for the entire family. Oh, but here is the dilemma for dad and his family fishing converts – just what type of fish will you fish? The small creeks contain cutthroats and brookies as do the mountain lakes, the Clearwater River holds nice browns and the Swan River is home to both cutthroats and bull trout. The Seeley Lake chain offers kokanee salmon, rainbows, cutthroats, yellow perch and the notorious pike.

From Summit Lake down to the town of Seeley, and then down to Clearwater Junction, the watershed is a tributary of thc Blackfoot River, which in turn is a tributary of the Clark Fork. At Summit Lake, Highway 83 crests on a small divide which begins the watershed for the Swan River that runs north to Flathead Lake. Throughout this recreational wonderland are numerous forest service campgrounds, Montana state park campgrounds and many unimproved camping sites on both Plum Creek logging land and in the Lolo and Flathead National Forests. Backpackers will find that the Bob Marshall Wilderness offers over a million acres to explore.

The Bob is 60 miles in length and joins the Scapegoat Wilderness to the south and the Great Bear Wilderness to the north, which reaches all the way up into the Glacier National Park. On the eastern side of the valley, the Mission Wilderness encompasses over 70,000 acres of jagged peaks, small glaciers and many mountain lakes and streams. All of this country is easily accessed from Highway 83, and every mile marker beckons the fishermen to a new piece of water.

Joe Bender of High Basin Sports in Seeley recommends 1/4 ounce Rooster Tail lures in the Rainbow, Chartreuse and Brown trout colors as well as 1/8 and 1/4 ounce Panther Martin lures in all gold or silver. He also recommends the yellow and red pattern and the black and red pattern. Joe said, "This country is where the fly fishers and the night crawler fishermen co-exist in harmony. There is just so much variety to choose from. In addition to the lures and spinners, one popular method of fishing from a canoe is to simply troll with a bobber and a piece of night crawler on a six-foot leader.

For the fly fishermen I generally recommend nymphs, unless they are rising to a hatch. I generally use a sinking tip with a Prince or a bead head pattern or an olive or black wooly bugger or leech pattern." When fishing for kokanee, Joe recommends a leaded line with cowbells plus a three foot leader and a Wedding Ring with a piece of white corn or a night crawler. Expect to catch kokanee from 8 to 13 inches.

Hyperbole and verisimilitude quite often tend to enter into discussions with fishing outfitters and shop owners. Joe is a refreshing anomaly. The evening before I met him I had hiked down to Clearwater Lake. Walking up the trail were three float-tube fishermen. They had fished all day and were quite pleased with the results, whenever the wind had died down. One of the fishermen good naturally boosted of the catch of the day, a 20" cutthroat. I told Joe I was a little skeptical. After 15 years as a guide, I am accustomed to some gross misjudgments for length and poundage of trout. Year after year I have had clients innocently proclaim that an 11 inch trout was a 14 incher. And when it comes to poundage, I have always marveled at full pound increments. When I do hear someone split the difference and call the catch a 4 and a 1/2 pounder, my imagination soars with the possibilities.

Joe confirmed that the lake contained many such specimens, but the lake was frustrating at times as it lacked consistency. "When it's hot, it is one of the best fishing spots in the region, but I have spent a half a day fishing and gone home skunked." The mere word skunked is an anathema rarely spoken but in private moments with one's most intimate friends or spouse. I took an instant liking to Joe. Comfortable with Joe's enthusiasm for the region's fishing and his open candor, I pressed him for his view's on Seeley's own Loch Ness Godzilla, the notorious pike.

Brought in by bucket biologists, the pike introduction is the bane of trout fishers. According to Joe the pike explosion has been a boon to the Seeley area as it draws in pike fishermen from all around the country. "Prior to the pike fishing, Seeley Lake was crap fishing for planted rainbows, sun fish, suckers and a few bass. It was the pits. Last year the largest pike that I know of being caught was a 25 pound 46 1/2 incher. Now, that's a fish with an attitude."

What most fishermen come to realize is that, unlike the pike up in Canada who often feed on themselves due to the scarce food supply, Seeley Pike are not aggressive feeders as they have large numbers of sun fish and trash fish to feed on. Joe recommends 1 ounce red and white Dare Devils, big buzz baits, and large-jointed Rappalas. At the very minimum he suggests using 12 pound line. Other popular lures are Rappala Magnums, weedless rubber mice, Jaw Breakers and spinner bait. Joe forewarns those who fish the lily pads, "Plan on actually landing about 10% of the fish you catch."

Fly fishers wishing to fish for pike should use wire leaders and deer hair mice. If you are fishing from a belly-boat or float tube, be sure to bring along a pair of pliers and gloves. When releasing a pike, be sure to turn them belly up so that they become motionless. When I asked Joe what his predictions were regarding the explosion of pike in the basin, he replied, "I think they are here to stay. According to a number of knowledgeable sources, the pike will peak in numbers and then decline. When this happens, they will move into pike zones which we are seeing already. Once this happens the trout population will stabilize as well. The major detriment to the introduction of pike has been the decline of Kokanee salmon, but in spite of this loss, I'm glad they are here."

Joe's store, High Basin Sports, is located on Highway 83 in Seeley Lake.

Highway 83: Mile-Marker 0 / Clearwater Junction (Highway 200)

MM 1: Harper's Lake and Blanchard Lake: Harper's Lake and Blanchard Lake are right next to each other. Both lakes are a 1/4 of a mile off the highway and provide access to the Clearwater River and a nice campground, especially for a family who has brought along a canoe. The campground is suitable for trailers and offers shade and an ideal spot for family recreation. Harper's Lake prohibits boats with motors. The lake is planted with trout each year as well as some retired brood stock. A small 18-acre pothole lake, Harper's Lake is separated from Blanchard Lake by the access road. Blanchard Lake is a misnomer as it is actually a 10 acre flooded oxbow of the Clearwater River. Blanchard Lake offers a potpourri of small trout, perch, bass, whitefish and rough fish.

MM 6.5: Salmon Lake State Park: Fee area. Salmon Lake State Park campground has been updated and provides new lavatories with coin operated showers. The campground has a boat launch and a picnic area as well as an amphitheater where they bring in guest speakers to talk about the wildlife as well as educational seminars sponsored by Montana Fish Wildlife and Parks. Native Americans also give presentations on their cultural heritage and history. Salmon Lake is a popular lake for all of the trout species and kokanee salmon.

The Clearwater River above Salmon Lake is a popular fishing area for browns. This short section to the Placid Lake turn off is a challenge, however, as it is braided swampland crowded with willow and tag alder.

MM 10.1: Placid Lake State Park / Owl Creek (Jocko Lakes): Right after you exit the highway, you will cross the Clearwater River, which has a campsite and a fishing trail both upstream and downstream. About a half of a mile further are some nice unimproved Plum Creek campsites on Owl Creek, the outlet creek for Placid Lake. Placid Lake State Park is three miles from the highway and charges a fee. The park has recently been upgraded and improved with coin operated showers and handicapped accessible rest rooms with hot and cold water. Placid Lake also has a boat launch. Popular with water skiers, the lake doesn't offer much for quality fishing, although it is loaded with small kokanee.

Owl Creek parallels the road and offers small cutthroats and brookies. Bring plenty of mosquito repellant if you plan on fishing the Clearwater River area where is joined by Owl Creek. **Jocko Lakes:** Ignore the signs to Jocko Lakes. The road takes off from the campground entrance. The lakes are high up in the Mission Mountains on the Flathead Indian Reservation. They are closed to fishing. The outlet, Jocko River, is an excellent high country stream. However, you will need a tribal permit to fish so you would need to continue driving to Arlee, Montana. From the highway to the fishing area on the Jocko is approximately 25 miles.

MM 14: Seeley Lake, Montana: (1,025 acres with a maximum depth of 70 feet) Just after mile-marker 14 look for Boy Scout Road on the left. The road swings around the east side of Seeley Lake and rejoins Highway 83 above the town. **River Point Campground** is 2.1 miles. 26 campsites. Cold drinking water. U.S. Fee Area. River Point Campground (USFS) offers swimming, camping and picnicking and is a fee campground. Providing lots of shade, the campground also has a good swimming area.

Seeley Lake Campground is 3.3 miles. Seeley Lake Campground, Lolo National Forest, is also a fee campground right on the lake. Shaded by larch, the campground also offers a nice concrete boat launch and a beach with a roped in swimming area. Public pay phones are available, but the campground does not offer showers. 29 campsites. Flush toilets. Cold drinking water. Boat launch. Seeley Lake provides lots of fishing opportunities for perch, stocked rainbows, cutthroats and pike, not to mention some hefty 5-10 pound brood stock from the Arlee hatchery. Yellow perch are best caught with a rubber jig with a piece of night crawler. The best pike fishing is found at the outlet of the lake.

MM 15-16: Seeley Lake, Montana

Seeley Lake Campground, Morrell Creek, Morrell Falls, Morrell Lake and Cottonwood Lakes (Road 477): Just as you reach the outskirts of the town of Seeley, look for Morrell Creek Road which heads east. Morrell Creek is first crossed 2 miles from the highway. The creek offers small cutthroats, brookies and the occasional brown spawner in the fall. **Cottonwood Lakes and Seeley Trailhead Campground:** The campground is one mile from the highway and not to be confused with the lakeside campground. Cottonwood Lakes are 8.4 miles from the campground, although there is only one real lake which is the middle lake. The other two "lakes" are shallow mud ponds. The middle lake is a narrow 15-acre lake, and it is only fished out of a canoe or small boat. The lake is stocked with Arlee rainbows, and it is a popular lake for fishing cutthroats and brookies as well. The lake offers a number of unimproved campsites. This is "pack it in – pack it out" country. Morrell Creek Road is actually a loop that comes out at Kozy Korner three miles from Highway 83. Take Woodworth Road just past Salmon Lake State Park.

MM 17.9: Seeley Lake Ranger Station

MM 19.4: Boy Scout Road: This is the loop road which swings around the west side of the lake and re-connects at Mileage Marker 14.

MM 20: Clearwater Lake Loop (Refer to Mileage Marker 28.)

MM 22.5: Lake Inez: (293 acres with a maximum depth of 70 feet) Fishing is similar to Seeley Lake. Lake Inez and Lake Alva have USFS non-fee campgrounds running along the shore of the lake right beneath the highway. Some of the sites are squeezed between the water and the access road with the highway up abovc it.

MM 24: Lake Inez Campground access

MM 25: West Fork of the Clearwater River / Marshall Lake: As soon as you turn off the highway, you will cross the Clearwater River. Right along side of the creek and the road are two grassy unimproved campsites. The West Fork of the Clearwater River is a brushy, little creek with scarce few fish. The road to Marshall Lake is 6.4 miles and offers a stunning view of the valley. Narrow and bumpy in places, I would recommend pulling only a tent trailer. When I got up to the lake, however, I was surprised to see a 19' trailer. When I talked to the camper, he had a harrowing tale about backing up his trailer on a windy cliff-side road when he ran into a gate. Marshall Lake has one campsite and a place to launch a boat although there are a couple of unimproved campsites on the creek about a hundred yards from the lake. The road forks just above the campsite and follows the side of the mountain up above the lake where a gate blocks further travel. Vandals had removed the warning sign. The father said that it had taken hours to back the trailer down the narrow, windy road, and his two young sons were terrified.

Marshall Lake froze out a number of years ago. All that is left are a few five-inch cuts. The creek also froze out and offers poor fishing in the upper reaches.

MM 26: Lake Alva: (approximately 300 acres with a maximum depth of 90 feet) Lake Alva is the most popular fishing lake among the locals. Offering good catches of kokanee, trout and the occasional bull trout, the lake also offers perch and pike. Similar to Lake Inez, Lake Alva has a non-fee USFS campground that runs along the water's edge just short of Mile-Marker 25, but it is more suitable to tents and truck campers.

Lake Alva Campground is a self-serve fee campground with no showers. 41 campsites. Cold drinking water. U.S. Fee Area. During the ice-fishing season, a 27-pound pike was speared in the lake. The campground has an excellent boat launch and a small beach with a roped off area for swimming.

MM 27: Rainy Lake: (70 acre shallow lake) Rainy Lake is popular fishing for 12" cutthroats. Rainy Lake has the largest population of bull trout and is free of pike.

MM 28: Clearwater Lake Loop: The dirt road is surprisingly smooth, and the view of the Bob Marshall Wilderness peaks are stunning. Clearwater Lake is 7 miles from the highway. You will find a parking spot with a 1/2-mile trail down to the lake. (Seemed much shorter than a half mile.) Don't waste your time trying to fish this lake from the shore. The lake is extremely shallow around its entire length. The lake is rich in leeches and fresh water shrimp with good hatches so the cutthroats are sometimes uncooperative. The lake is best fished from a belly boat or a canoe. The best fishing is in the northwest end of the lake. Joe Bender, owner of High Basin Sports, recommends olive leeches, bead-head nymphs and hoppers in August. The lake offers a number of pack-in camping sites.

MM 31: Summit Lake: Summit Lake is a small, brushy lined lake that freezes. It is rarely fished. The few rises that you see are smaller cutthroats moving up or down from Bertha Creek. Bertha Creek is so over-grown it is not worth the effort to fish it. Summit Lake is the dividing line for the Clearwater that drains south to the Blackfoot River and the Swan River drainage that flows north to Flathead Lake.

Cry of the Loon: (USFS) "The cry of the loon is no laughing matter. The common loon is becoming uncommon. Nearly 200 loons take up summer residency in Montana. Of the sixty nesting pairs, only about 30 chicks survive. Loons are very sensitive to human presence. If a loon is forced off her nest, the eggs will cool or predators will eat them. If you see a single bird in the water in May, she is probably off her nest near the shoreline. Leave the area immediately."

MM 34.3: Lindbergh Lake, Bunyon Lake, Meadow Lake, Crystal Lake, Glacier Lake:

Lindbergh Lake: (725 acres with a maximum depth of 125 feet) Within a half of a mile of exiting Highway 83, the road crosses the Swan River. The campground is 4.5 miles from the highway and offers only a few camping sites, a picnic area and a boat launch. The lake is surrounded by summer homes. The campground only offers four sites suitable for camping trailers. Half way up the road is a road to the right leading to **Bunyon Lake.** It is a distance of 7 miles. Bunyon Lake is a high elevation lake with no camping facilities unless you are willing to pack your gear down to the lake, a distance of 200 yards. This is not a road for trailers!

Bunyon Lake fishes very well for small cutthroats. For every four, 6" fish that you catch, you'll land a 10 or 12 incher. This is a beautiful little lake a bit short of ten acres. It would be the perfect spot to launch a belly-boat and just cruise around catching hungry little cuts. Less than a mile away lies **Meadow Lake.** Meadow Lake is only slightly bigger. Somewhat swampy, the lake is blocked by a gate so you must walk a short distance to the lake for 8 – 12" cuts. **Crystal Lake** (186 acres) may be reached from a trail at Meadow Lake, the southern end of Lindbergh Lake, or a trailhead may be taken from Beaver Creek Road which is just above Summit Lake. A relatively large lake, the lake seems to be declining in both the numbers of fish and the size of the fish.

Glacier Lake: In my sojourn through this country, I didn't get a chance to hike in and fish Glacier Lake. However, when I hiked down to Bunyon Lake, I ran into a family who had just fished Glacier Lake. It was their first choice from all the lakes that they had fished. Although they never caught anything larger than 12 inches, they watched a lone fisherman pulling in some hefty 14 inch cuts, but by the time he headed out, it was time for them to leave as well. Follow the Glacier Creek Road. Plan on an hour's hike to reach the lake.

MM 35.6: Holland Lake: (416 acres with a maximum depth of 150 at the east end of the lake.) Holland Lake offers two large USFS fee campgrounds and a boat launch and a roped swimming area. Campsites line the shore with spectacular views of the waterfall at the east end of the lake. Fishing is generally good for cutthroats, rainbow trout, kokanee and a few bull trout. Be prepared for lots of boating activity and jet skis. The outlet creek is good fishing for small trout.

MM 43: Flathead National Forest Work Center (Information)

Swan River

Floating on the scenic Swan River

Originating out of Lindbergh Lake, the Swan River rushes 35 miles to Swan Lake. Although not as fertile of a river as other rivers in western Montana, the Swan River, nonetheless, produces good numbers of westslope cutthroats, rainbows, bull trout and mountain whitefish. The great advantage of the Swan is that it is relatively isolated with less fishing pressure. The challenge is two-fold from Mother Nature. The mosquitoes and flies feast on fly fishers who defy the tangled, dense foliage along the shore. The greatest challenge, however, lies waiting for the rafters and canoeists. Good luck!

Rafting the Swan is similar to rafting on Rock Creek. The oarsman must be ever vigilant, and their fly casters can not be contemplative or inaccurate in their casting ability. The water is especially swift early summer and appears to be one long riffle, punctuated by occasional pools and eddies. The best cover for the trout is under the logjams and downed trees, and it is these obstacles which make the Swan River risky. After a record rainfall for June, 1998, I launched my one-man drift boat at Piper Creek and floated down to my campsite at Cedar Creek Campground on the Fatty Creek Road. I had received information on a large logjam, but I didn't listen carefully. Left or right? I went right, and it was the wrong decision as I came around a swift bend and encountered an incredible 20-yard logjam. If I had been floating in a raft, I would have been faced with an extremely difficult decision, as there was no going back upstream due to the fast current. Luckily I found a narrow opening to follow, and I only had to drag my little boat over two logs.

Normally, I am fairly adept at floating while I am tying on a new fly. Not so for the Swan. Because I wanted to fish Jim Lake that evening, I just fished without stopping. What a rush it was for speed, scenery and fishing. I started out with a size 12 Royal Humpy and went a 100 yards without catching a fish. Oh, oh, I thought. But then they started coming up to my fly one after another. I must have caught over 15 rainbows and cuts, all under 9 inches. Due to the speed of the water, I knew I was missing good pocket water and sheltered downfall. Rowing and casting without stopping is not the way to fish the Swan.

I switched to a girdle bug and didn't have another fish on for over an hour. I thought to myself, okay you've caught the river's dinks, now let's put on a Muddler and pull up some of those bigger guys. With about a mile to go to my campsite, I tossed out an un-weighted Muddler. The deer-hair collar kept the large Muddler floating high and dry. One dink after another rose to hit the Muddler even before I had a chance to strip it under the water. When I got off the river, I walked up to Eric Bjorge, who is a river guide and owner of *Two River Gear* store in Bigfork.

"Well, all I've caught is dinks today," I said.

"Pretty typical for the first day on the Swan," he replied. "If you want the big guys, you've got to work a nymph."

"What can I expect from this river?" I asked.

"24-30 inchers," he retorted.

"Bull," I said.

"Yeah, bull trout, but I've caught a lot of 18 to 20 inch rainbows on this river."

Swan River trout average between 8 and 12 inches. In talking to Eric further, he suggested that if you are going to fish the Swan, "Go big or go home." The Swan has a long and steady hatch of Isoperla stoneflies so stimulators or large yellow Humpies will work well.

Access is restricted from Lindbergh Lake crossing all the way down to Cold Creek. Many roads cross the river, but for the most part the property is posted and there is no place to park. The following information was excerpted from the pamphlet "Fishing Waters of the Swan Valley" a joint publication sponsored by the United States Forest Service for the Flathead National Forest and the Montana Department of Fish, Wildlife and Parks. **Upper Section:** "From Lindbergh Lake Road to Condon the upper river is relatively shallow and wadable, containing numerous riffles and runs. Water temperatures warm by mid-summer and smaller brook trout and rainbow trout favor the area. Floating is difficult due to low water, logjams and split channels on the lower end. General stream regulations apply (see fishing regs). **Middle Section:** The section from Condon to Piper Creek Road is characterized by smaller flows, a diversity of channel conditions and pools formed behind log jams and fallen trees. Good-sized rainbow trout are common along with bull, Cutthroat and brook trout and abundant mountain whitefish. Logjams hamper floating above Cold Creek and skilled rafting is recommended below this point. General stream regulations apply upstream from Piper Creek Bridge (see fishing regs). **Lower Section:** From Piper Creek Road to Porcupine Creek Road this section contains the greatest diversity with respect to depth, cover and water volume. Stream banks are fairly open after spring high water and there is some channel splitting. Experienced canoeists and rafters navigate this section, but caution must be exercised due to fallen trees and logged jams. Catch and release regulations for rainbow and cutthroat trout apply from Swan Lake up to Piper Creek Bridge." USFS

Swan River by Cedar Creek Campground

MM 46.7: Cold Creek Road Fishing Access for the Swan River plus access to high elevation lakes: The Swan River access has good parking on both sides of the bridge. (Peck Lake 6 miles; trailhead to Cold Lakes 7 miles; Jim Lake 10 miles): **Peck Lake:** Peck Lake access is 6 miles from the highway.

Watch for the sign, as you will make a right turn. Peck Lake can be accessed close to the road. The lake is a shallow, swampy lake with stocked trout. **Upper and Lower Cold Lakes:** Nestled close to the Mission Mountains divide, both lakes are reached within 2.5 miles from the trailhead, and each have healthy populations of cutthroats from 12 to 16 inches. At 2.9 miles from the highway, the road to Cold Lakes and Jim Lakes turns to the right. At 5.9 miles the road forks to the left for the Cold Lakes trailhead. From the turn-off to Cold Lakes continue 4 miles to Jim Lake. The last four miles is a second gear pull, and the road is bumpy and should be attempted only by high clearance vehicles. The **Jim Lakes** basin is a photographer's dream. Even in July there were slivers and patches of snow on the mountain rims over looking Jim Lakes. Be forewarned that the narrow and bumpy entrance to the lake is strictly for trucks. The primitive road jack-knifes down to three compact camping sites on the lake. To make the turn I had to back up a few times, and I was tempted to put my truck in four-wheel drive. The lake offers excellent scenery and good fishing. Just after you cross the bridge over the outlet creek, there is a turn-around and parking area for non-four-wheel drive vehicles. From that point to the lake is only a half of a mile.

MM 50.8: Salmon Prairie Road: Good river access less than a mile from the highway. Most floaters float to Fatty Creek.

MM 52: Lion Creek Road (Lion Creek is closed to fishing.)

MM 53.6: Piper Creek Road: Access is 3/10 of a mile from the highway, but it has limited parking.

 **MM 54.5: Van Lake Road #9882:**
(58 acres with a maximum depth of 40 feet)
Van Lake is a popular local fishing lake, but you need a pick-up truck and a small boat as the shoreline is difficult to fish. At two miles stay left. The lake has primitive camping sites.

MM 58.5: Fatty Creek Road: (Metcalf Lake, Shay Lake, Fatty Lake and Cedar Lake, Cedar Creek and Fatty Creek) The bridge is 3/10 of a mile from the highway and offers a boat launching access. Across the river is Cedar Creek Campground which offers drinking water and toilets. On the far side of the bridge is a bumpy road which leads to a nice picnic area with tables right on the river about 100 yards down from the bridge. Cedar Creek is crossed right after the campground, but it offers only very small cutthroats. From the highway 6/10 of a mile, you will note a fork to the left. This road will lead to **Shay Lake**. Caution: Shay Lake should be driven to only in a 4x4 rig that has already received abuse through the years as the road is overgrown in parts.

If you have a new paint job, plan on scratches! At one mile and four tenths the main road forks to the left.

Metcalf Lake is 2.2 miles from the campground. Make the first right turn off of Fatty Creek Road, and then make another right turn to the lake. There are no signs for the second right turn except a "Pack it in-Pack it Out!" sign. The lake may be reached by a car to within 3/10 of a mile. Only a truck should attempt the last portion. The lake is popular with local young adults. They have built a high swinging rope above the lake. The lake is shallow except for the small portion by the swing. The lake is being managed for trophy trout, but I would advice belly-boaters to arrive early or stay late to avoid the swing divers.

Fatty Creek is crossed 3.6 miles from the highway. The Fatty Creek Road to the Cedar Lake trailhead is exactly nine miles from the highway. The road is an ear popping, second gear road as it climbs high up in the Mission Mountains. From 4.1 to 4.2, as of the summer of 1998, the road is rutted and very bumpy. I would not recommend a low clearance vehicle. **Cedar Lake** trailhead has a large turn around. The lake is about a four mile hike, and keep in mind that you are in grizzly country, so if you are traveling alone or in a group, pepper spray may be a prudent purchase. Camping at the lake is designated as no-impact camping. **Fatty Lake** is accessed by a hunter's trail about 1.5 miles before the trailhead. I could not find it. Although it reportedly fishes well, I would recommend the established trail to Cedar Lake, which has a healthy population of cutthroats.

MM 63.5: Point Pleasant Campground: The campground offers a boat access, but it is very over-grown and easily missed. This is a beautiful non-fee campground right on the river.

MM 66.7: Road #10161: Easily missed, this site offers a great access to the river as well as a take-out for rafters. Camping is allowed on a "Pack it in-Pack it out" basis.

MM 68.2: Porcupine Creek Road: The Swan River is crossed one mile from the highway. Access is good for wade fishermen, but you will have to drag your raft or canoe up a 15' bank to the road.

MM 71-72: Swan Lake, Montana

MM 71.9: (USFS) Swan Lake Campground: 36 campsites for trailers, RV's and tents. Fee area. Water available, vault type toilets, swimming beach, boat ramp.

MM 82.5: Junction: Montana State Route 209 heads west five miles to the town of Bigfork and Highway 35, which is the west side route along Flathead Lake beginning at Polson and ending at Kalispell.

MM 86: Echo Lake: The highway now turns due east (Follow the signs to Echo Lake. The lake is popular for water skiing and summer homes, but it does have fair fishing, nonetheless.)

MM 88.6: Jewell Basin Hiking Area:

The Jewell Basin Hiking Area is at the north end of the Swan Mountain Range between Kalispell and Hungry Horse Reservoir. It is 17 miles east of Kalispell and 18 miles southeast of Columbia Falls. To reach the Jewell Basin hiking area, follow State Highway 83 to the Echo Lake Road; follow the Echo Lake Road north approximately 2 miles to a T intersection. Turn right. This road leads to a junction with the Jewell Basin Road (#5392). Follow the Jewell Basin Road approximately 7 miles to the trailhead and parking area. The last 5 miles are steep and contain drive-through drainage dips. Caution is advised if traveling with low clearance vehicles. Trailers are not recommended.

The Jewell Basin Hiking Area is a specially designated backcountry use area consisting of 15,349 acres of high mountains. It includes 27 alpine lakes, many picturesque mountain streams, mountain meadows, rocky peaks, sub-alpine timber and a variety of flowers. Elevations with the basin range from 4,240 feet on Graves Creek to 7, 542 feet on Big Hawk Mountain. Thirty-five miles of trails connect most of the lakes. The average hiker in good physical condition can travel 2 to 3 miles per hour.

Fishing is generally excellent in the lakes and creeks, although like all fishing it is subject to the whims and fickleness of Mother Nature. Camping in the Jewell Basin is on the basis of "no impact." Be cautious, as this is Grizzly country. Bears are unpredictable and, in certain circumstances, can be very dangerous. Additional information on how to camp in bear habitat is available at any of the five District Offices or the Forest Supervisor's Office in Kalispell.

MM 91: Junction with Highway 35: You are 2 miles to Bigfork or 17 miles to Kalispell.

Saga: Crick Fishing

Years ago when I worked out of a local fly shop, I wouldn't hesitate in suggesting a guided instructional trip to one of our local creeks. I fondly recall many days when instruction was immediately reinforced with fish after fish rising to take a swat at my client's Royal Wulff or bushy Humpy. If you are new to the sport of fly-fishing, spend as much time as you can on mountain creeks. You will be delighted with the action as well as your accelerated mastery of requisite skills. Having spent 15 years behind the oars as a fly fishing guide, I would also recommend as many days on the river with a guide as you can afford! A good guide will not only help you catch fish, he will instruct you in the nuances of the sport.

The size of a trout is relative to the conditions of its environment. High elevation, canyon creeks do not produce large trout, but they do provide a respite from the summer heat and an intimacy with the water and flora of a mountain stream. Best of all, they produce an abundance of small, hungry trout. And when you catch a 10 incher, it is akin to landing a 16 incher on the river. If you are new to fly fishing, start out on a creek. Besides offering lots of fish, it will teach you many skills in a short amount of time. A creek-fishing trip will teach you that a short cast is all you need. Get right out in the middle of the creek and fish directly upstream on both sides. Make short casts, and control your line. In most cases you merely have to hold your rod tip up and keep the line out of the water!

Regarding your choice of fly patterns, big is better on a creek. Use size 10 and 12 common attractor patterns. If the water is heavy, and you have to stay to one side of the creek, use a Girdle Bug or a Yuk Bug. Fish these bugs just as you would a dry fly. Allow them to sink under the surface and watch for the strike. Learn where the fish hide as it is much the same on the rivers. With lots of action, you will learn to read the water, anticipate the strike, and set the hook.

I always proclaim that I am an expert when it comes to fishing a creek even though expertise can be acquired with just a few creek experiences in late July or August. One summer I was taking out a father and his son to teach them "crick fishin." Looking up the trail, I spotted a lone fly fisherman walking down the trail. "I'll bet he had lousy fishing," I whispered to the young boy. "Let's find out." Sure enough the man had caught only a few small cutthroats, and it was obvious he was disappointed.

When he was out of hearing, the father looked at me quizzically, and the young boy asked, "How did you know?"

"Simple," I replied. "He had dry pants and dry sneakers!"

Follow these four rules for successful creek fishing: (1) Get wet! Position yourself in the middle of the creek, and keep moving upstream in the water. Better yet, keep your fly along the seams and in slow pockets at a slower speed. (4) Unless you are using a hopper, present your fly gently on the water.

Once you have caught a dozen fish, the stress of your daily life will slip away as you sit on a rock contemplating what fly you will use next. Resting your feet on the gold, pebbly bottom, you will probably take in a breath of cool mountain air and think, "This is what it is all about."

Southwestern Montana

Southwestern Montana Accommodations and Services

The southwestern region is quite large. I have included only accommodations that are reasonably close to good fishing. For a complete regional listing and descriptions of accommodations and services, request a free travel planner from Travel Montana, Department of Commerce, P.O. box 200533, Helena, Montana 59620-0533, or telephone: 1 800-847-4868. For Travel Montana Internet Information: http://travel.mt.gov.

Anaconda Private Campground: Fairmont RV Park, Exit 211 from I-90; 86 RV sites, next to Fairmont Hots Springs (406) 563-6030

Big Sky, Montana:
Best Western Buck's T-4 Lodge, P.O. Box 160279 Big Sky, Montana 59716
1 800-822-4484 Fax: 406-995-2191 Email: buckst4@mcn.net
www.buckst4.com

East Slope Anglers, Box 160249, Big Sky, Montana 59716 1 888-359-3974
Gallatin River

Gallatin Riverguides, Box 160212, Big Sky, Montana 59716 (406) 995-2290
www.montanaflyfishing.com

Bozeman Fly Shops and Sporting Goods:

Montana Troutfitters, 1716 W. Main, Bozeman, MT 59715 (406) 587-4707
www.troutfitters.com
Powder Horn Outfitters, 35 East Main, Bozeman, MT 59715 (406) 587-7373
RJ Cain & Co., 204 E. Main Street, Bozeman, MT 59715 1 800-886-9111

Bozeman Area Private Campgrounds:

Bear Canyon Campground, 3 mile east of Bozeman, I-90 Exit 313
1 800 – 438-1575 Heated pool, clean restrooms, pull-through sites

Bozeman KOA, 8 mile south of Belgrade (406) 587-3030: Natural hot spring pools, Kamping Kabins and tepees

Butte Fly Shops and Sporting Goods:

Bob Ward & Sons, 1925 Dewey, Butte, Montana (406) 494-3445
Fish-On Fly & Tackle, 3356 Harrison Avenue, Butte, MT (406) 494-4218

Butte Area Private Campgrounds:

Butte KOA, 1601 Kent, Butte, MT 59701 (406) 782-0663 Playground, fishing and swimming

Cameron, Montana: Beartooth Flyfishing, 2975 Hwy. 287 N., Cameron, MT 59720 (406) 682-7525

Dillon Fly Shops:

Fishing Headquarters, 610 N. Montana Street, Dillon, Montana 59725 (406) 683-6660
Frontier Anglers, 680 N. Montana Street, Dillon, MT 59725 (406) 683-5276

Dillon Private Campgrounds:
Dillon KOA, 735 West Park, Dillon, MT 59725 1 800 KOA-2751 Pool, fishing, playground, cabins
Skyline RV Park, 3 mile north of Dillon on Hwy. 41 (406) 683-4692 Fishing, golf course within 3 miles

Emigrant Bed and Breakfast: Yellowstone Country Bed and Breakfast (30 minutes from the north entrance to Yellowstone National Park.)
(406) 333-4917 (800) 459-8347 www.j-tech.net/yellowstonecountry

Ennis Fly Shops:

Headwaters Angling, Box 964, Ennis, MT 59729 (406) 682-4263
Madison River Fishing Co., P.O. Box 627, Ennis, MT 59729 (406) 682-4293
The Tackle Shop, 127 Main, Ennis, MT 59729 (406) 682-4263

Ennis Private Campgrounds:
Camper Corner, 1 800 755-3474 Walking distance to Main Street, cable

Elkhorn Store and RV Park, (406) 682-4273 Gas station, store, tackle
Lake Shore Lodge, (406) 682-4424 Marina, rentals, cabins, shade

Gardner Private Campground: Rocky Mountain Campground, 14 Jardine Road, Gardner, MT (406) 848-7251 Playground, mini-golf, bus tours

Livingston Fly Shops:
Dan Bailey's Fly Shop, 209 West Park Street, Livingston, Montana 59047
(406) 222-1673
George Anderson's Yellowstone Angler, P.). Box 660, Livingston, MT 59047
(406) 222-7130
Montana Master Angler, 107 South Main, Livingston, Montana 59047
(406) 222-7437
Livingston Area Private Campgrounds:
Paradise Livingston Campground, 1 block N on US 89, (406) 222-1122
Paradise Valley KOA, 163 Pine Creek Road, Livingston 1 800 KOA-2805
Yellowstone's Edge RV Park, Hwy. 89, 18 miles south 1 800 865-7332

Melrose Fly Shops:

Montana Fly Co., P.O. Box 29, Melrose, MT 59743 (406) 835-2621
Sunrise Fly Shop, P.O. Box 85, Melrose, MT 59743 (406) 835-3474

Pray, Montana / Fly Shop: Knoll's Yellowstone Hackle and Flyshop P.O. Box 76, Pray, MT 59065 (406) 333-4848 Email: knoll@avicom.net/knoll/
http://www.avicom.net/knoll/

Sheridan, Montana Fly Shop: Harman's Fly Shop, 310 S. Main, Sheridan, Montana 59749 (406) 842-5868

Twin Bridges Fly Shop: Four River's Fishing Co., 205 S. Main, Twin Bridges, Montana 59754 (406) 684-5651

West Yellowstone Fly Shops:

Blue Ribbon Flies, P.O. Box 1037, West Yellowstone, Montana 59758
(406) 646-7642
Bud Lilly's Trout Shop, 39 Madison Avenue, West Yellowstone, MT 59758
1 800 854-9559
Madison River Outfitters, 117 Canyon St., West Yellowstone, MT 59758
(406) 646-9644
R.J. Cain & Co., Box 1450, West Yellowstone, MT 59758 1 800-35-TROUT
West Yellowstone Private Campgrounds:
Yellowstone Grizzly RV Park, 210 S. Electric Street (406) 646-4466
152 RV sites 4 blocks from West Entrance to park

Yellowstone Park KOA, 6 miles west on Hwy. 20 1 800 562-7591
188 sites, pool, hot tub, game room

Wise River Fly Shop: Complete Fly Fisher, Hwy. 43, Wise River, Montana 59762 (406) 832-3175

Yellowstone National Park / Amfac Parks and Resorts (307) 344-7311
Bridge Bay Campground, 420 site / Canyon Campground, 280 camping sites / Fishing Bridge RV Park, 345 RV sites / Grant Village Campground, 414 sites / Madison 292 sites
13. Exit numbers roughly correspond to mileage markers.

Interstate 90 East from Rock Creek to Livingston

Exit 126: Rock Creek (see page 95)

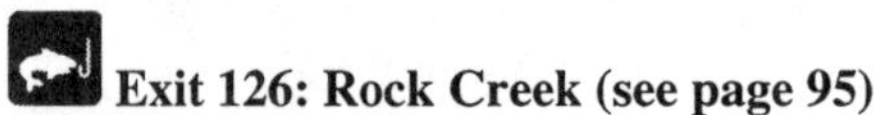 **Exit 130: Beavertail State Campground:** Twenty six miles east of Missoula, Beavertail State Campground includes a half-mile of frontage on the upper Clark Fork River under a canopy of tall cottonwoods. The campground has 26 camping sites with toilets, water and a hand-launch boat site.

MM 143: Rest area

Exit 153: (Side Trip): Drummond, Montana (Anaconda, Georgetown Lake, Phillipsburg): If you are not in an "interstate hurry", the scenic route to Anaconda via Georgetown lake provides spectacular scenery along with great fishing opportunities if you want to add a few extra hours to your trip. Make it a full day. You deserve it. Exiting the Interstate in Drummond, the mileage markers begin with mileage marker 64 and work backwards six miles north of Anaconda where Highway 1 meets the interstate again at mileage marker 0. From the interstate at Drummond, Phillipsburg is 27 miles. If you arrive in early June or in the fall, you may want to wet a line on **Flint Creek**. At mile marker 63, turn left. Drive one mile and enter Drummond City Park and Rodeo Grounds.

The park offers a nice shaded picnic site right along the upper Clark Fork River. Camping is permissible for a daily fee of $10. At the back of the park you will note a train trestle. Walk under the trestle and follow the Clark Fork River for a ten-minute walk to where Flint Creek enters the river. This section fishes poorly during the heat of summer, but fair size browns enter the creek during the fall.

Flint Creek fishing improves further towards Phillipsburg. Look for county roads off of Highway 1 which cross Flint Creek. Two such access points are located at mile marker 54.9 (Douglas Creek Road) and at mileage marker 51.7 (Henderson Creek Road). A few miles from Phillipsburg, Flint Creek travels through a narrow valley. The creek lazily cuts and winds through willow lined-banks and produces good catches of 10-12 inch browns. This section is mostly un-posted and located between mileage markers 42-47.

A few miles past the charming, old mining town of Phillipsburg, Highway 1 intersects with Highway 38. Highway 38 will take you over Skalkaho Pass and then on down to Hamilton, Montana to the Bitterroot River, or you may want to follow Highway 38 a few miles to the upper end of Rock Creek. This loop will take you around to the interstate again at Exit 126, a few miles from Missoula.

From Phillipsburg, continuing on Highway 1, the highway passes by Flint Creek Campground at mileage marker 30.3. The campground offers 16 camping sites, some of which are just large parking areas for trailers. Some of the camping sites lack tables. Although the campground is old and somewhat run down, it is a good place for older children who want to play in the creek, as Flint Creek at this point is very small. From the campground Highway 1 climbs up the mountain to meet the reservoir dam for Georgetown Lake.

Georgetown Lake is a shallow, weed infested meadow lake. A little over four square miles, the lake sits at an elevation of 6,350 feet. Bordered by meadow grassland and alpine hillsides, Georgetown Lake is picturesque by any standards. A popular recreation lake during the summer, Georgetown Lake is renown as a prolific aquatic lake in both insect production and fish growth. Although whirling disease has impacted the native runs of rainbows, stocking programs have minimized losses. Arlee rainbows, kamloops and Eagle Lake rainbows average 14 inches with impressive numbers of 16-18 inchers. Although less in numbers, brook trout grow to impressive size, and, yes, trophy trout abound.

Late spring and early summer bring about heavy hatches of Callibaetis. By mid-summer, look for emerging damselflies followed by prolific hatches of caddisfly. Because of the gradual gradient along the shore, most fishermen prefer to fish from boats or float tubes. Smaller tippets, heavy fish and thick weed beds creates a fun and challenging fishing experience in a beautiful setting. The lake is easily accessed around its entire length, and the immediate area offers numerous campgrounds, boat launches, picnic sites and swimming.

(USFS) **Phillipsburg Bay Campground:** The campground has 69 campsites which accommodate trailers up to 32 feet. The boat launch is suitable for trailers and two-wheel drive vehicles.

(USFS) **Piney Creek Campground:** The campground has 49 campsites and can accommodate trailers up to 48 feet. The boat launch is suitable for trailers and two-wheel drive vehicles.

MM 27.1: Georgetown Lake Picnic Site

MM 24.8: Grassy Point Boat Launch

MM 19.5: Spring Hill Campground (picnic): Spring Hill Campground offers 15 campsites with 22' trailer space. The campground is 11 miles northwest of Anaconda on Highway 1.

MM 8: Anaconda, Montana

MM 5: Lost Creek State Park: Take Route 273 north from Highway 1 and then follow the signs six miles to the campground. Lost Creek tumbles over a fifty foot ledge, which makes this one of the more scenic campgrounds in the area. The campsite provides 25 campsites with water and toilets. Lost Creek is a small creek offering fair catches of smaller brook trout and cutthroats.

MM 4.4: Road to Wisdom, Montana (Big Hole River)

MM 0: I 90 -- End of the scenic route from Drummond to Anaconda

Return to Interstate 90 at Drummond, Montana Traveling East to Anaconda and Butte

MM 169: Rest area

Exit 171: Fishing access to upper Clark Fork River

Exit 174: Garrison Junction and the **Little Blackfoot River:** The Little Blackfoot River is really no more than a creek, but it is well worth fishing. Although no public access points are available, numerous pull-over spots may be seen from the highway on the way to Helena, a distance of 44 miles. Most of the land is not posted, and the creek runs parallel to railroad tracks for a number of miles north of Garrison. Although some sections hold larger browns, a typical brown runs 8 to 12 inches.

 **Exit 179: Beck Hill Fishing Access**

Exit 184: Deerlodge, Montana

Exit 187: Deerlodge Information Center

Exit 197: Galen Fishing Access

Exit 201: Warm Springs Wildlife Management Area: Warm Spring Ponds, one of the largest superfund clean-up sites in the country, has been transformed into a wetlands management area for wildlife and trophy trout management. After a century of copper mining and milling contamination, the area became barren. Arco and the Anaconda Company have spent millions of dollars to prevent metal seepage from Silver Bow Creek. Today fly fishers stalk trophy browns and rainbows in these ponds. The most popular method, however, is fishing from a float tube. Brochures and fishing regulations are placed at the entrance. Camping is non-designated camping, and you will need to bring your own water. (Pack it in – Pack it out) The trout average two pounds, and there are still some monsters that cruise along the bottom. The problem, however, is that they are satiated from an abundance of aquatic insects and great populations of scuds and leeches.

I have fished it only once in 1983 with Charlie Miller who owned a fly shop in Hamilton. I have bitter-sweet memories of that day. I broke a Sage rod on the first cast. Earlier in the morning I had leaned my rod on the hood of the truck, and the wind had blown it down. Charlie inadvertently stepped on it, but the only damage we could detect was a tiny chip in the enamel. One cast and it exploded. I borrowed Charlie's spare rod, and we fished all day in one pond. Finally, I landed a 24" brown. Just before the end of the day, I landed one more fish. How hard are you willing to work for a trophy trout?

The best time to fish is in the spring and fall. Be sure to read the special regulations.

Exit 201: Anaconda, Montana
Exit 219: Junction with Interstate 15 to the Big Hole River and the Beaverhead River: (See pages 155-165)

Interstate 90 from Butte to Livingston

Exit 249: Whitehall, Montana and the Jefferson River: Having spent a number of days fishing the Jefferson the one year I lived in Whitehall, I can with a clear conscience steer you away from this one. Even before the days of Whirling Disease, the Jefferson presented a challenge. Primarily a brown trout stream, the Jefferson river flows 80 miles through farm land which adversely impacts late summer stream flows. Locals, like my former high school principal Nick Holmes, know how to reap the bounty of the Jefferson, as do most of the ranch kids. If you are traveling through the area and short on time, pass this one up as you are real close to the Madison, the Big Hole and the Beaverhead!

 **Exit 256: Cardwell, Montana and the Boulder River**

Lewis and Clark Caverns: Located in the rugged Jefferson River Canyon, Lewis and Clark Caverns features one of the most highly decorated limestone caverns in the Northwest. Naturally air conditioned, these spectacular caves are lined with stalagmites and columns. The Caverns—which are part of Montana's first and best known state park—are electrically lighted and safe to visit. To avoid peak use periods, call the park for suggested visitation and tour times. (406-287-3541)

Montana State Parks brochure

Exit 274: Exit to Ennis, Montana (Madison River – See page 145)

Exit 278: (Side Trip – Madison River) Three Forks / Route to Yellowstone National Park via the Madison River to West Yellowstone Entrance (Hwy 287)

Note: Skip to page 150 to continue on Interstate 90.

Madison River

Deemed one of the most abundant trout fisheries in the world, the Yellowstone River has a challenger less than four hours away. Montana's second crown jewel is still a show case. Having been ravaged by whirling decease during the early part of this decade, Madison loyalists watched the number of rainbows plunge from 3500 a mile down to 500 to 600 per mile. Juvenile populations dropped 90% in a few short years. Clearly the Madison fishing frenzy has waned. No longer do wade fishermen curse the steady stream of drift boats. But newcomers will find no memorial markers with epitaphs lamenting the death of the Madison. The loss has been profound, but the Madison River is still one of the top fisheries in Montana. Browns average 1,500 to 1,800 per mile with a healthy population of trophy fish.

Research continues on solutions to mitigate the whirling disease impact on rainbows. One promising solution is looking at early spawning rainbows which would have less exposure to the WD parasite. In temperatures blow 50 degrees, the host worm actually produces very few spores. In an article published in the Missoulian August 6, 1998, Dick Vincent, Region 3 Manager, suggests that finding strains of rainbows and cutthroats that are predisposed to spawn early holds promise for the future. "We may be able to actually spawn fish in the wild, imprint the colder temperature on them, then put them back out there in the hope that they would imprint their young to spawn earlier."

What is not missing from the Madison River today is the opportunity to fish a great brown stream that offers pristine settings and some of the most beautiful water in the world. Whether in the park or in the Ennis area, the Madison River deserves respect having only slipped from runner-up to second place.

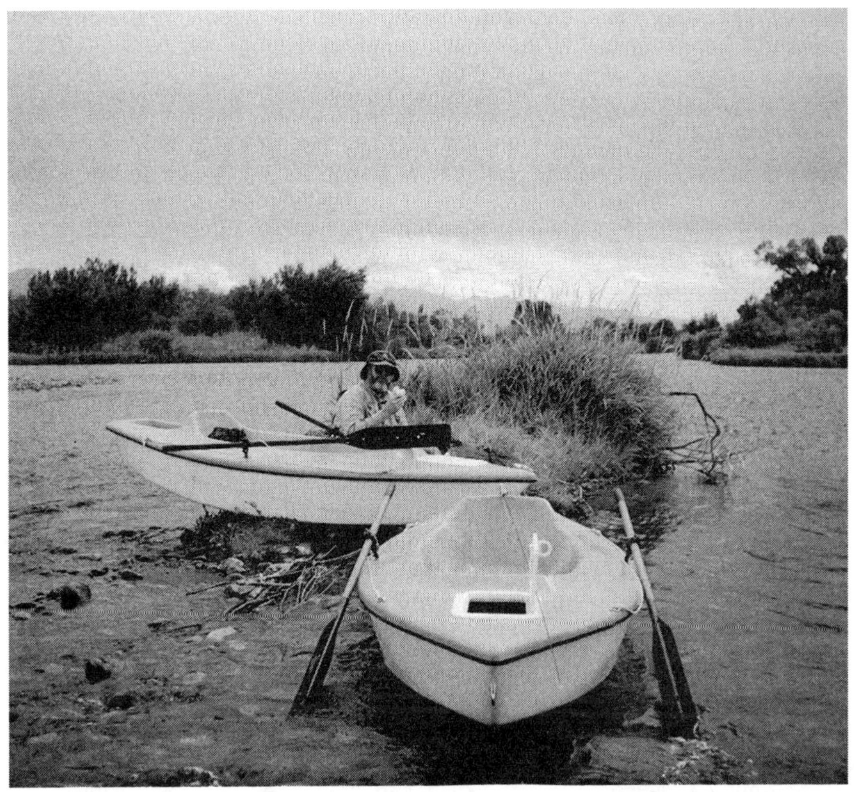

The author taking a break on the Madison River near Ennis, Montana

The Madison River originates fifteen miles inside the Park from the West Yellowstone Entrance. Just above the National Park Meadow, the Gibbon River joins the Firehole to begin the Madison's journey for over a 130 miles to Three Forks, where it joins the Gallatin and the Jefferson to form the Missouri River. Although the park section is fished throughout the summer, the best fishing occurs in June during the Salmon Fly hatch and the Green Drake hatch. Migratory trout spawn in this section both during the spring and fall. The fall receives heavy pressure as anglers anticipate the fall brown spawning runs out of

Hebgen Lake. Heavy duty streamer patterns work best, but fishermen are also successful using nymphs and egg patterns.

Keep in mind that by mid summer the park section water begins to rise in temperature due to the summer heat combined with the thermal activity in the Firehole region. An additional challenge is that Madison River trout are hammered all year long, and they become vary educated. Just inside the park boundary, fishermen can take a left on a dirt road to Baker's Hole area if they want some semblance of solitude. With the advent of fall and the anticipation of brown spawning runs, the area becomes quite a popular gathering spot. Regardless of the season, be cautious in disturbing wildlife, especially bears.

Leaving the Park, the Madison takes a short run and enters Hebgen Lake. Hebgen Lake runs 16-miles long and the area provides a number of campgrounds. Most of the arms of the lake offer good fly fishing for float tubers. For camping information contact the Hebgen Lake Ranger District, PO Box 520, West Yellowstone, MT 59758 or call (406) 646-7369. All Hebgen Lake Ranger District fee sites are available to reserve on the recreation reservation system by calling 1-800-280-2267. Hebgen Lake offers seven campgrounds. Rainbow Point Campground and Baker's Hole campground exclude tent camping because of bear activity. Baker's Hole Campground is right on the Madison River just above where it joins the Madison Arm of Hebgen Lake. Anglers will find a white stake denoting the Park boundary.

At the outlet of Hebgen Lake, Quake Lake was formed during the 1959 earthquake. Below Quake Lake to the Junction with Highway 87, the scared remnants of the quake make floating this section of the river extremely dangerous, and even experts shun this short section. The junction with Highway 87 begins the mileage markers. Ennis, Montana, is 41 miles downstream.

MM 0: Highway 287 junction with Highway 87 to Henry's Lake, Idaho. The water from Quake Lake to the junction with Highway 87 is both sobering and challenging. The 1959 quake registered 7.8 on the Richter Scale, and an entire mountain slid down on one of the most productive stretches of the Madison for large trout. A campground was buried, and many lives were lost. Almost forty years later, gray pine tree stalks slant from the river, and the boulder strewn heaps of piled high gravel and rock testify to this horrific event. The water looks barren above the junction, but dedicated nymph fishermen take fish in the fast foam and surface film. From the junction to Ennis, a distance of approximately 50 miles, this famous section of the Madison has been described as a 50-mile riffle.

The best time to fish this section of the Madison is early summer and fall. The first awaited hatch is the prolific caddis hatches of late May and June, but the Madison River's Salmon Fly hatch is justifiably famous and eagerly awaited. But like the Big Hole and Rock Creek, making flight reservations and motel reservations six months in advance can lead to great disappoints when you are confronted with lingering storms, late run-offs, or heavy or late snow accumulations. Hitting it just right is a crap shoot, but if you have the time and the money, it is more than worth the gamble. Traditionally, the hatch starts during the last week of June through mid July followed by the presence of golden stoneflies. With the announcement of, "Gentlemen, start your engines," an interesting rush to the water takes place. Nymph fishermen head upstream above the hatch to chuck 2 inch weighted Bitch Creeks and various other stonefly nymphs into the cold water. Dry fly enthusiasts rush around probing the river and chasing guide rigs. And the leisure set move behind the advancing hatch knowing that trout have orange memories and rise readily to smaller yellow and orange stimulators.

The dog days of August calls for terrestrials, but those enticements are often ignored. One popular and effective technique is to add a bead-head Prince as a dropper. Realistically, during the heat of August, expect to catch smaller fish. By all means pound the water mid day with hoppers, beetles and ants, but do not ignore early morning nymphing techniques and evening hatches of Blue-wing Olives. September and October bring about a change of tactics with heavy streamers.

Wade Lake and Cliff Lake: Wade Lake and Cliff Lake turn off is just downstream from the junction. Both lakes are fairly large and may also be reached from the West Fork Bridge access at mile marker 9.6. Both lakes have campgrounds, but fishing from shore is somewhat difficult due to the steep shoreline. The lakes support healthy populations of 10 to 14 inch trout. Wade Lake Campground offers 30 camping sites, Hill Top Campground offers 20, and Cliff Point offers 6 sites and a trailer boat launch

MM 9.6: West Fork Campground: The West Fork Campground offers seven shaded tent camping sites right along the West Fork of the Madison, which is a beautiful stream in its own right, offering fair catches of rainbows and browns. The West Fork may be accessed for almost fourteen miles on a dirt road. The West Fork blows out early during spring run-off and after a heavy storm. Above the West Fork the river clears earlier due to both the nature of the Park and the addition of Hebgen Lake, which tends to settle the silt. Next to the West Fork Campground is the West Fork Cabin Camp and RV Campground.

MM 15.7: Lyon Bridge Recreation Area: Boat launch and picnic area

MM 22.7: Palisades Campground: One mile off the highway, Palisades Campground offers 7 camping sites along side of the river with a towering bluff on the other side.

MM 30.8: McAttee Bridge: McAttee bridge has a day use site as well as a boat launch. Three miles down a well maintened road is the Wall Creek Wildlife Management Area and **West Madison Campground.** If you like sage brush and full exposure to the sun, then this campground provides 22 camping sites and a boat launch.

MM 38: Cameron, Montana: Cameron has a post office and the Blue Moon Store and RV Park.

MM 40: Varney Bridge (campground): The road to Varney Bridge is over three miles on some rough road. Although the campground has a self-deposit fee requirement, it is somewhat old and run-down. Nonetheless, the five or six campsites are on the river bank with mature cottonwoods providing welcome shade. Most locals take the secondary road out of Ennis on the west side of the river to Varney Bridge.

Floaters can choose a half-day float and spend more time out of the boat fishing by taking out at the Eight Mile Ford boat launch, or they may float down to Ennis Campground. The stretch from Varney Bridge to Ennis Campground, unlike the water upstream, separates into many braided channels and islands. Even with this separation of water, the Madison flows swift against undercut banks and tiny islands. This section has traditionally maintained the largest browns.

Ennis Campgrond: Just across the bridge from Ennis, Ennis Campground is a shaded campground on the river. The campground is a Fish, Wildlife and Parks campground with 25 camping sites with mowed grass. Before the bridge crossing, look for the turn off to **Valley Garden Campground** which is on the secondary road leading to Bear Trap Canyon. Float fishing from Ennis Campground to Ennis Lake is closed.
Ennis, Montana

The Madison River from Ennis to Three Forks:

Ennis Lake: The lake is shallow, no more than 20 feet in most places. Solar heating of the lake, often reaching close to 80 degrees during the heat of summer, threaten both the trout in the lake and the trout downstream. In spite of this, healthy populations of three to five pound Eagle Lake rainbows and browns entice boaters and float tubers.

Ennis Lake Outlet to Three Forks: The outlet of Ennis Lake picks up speed as it drops down through the Lee Metcalf Wilderness in Bear Trap Canyon. Bear Trap Canyon is wicked whitewater country and should be avoided unless you are knowledgeable about the vagaries of this rushing canyon water. For floating information contact the Bureau of Land Management, Box 3388, Butte, MT 59702.

Highway 287 splits at the town of Norris and heads to Cardwell and Interstate 90. The Madison River is reached again by taking Highway 84 to Warm Springs and then to the outlet of Beartrap Canyon. A secondary road, Madison Road, follows the river to Three Forks. The lower Madison is broad and much warmer as a result of the shallow water of Lake Ennis. Lower in elevation, the lower Madison's water temperatures by mid-summer slows down the fishing. Released fish are highly stressed and frequently die. Spring and fall are most assuredly the best time to fish the lower Madison.

Side Trip: The Ruby River

Follow Highway 287 out of Ennis to the restored mining towns of Virginia City and Nevada City to the town of Twin Bridges where the Ruby River and the Beaverhead join to form the Jefferson River. The Ruby River may be a misnomer as it really looks more like a large creek than a river, especially late in the summer. While populations of grayling increase, rainbow populations seem to be decreasing. Even with stream access laws, the Ruby offers few public access points with the exception of three or four bridges. Similar to the Beaverhead, the Ruby meanders down through a willow-lined valley. Unless you have access on private property or a lot of free time to seek out those few and far-between public penetrations, my advice would be to turn south on Highway 41 towards Dillon and fish the famous Beaverhead. (See the Beaverhead River on page 178.

Returning to Interstate 90 heading east towards Bozeman

Exit 278: See page 145
Exit 283: Madison Buffalo Jump State Park: Prior to the introduction of the horse to the Indians of the Northern Great Plains, the Blackfeet, Flathead and Shoshone tribes stampeded herds of bison over this precipice in order to secure the necessities of food, shelter, and tools. The top of the jump affords impressive views of the Madison River Valley and surrounding mountain ranges.

Montana State Parks brochure

Exit 288: Manhattan, Montana

Exit 298: Belgrade, Montana

Exit 305: Bozeman, Montana / Route to Yellowstone National Park via the Gallatin River along Highway 191 to the West Yellowstone Entrance

Gallatin River

Note: For a camping and picnic guide to Gallatin National Forest along the Gallatin River, call (406) 587-6920 or write Bozeman Ranger District, 3710 Fallon Street, Suite C, Bozeman, MT 59718.

Float fishing is prohibited on the Gallatin inside the park boundaries to the East Gallatin River. The only section open to float fishing is from the East Gallatin River down to Logan Bridge on Highway 205 or further down to Missouri Headwaters State Park. The Gallatin during spring run-off challenges floaters with Class III and IV whitewater. If you are going to float even during the summer, I would recommend buying the Gallatin River, Montana Afloat map which may be purchased in any fly shop throughout western and southwestern Montana. It would also be prudent to stop by one of the local fly shops in Bozeman or the Gallatin Valley for current river information.

About forty years ago in the Mono Lake Basin, I picked up my father's South Bend fly rod. I had no use for a tapered leader. Four feet of stout monofilament attached to an Eagle Claw hook with garden hackle or a salmon egg was all I needed. Carrying an old set of rusty pliers and a pill box of split-shot, I was ready to meet the challenges of the day. Steep timbered mountains, towering crags and the fluttering silver dollars on aspen trees imprinted my boyhood with a transcendentalist view of nature. The Gallatin is equally inspiring.

Unlike the Madison River, which is surrounded by bench land sage brush, the Gallatin Canyon section inspires that same boyhood sense of wonderment. The Gallatin River from the Park boundary to Taylor Creek primarily holds small rainbows. Still resembling a creek, the water is easily waded and easily assessable with many pull-outs along the highway. Taylor Creek is renown for mudding up the river. Spring run-off "generally" subsides the last week of June.

From Taylor Creek to the West Fork of the Gallatin, and the junction with Big Sky Resort, harbors an astounding number of 10 to 12 inch rainbows with estimates from 3,000 to 5,000 per mile! This section can only be described as just fun fishing. Drive along the river and pick the type of water you enjoy fishing. Riffles, pockets, pools and boulder-strewn sections provide a diversity of habitat for both dry fly fishermen, nymph fishermen and spin fishermen. The best part of this fun fishing is the fact that the fish readily rise to attractor patterns in the fast waters. Leaving the red sandstone cliffs and the canyon behind, the Gallatin enters agricultural bottomland.

Heavily agriculture use leaves a scarcity of water in some parts of the braided bottomland. Access is difficult with the exception of public bridge crossings, which are numerous above and below Four Corners. Be sure to stay under the high-water mark, and you are perfectly legal. During the heat of summer, this section is difficult to fish with the exception of pools and banks which often hold good size browns. If you are visitor with a limited time to fish, skip this section of water. From the Logan Bridge on Highway 205 at the junction with Logan-Trident Road to Missouri Headwaters State Park, the river is open to float fishing. This is an especially popular section during the fall for spawning runs from the Missouri River.

Gallatin River

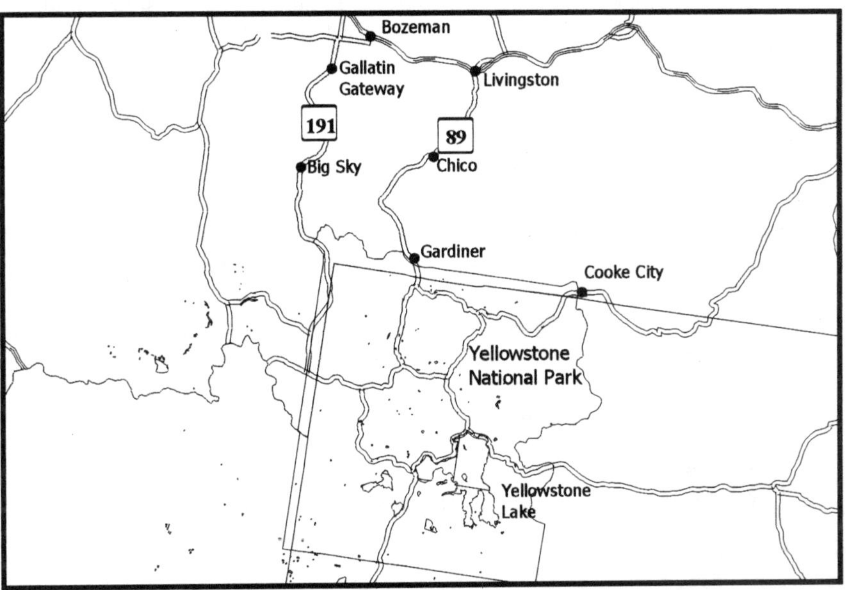

Side Trip: West Yellowstone to Bozeman Via the Gallatin River

MM 1: Access road to **Baker's Flat Campground:** Located three miles north of West Yellowstone, the campground has 72 camping sites and is restricted to **hard-sided campers only.**

MM 2.8: Access to **Rainbow Lake Campground:** Located five miles north of West Yellowstone, take Road #610 west three miles, and then turn north on Road 6954 two miles to the campground. The campground has 85 camping sites and is restricted to hard-sided campers only.

MM 11.1: Grayling Creek: Grayling Creek is an over-grown, swampy creek holding fair numbers of trout, but bring along plenty of mosquito repellant and pepper spray for the bears!

MM 20: Gallatin River inside Yellowstone Park Boundary

MM 22: Fan Creek: Fan Creek is within Yellowstone Park Boundary and holds small cutthroats and rainbows. Fan Creek may be reached above the highway by taking a short hike up the Fawn Pass Trail.

MM 31: You are now exiting Yellowstone Park, and you will need a Montana State Fishing License.

MM 34: Taylor Creek: Taylor Creek is good fishing for fair size cutthroats.

MM 41.5: Red Cliff Campground: Located 48 miles south of Bozeman on Highway 191, the campground offers 68 camping sites and 4 picnic sites. Just below Red Cliff, the highway enters the Porcupine Wildlife Management Area that ends just short of the **West Fork of the Gallatin.** The West Fork of the Gallatin is a small stream, and it parallels the road leading to Big Sky Resort. The stream fishes well for 7 to 9" trout if you care to fish in a commercially developed playground.

MM 56.8 Moose Creek Flat Campground: Located 32 miles south of Bozeman, the campground has 14 camping sites

MM 57: Swan Creek Campground and Greek Creek Campground: Greek Creek Campground is on Highway 191 thirty-one miles south of Bozeman and has 14 campsites. Swan Creek Campground is one mile east of Highway 191 on Swan Creek Road with 11 camping sites.

MM 65.3: Squaw Creek Bridge / Spire Rock Campground: Spire Rock Campground is located 26 miles south of Bozeman off Highway 191. From the highway take Squaw Creek Road two miles. The campground has 10 camping sites and is a non-fee campground. **Squaw Creek** is a fast, tumbling creek, and it provides good fishing for rainbows, cutthroats and brookies. A few miles down Highway 191, **Spanish Creek** enters from the west. Spanish Creek is also good fishing for smaller brook trout.

Interstate 90: Livingston, Montana

Exit 333: Livingston, Montana / Route to Yellowstone National Park via the Yellowstone River to the town of Gardiner (North Entrance)

Yellowstone River from Livingston to Yellowstone National Park

The legendary Yellowstone River inspires awe and reverence. From its source waters high in the Absaroka Mountains to its rendezvous with the Missouri River in North Dakota, the great Yellowstone River remains an uninterrupted, free-flowing river for over 600 miles.

Outside the park the river affords excellent fishing opportunities from Livingston to Gardner for both wade fishermen and float fishermen. Below Livingston, the Yellowstone River offers excellent fishing to Big Timber. One disadvantage of this section is that the float fishing access points are further apart and access to the river is more restricted. For the most part, the Yellowstone River is an easily navigated river.

However, the three-mile section of water from Gardner to McConnell Landing is a whitewater section as is the section from Joe Brown to Yankee Jim Canyon. This section requires an experienced whitewater oarsman. From the East River Road to Livingston is relatively easier to float although braided channels, sharp turns and sweepers require the usual vigilance. Mayor's Landing on 8th Street is the last Livingston take-out.

Yellowstone River in the Park: Since the mileage marker 0 begins at the park entrance and ends at mileage marker 60 in Livingston, I have decided to work backwards on the chance that you may be traveling to the park from Livingston. Shuttles may be arranged through the fly shops.

MM 60: Livingston, Montana

 **MM 51: East River Road Fishing Access**

MM 50: Carter Bridge: Carter Bridge has a good boat take-out and is a good spot for wade fishermen.

 **MM 45: Trail Creek fishing access**

MM 43.3: Pine Creek: Take the Pine Creek road 1.4 miles to the bridge fishing access and boat launch.

MM 41.4: Mallards Rest Campground: The campground is a fee campground and offers 20 sites on a "Pack it in – Pack it Out" basis. The campground also offers a boat launch and good access for wade fishermen.

Note: From Carter Bridge to just above Point of Rocks, the East River Road parallels the river. The East River Road has Loch Levin Campground. Loch Levin is 9 miles south of Livingston. Take the Pine Creek Road and head south again to the campground. Loch Levin Campground has 30 campsites, water, toilets and a boat launch.

MM 37.2: Mill Creek Bridge: Mill Creek Bridge has a private boat launch that is not posted. The gate is open, but I would skip this access unless you have a 4-wheel drive vehicle. The launch is steep and rocky with little room to maneuver. Take the Mill Creek Road 11 miles to **Snowbank Campground** which has 12 camping sites.

MM 33.4: Fishing access

MM 31: Emigrant, Montana: Take the road to the river and cross the bridge. On the other side of the bridge is a day use site with a good boat launch as well as good access for wade fishermen.

MM 25.5: Fishing access

MM 23.8: Meditation Point: Here is a rest area and picnic site large enough for the largest RVs with good fishing access to the river.

MM 21: Point of Rocks: Point of Rocks has a boat launch.

MM 19.7: East River Road

MM 18: Carbella Campground: Carbella is an unimproved campground 1 mile west of the Tom Miner Bridge. It has five campsites.

MM 13: Yankee Jim fishing access. Just upstream from Yankee Jim is the Slip and Slide access, but you will need to carry your boat to the water's edge.

MM 7.1: Corwin Springs Boat Launch

 **MM 6.3: LaDuke Spring Picnic Site**

MM 3: McConnell Landing

MM 0: Gardiner, Montana

Yellowstone National Park

Fishing Fact: Larger than Rhode Island and Delaware combined, Yellowstone National Park is immense, covering 3,472 square miles. Yellowstone Lake itself covers 136 square miles. The world's first national park, it no doubt vies for the title, "World's Greatest Trout Park." If you are limited to less than a week to both explore and fish the park, then this book will suffice. However, if you have planned an extensive vacation in the Park to fully fish its riches, then I would recommend purchasing The Yellowstone Fly-Fishing Guide, written by Craig Mathews and Clayton Molinero.

Yellowstone Campground Information

(Park hand-out – Yell 361, 1998)

"Campsite availability is first-come, first serve at the following campgrounds: Mammoth, Norris, Indian Creek, Pebble Creek, Slough Creek and Tower Fall. During peak camping season (late June to mid-August) all campgrounds may be filled by 11:00 a.m.; arrive early to obtain a site. [Slough Creek often has vacated campsite filled by 9 a.m.] **Reservations** can be made for Canyon, Bridge Bay, Madison, Grant Village, and the Fishing Bridge RV Park by calling (307) 344-7311. Overnight camping of any type (tent, vehicle, or RV) outside designated campgrounds is not permitted.
Hookups are available at the concession operated Fishing Bridge RV Park, which is open from late May to early October. The RV Park provides water, sewer, and electrical hookups. The RV Park is restricted to hard-sided camping units; tents and trailers are not allowed.

Showers and Laundry Facilities are provided by a concession service for an additional fee. They are located adjacent to the campgrounds at Canyon, Grant Village, and Fishing Bridge RV Park (showers and laundry are located within four miles of Bridge Bay campground)."

Fees generally average between $10 and $15 except at the Fishing Bridge RV Park which charged $27 during the summer of 1998.

The park entrances are the South Entrance above Jackson, Wyoming, the West Entrance in the town of West Yellowstone, the North Entrance below the town of Gardiner, Montana, the northeast entrance a few miles from Cooke

City, Montana, and the East Entrance leading to Cody, Wyoming. All entrances lead to Yellowstone Lake, and a loop connects all the entrances.

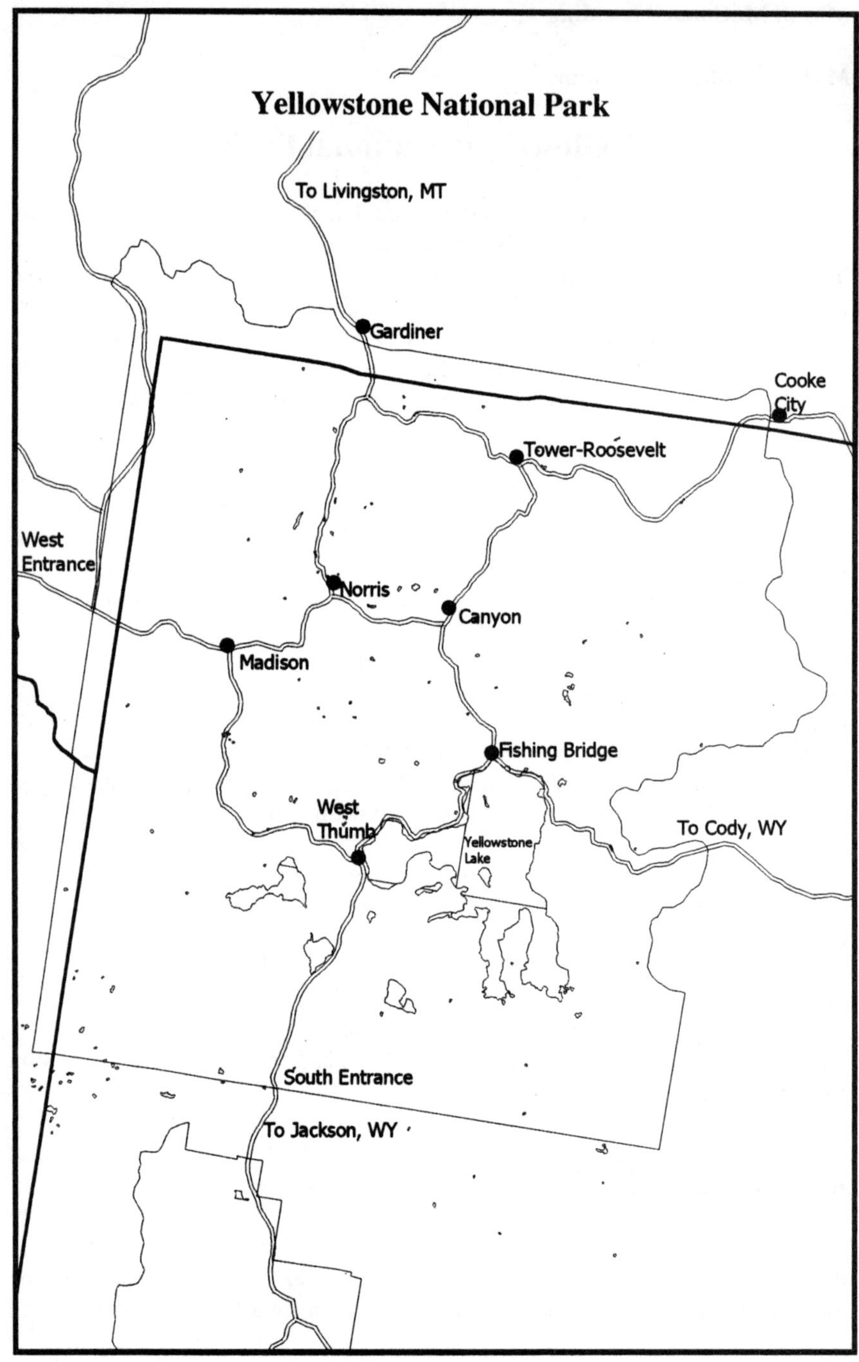

In keeping with the spirit of this highway fishing guide, I have included only those rivers, streams and lakes which can be reached by vehicle or in a short day hike. Since the Park does not employ mileage marker signs like the state of Montana, I have concentrated on the park entrance roads and the Grand Loop Road.

Gardiner Entrance

From Mammoth to Tower to Cooke City

Gardner River: A special bait section for children provides excellent fishing for small brookies above Osprey Falls close to the Indian Creek campground. Below the falls, the Gardner plunges down a canyon on its course to the Yellowstone River. The next access is the Mammoth-Tower Bridge a few miles east of Mammoth. Upstream from the bridge the canyon impedes progress, but this short section holds numerous 6 to 10 inch rainbows and brookies. Below the bridge the Gardner River is joined by Lava Creek. Standing on the Mammoth side of the bridge, you can look down to where Lava Creek joins the river. Hiking down below this section provides good fishing for cutthroats and brook trout although be prepared for some of the choice waters to come up empty. Rather than turning the corner and heading upstream to the bridge again, take the time to fish the first half mile of Lava Creek. Lava Creek is strictly dabbing your fly in small pockets, but when I last fished it during August of 1998, the rainbows were averaging 10 inches and fat. This section, extending for three miles, can be hot during August so tie on a bead-head Prince as a dropper.

Yellowstone River in the Black Canyon (trail access): The Black Canyon may be reached by hiking across sage brush, bench land and down to the river. From the bridge above Tower, near the confluence with the Lamar River, down to Blacktail Deer Creek, the distance to the river may vary from two to fours miles. I especially enjoy this rugged canyon fishing on big water. Concentrated nymph fishing is so much easier than training my trifocals on a size #18 dry at Buffalo Ford. On my last trip down into the canyon, I landed a measured 18 inch cutthroat. But hiking in and out unnerves me as I am too cheap to invest $40 for pepper spray, and I almost always fish alone. Somehow I never remember to make noise. I huff and puff up the slope furtively glancing behind me.

Mammoth-Tower Bridge: Access to the Gardner River and Lava Creek

Lava Creek Picnic Site: The fishing is somewhat difficult both upstream and downstream due to brush and trees, but the fishing is good for small trout.

Blacktail Deer Creek: Blacktail Deer Creek crosses the Mammoth-Tower Road above Lava Creek crossing. The creek cascades down the mountain four miles to meet the Yellowstone River. The creek offers good fishing for brook trout above and below the road.

Blacktail Ponds: A small pond a short distance from the road, Blacktail pond is void of shrubbery or brush, although it is very boggy for most of the shoreline. It is rare to pass by this pond at dusk without seeing at least one nymph fisherman working the pond for 10 to 14 inch cutthroats and brook trout.

Tower Creek: A good size creek, Tower Creek may be reached from the Tower Creek Campground. Fishing is good for small rainbows and brookies. A section of the Yellowstone River may also be fished by Tower Falls

Yellowstone River above Tower (the confluence with the Lamar River is a mile downstream): Just as you cross the bridge, there is a picnic site and parking area. A trail leads down to the confluence of the Lamar River and the Yellowstone River. The Lamar section consists of heavily silted pools and steep banks, but from the Lamar upstream for a half-mile offers rough and tumble nymph water. It is too small of a section to share.

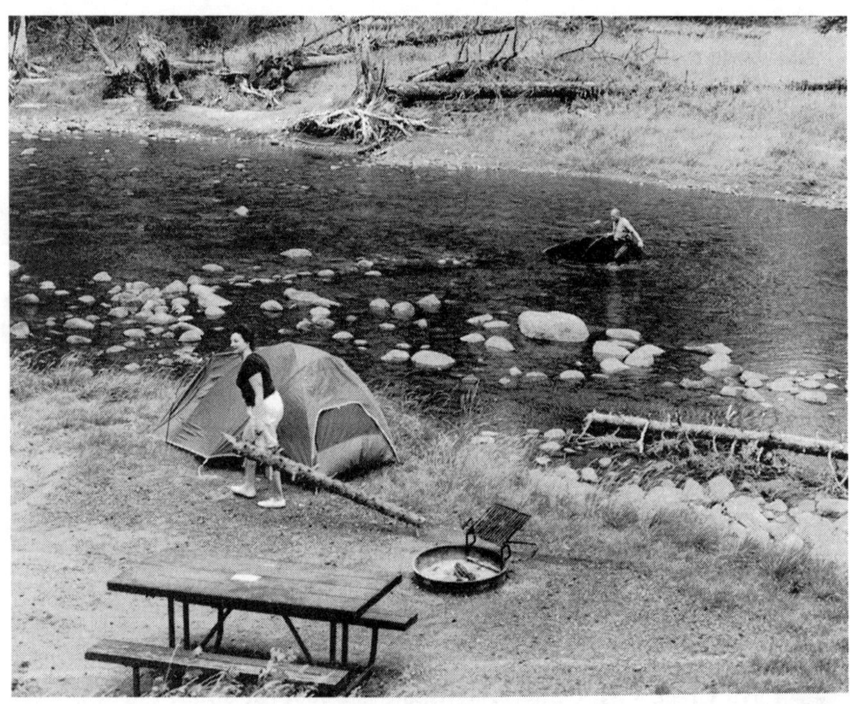

A gust of wind blows a tent into Slough Creek.

Slough Creek: Over twenty years ago when I lived in Wyoming, I heard near reverent praising of Slough Creek. As I recall at that time, only trailers were allowed in the campground so I passed it up for more favorable fishing in other areas of the park. In finalizing this book, I headed for Slough Creek as soon as I entered the Park. Pulling a 15-foot, 1984 Komfort, I was prepared. I arrived to a gala of colorful tents at the campground at 9 a.m. and watched two families depart. Slough Creek Campground is off the beaten track, actually only 2.3 miles of washboard road from the Cooke City Road, but it is a long ways from the Interstate for travelers heading home. By 9:30 the three vacated sites were full.

During that first day, I returned to fish the Gardner again. Returning to the campground, the sky clouded up and in no time at all, my windshield wipers were on high, smearing and skipping across bug splats. The next day I fished the Lamar for the first time. Because of the heat spell, it had been fishing very slowly. When I arrived at a secluded spot, the water was somewhat roiled, but the off color was not enough to concern me. I fished for an hour and a half to no avail. Having been skunked, I headed for the confluence of the Lamar and the Yellowstone determined to catch a fish on the Lamar --nothing. Catching a few hefty cutthroats on the Yellowstone River, I headed back to Slough Creek for an early dinner and then a up the trail to the first meadow.

The trail to the three meadows of Slough Creek does not begin in the campground as a narrow canyon impedes progress. The first meadow is notoriously tough from what I had read and from what I heard in camp. Everyone advised me to pass up the first meadow and fish the second meadow, which is about five miles up from the trailhead. By the time I had hiked in to the first meadow, I realized that I had only about two hours to fish. I walked up to the first bank and peered into the softly flowing creek. I put on my Polaroid glasses and in doing so looked down to see a 16" cutthroat slurping on midges oblivious to my presence.

I crawled through the grass to the next run and spotted a 17 or 18 inch cut gently fanning his tail and sipping bugs right next to the bank less than ten feet in front of me. Ten offerings later, I stood up. The cutthroat moved one foot over and two feet up and continued slurping a #22 white midge. Slough Creek cutthroats are like the elk and buffalo. If you don't get too close, they just ignore you and go on chewing their cud, or in this case sipping the midges. For the second time in one day I had been skunked!

Most of the fishermen I spoke to that evening said they had poor to fair fishing at the second meadow and excellent fishing for smaller trout at the third meadow, which is 8-miles from the trailhead. Next time I am going right back to that first meadow with 7X tippet and an assortment of midge patterns.

Slough Creek offers excellent fishing from the campground to its meeting with the Lamar River, but it is similar to a spring creek and requires skill and patience. Surprisingly, few people actually fish this section while upwards of a hundred fishermen a day hike up to the meadow sections.

Lamar River: Another day! Regardless of my dismal introduction to the Lamar, the river offers excellent fishing for cutthroats and rainbows once the river has cleared (later than most). Craig Mathew in his book The Yellowstone Fly-Fishing Guide mentions the proclivity for Lamar cuts to migrate up and down the stream which, in turn, keeps anglers covering a lot of ground.

Gliding through open meadow land with towering mountain ranges in the background and sparse clusters of cottonwoods, it is easy to visualize what the entire region looked like prior to settlements. From its confluence with Soda Butte Creek to the canyon, a distance of six or seven miles, the Lamar receives lots of fishing attention. The expansive grassland, home to buffalo and antelope, hosts large grasshoppers and other terrestrials which find their way into the Lamar. The canyon, although more difficult to fish, offers slightly larger trout in the pools and pockets.

Soda Butte Creek: Gliding down a beautifully timbered canyon from Cooke City down to the Lamar flood plain, Soda Butte Creek offers quiet solitude and good fishing for cutthroats.

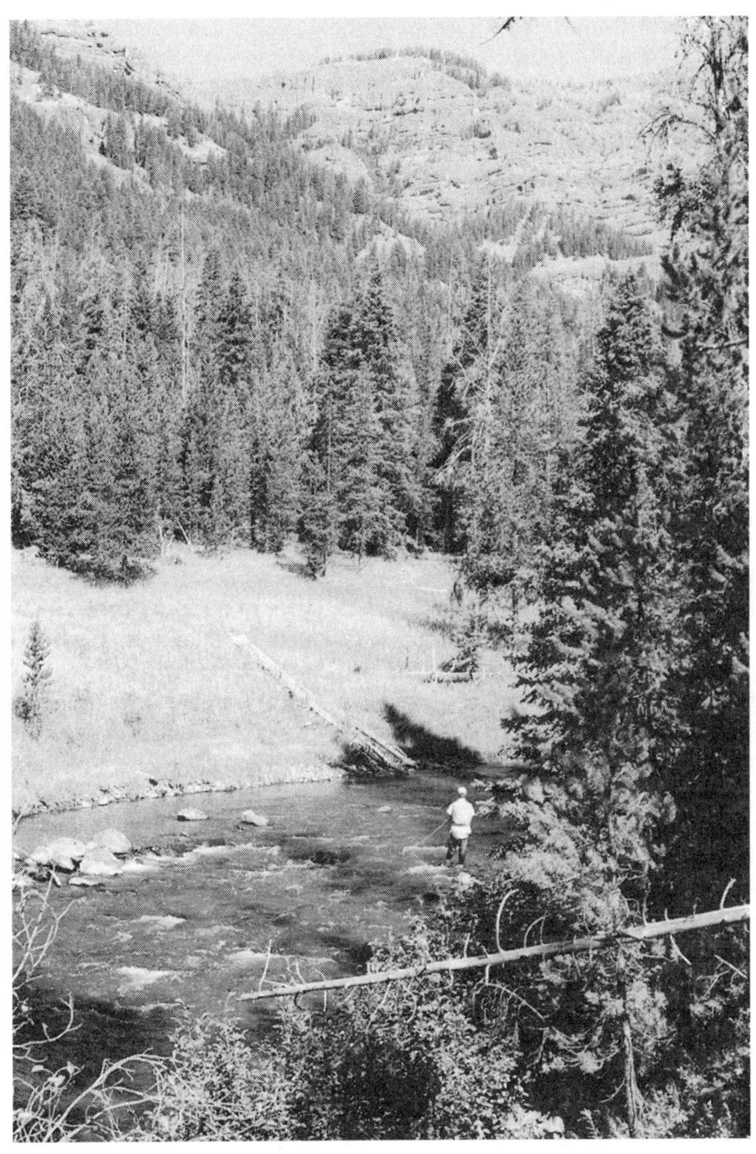

Gardiner Entrance

From Mammoth to Norris 21 miles
Norris to Madison Campground 14 miles

Indian Creek (campground): Sitting on a small rise eight miles south of Mammoth, Indian Creek Campground is surrounded by verdurous meadows and winding streams. Indian Creek joins the **Gardner River** near the campground and offers special bait fishing opportunities for children fishing for small brookies. **Obsidian Creek** joins the Gardner River in the vicinity of the campground and also offers good fishing for brookies and special regulations for children. By following the Bighorn Pass Trail near the campground, families may also fish **Panther Creek**, a small tributary of the Gardner River. For children and novice anglers, this campground offers wonderful fishing opportunities and good wildlife viewing prospects.

Twin Lakes: Although you will see people fishing these two shallow lakes, they are considered to be almost barren.

Norris Campground / Solfatara Creek: Entering the Gibbon River at Norris Junction and the campground, Solfatara offers fair to good fishing for smaller trout.

Gibbon River: From its source waters, Grebe and Wolf Lakes, the Gibbon River flows through timbered terrain until it crosses the Norris-Canyon Road and enters Virginia Meadows on its way to the Norris Campground area. Anglers can expect to fish for browns, rainbows and brook trout. Joining Solfatara Creek at Norris Junction, the Gibbon gradually gains stature along with wary browns. Down further lies the Gibbon Meadow followed by a nice section before Gibbons Falls. From Gibbon Falls, the Gibbon resembles more of a freestone creek until it reaches the meadow section and the confluence with the Firehole at Madison Campground. The best fishing period is the latter part of June and fall, but the river also responds well to a well-placed hopper during the heat of summer.

Yellowstone Saga

On my very first trip to Yellowstone Park in the early 70s, I stopped at Bud Lilly's Fly Shop in West Yellowstone. My two fly boxes in those days held mostly my own attractor abominations. I was eager to gain some good advice as I was camped at Madison Campground. My first day fishing produced pretty slim pickings. As a young man in my twenties, I was most familiar with fishing for rainbows and brookies on the eastern slopes of the Sierras. I had "Novice" written across my forehead.

The gentlemen who assisted me never gave me the bums rush when he found out that I was near broke and only planning on purchasing three or four flies. He dropped three huge Bitch Creek nymphs into the palm of my hand and told me how to fish them. I had never seen such leviathan monsters. I was incredulous. I wasn't even sure how well I could cast one. But oh, how sweet it was when I landed a 19 inch brown out of a meadow pool on the Gibbon River, a short hike from the campground. Later that evening I cast to the same trailing piece of grass, the exact same spot, and pulled in an 18 inch rainbow.

One of my sons was horrified a few years ago when he found the photographs of me holding up those bloody corpses. I explained to him the mentality of those days and quickly shared with him my conversion during that same year. I suppose as a final act of contrition I should burn the photographs, but I have put off that decision for later. Ten years later I would have another Yellowstone fishing experience, which I will always treasure. I back packed to the outlet of Heart Lake as a fishing guide and leader of five teenage boys.

The last trail hike I had made was as a Boy Scout. My pack was an old hand-me-down from my father, and it didn't have a padded hip belt. We had reserved the last campground at the outlet of Heart Lake. Getting a late start, we arrived at the ranger station on the lake and made arrangements to sleep at a mid-way campsite. One of my attendees had just leaned over the lake to scoop up a handful of water, and his sleeping bag fell into the lake, slowly expanding with water.

It was mid June and cold. During the day I had already lightened the load of one boy's pack, and I was exhausted. That night I lay in a small tent in my clothes. I was shivering. Giving up my sleeping bag to the youth was my responsibility, and I had no bitterness until early in the morning when I was shaking terribly from the cold. This homophobic young man in my warm sleeping bag wouldn't let me get near him!

The next day four of the boys pulled off the trail a mile from the campsite to fish the rises on the lake. I was stuck with the frail young man who by this time had passed on the remaining heavy items from his pack to mine. Arriving at the camp we were so exhausted all we could do was collapse to the ground. The youth was so exhausted he didn't bother extricating himself from his nearly empty pack. We were just a few feet away from the outlet creek. The boy turned to me and said, "I'll never do this again for the rest of my life. I'm sorry you had to carry all my stuff."

"It's ok," I said, "and just for the record, I've decided I'll never back pack again for the rest of my life. My feet are killing me, but I'm too pooped to even take off my boots."

Suddenly, a cannon ball dropped into the small creek. Thinking the troop was behind us up the slope, I yelled out, "Knock it off!" When the next rock slapped the water, we waited, but there was no response.

The young man, struggling out of his pack, looked up the slope and then gazed at the water. "Dave, those aren't rocks. They're fish. They're huge fish. They're feeding right in front of us, Dave."

"Go ahead, sport. They're all yours," I said.

"Maybe later," the lad replied. Within two seconds of this arcane conversation, we were both energized and racing to present the first cast. Within the next hour or two, we had both landed seven or eight spawners returning to the lake. All of these fish ranged in size from 18 to 20 inches. All of these beauties were caught on #12 attractor patterns. At the outlet, I caught a measured 24 inch male on a small Muddler. All of the fish were caught along a quarter mile, flat stretch of water before the creek plummeted down the canyon. The remaining young men boisterously appeared a few hours later bragging about catching a ton of 16 inch cuts along the shoreline. We nonchalantly told our tale, which earned nothing but hoots of derision.

For the next two days we caught the same fish and more. Each time one of us stalked the water's edge, we had to scale back our offerings until the last fish landed was caught on a #20 Adams. I will never forget those two days.

Madison Campground: Centrally located, the campground is bordered by the Gibbon River and the Firehole, and it is only 14 miles to West Yellowstone.

West Yellowstone Entrance

Park Entrance to Madison Campground 14 miles
Madison Campground to Old Faithful 16 miles
Old Faithful to West Thumb 17 miles
West Thumb to South Entrance 22 miles

Firehole: The Firehole, joining with the Gibbon River, begins the Madison River. Shallow wading water in an idyllic setting promise more than what the river will produce during the summer months when thermal heating drives the fish to cooler sanctuaries. The best time to fish the Firehole is during the spring and again in the fall.

Old Faithful: Faithful and never disappointing, the geyser symbolizes the power of nature.

Shosone Lake (trail): The second largest lake in Yellowstone Park with over 8,000 acres, the lake is huge, remote and accessed only by trail. When I taught in Jackson, Wyoming, my first summer fishing outfitter was Roberta Knapp. Roberta was one of the first woman outfitters in Wyoming. A tall, strong woman, this lady could fish and row a boat under any conditions. I learned a great deal from her, as she was a generous person and a passionate fly fisher. Driving out of the Gros Ventre one summer day, she shared with me all the great fishing stories she had of fishing big browns and lake trout on the channel between Shosone Lake and Lewis Lake. If you are fishing the park during the fall, be sure to take the Lewis Channel Trail, a seven-mile hike, or the trail just above it, which takes a straight line through the woods directly to Shosone Lake, a distance of 4.5 miles. Fishing heavy fall streamer patterns for big browns and lake trout in the fall has to be a wonderful experience, and I am sad to say I never made it.

Shosone Lake fishing is rated excellent during early summer with drys, nymphs, scuds and leech patterns. Later in the summer the trout retreat to deeper waters which are reached by canoeists paddling from Lewis Lake, through the channel and into Shosone Lake (with a one-mile portage at the end of the channel).

Lewis Lake: Lewis Lake allows motorized boats. Boat fishermen both spin and troll for large lake trout and browns. The lake's east shore parallels the road leading to the South Entrance. Fly fishermen fare well at both the inlet and the outlet to Lewis River.

West Thumb to Fishing Bridge Junction

(21 miles)

Yellowstone Lake: Looking at a map of Yellowstone National Park, Yellowstone Lake draws center attention at 87,450 acres. Famous for its staggering numbers of Yellowstone Cutthroat, the lake is presently under siege from the unauthorized introduction of nefarious lake trout. Thanks to some stupid, bucket-biologist, lake trout are expanding rapidly and preying on the young cutthroats. Regulations now require killing all lake trout caught.

Excellent fishing may be experienced right along the shoreline using small drys and nymphs. Anglers may keep two fish under 13 inches, but this is not always easy since most Yellowstone Cutthroat measure between 14 and 16 inches. Boating is allowed, but it requires a special permit along with special regulations for fishing in the arms of the lake. The most popular fishing from shore is between the Sand Point Picnic Site and the Gull Point area which is on the Grand Loop Road between West Thumb and the Fishing Bridge Junction. (Be sure to walk across the **Fishing Bridge** and gaze at all the fish.)

Yellowstone River to Gardiner, Montana

The river gathers her source water down through the meadows of the Thorofare to empty into the Southeast Arm of Yellowstone Lake. Only hikers with long strides and heavy packs reach the pristine fishing of the Thorofare where 16-inch hungry cutthroats snatch offerings rejected anywhere else. Only experienced hikers conditioned to arduous terrain, hordes of early summer mosquitoes, and the ominous presence of bears should contemplate planning a trip to the Thorofare.

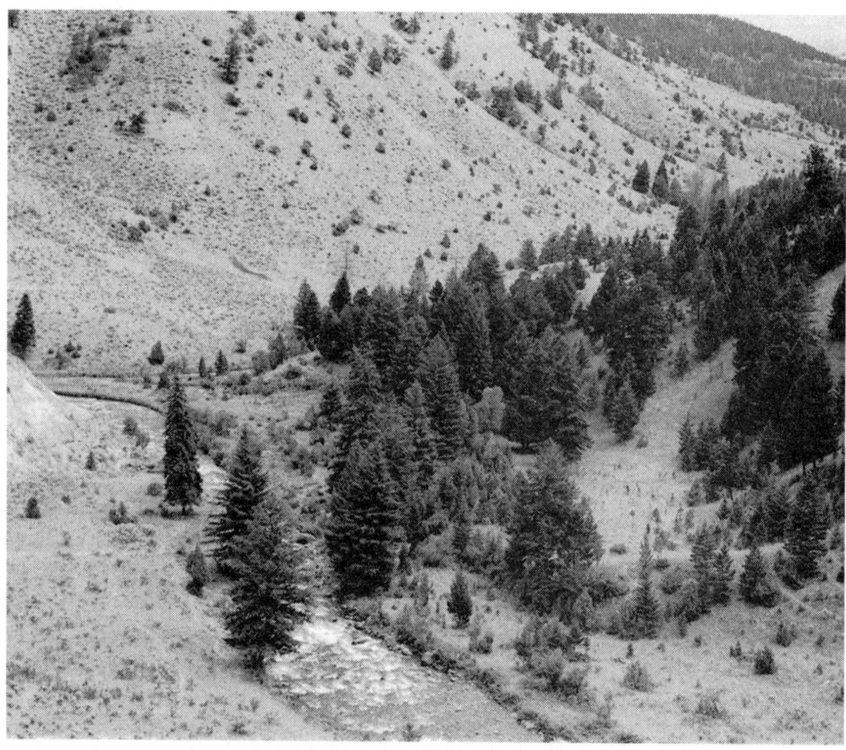

Looking down from the bridge at the Gardner River as it meets Lava Creek.

Although the outlet to Yellowstone Lake is closed the first mile, the next six miles of catch and release draw fly fisherman from around the world to test their skills against 16 and 18 inch Yellowstone Cutthroats. But into this zone of packed fishermen and multitudes of hefty cutthroats, Mother Nature levels the playing field with prodigious hatches. For the uninitiated, wading knee deep into the broad Yellowstone amidst what appears to be hundreds of sippers can be awe inspiring. After a fly fisher has changed flies a half a dozen times and added a section of 6 or 7X tippet to no avail, the river suddenly becomes daunting, more challenging than a spring creek. On my last visit to Buffalo Ford, I wandered the banks with only a Cannon AE-1 intent on catching a big one on film. My photographic experience, with the camera set on automatic, matched the expertise of the majority of young fly fishers eagerly casting over the water. After an hour of observing five or six casters, I realized that the light was fading fast and the prospects of photographing a landed fish was quietly fading.

I moved up the road to the next pullout and spotted my man. Ten feet from the bank, I spotted the flash of line splaying droplets of water across the darkening water. The rod arced and the pumping action told me he was about to land a nice cutthroat. Parking my truck, I quickly crossed the road and sat down on the bank behind him. Two friends were fishing below him with the same success, and their banter and jubilation frayed the nerves, I'm sure, of those frustrated fishermen in the general area who never did land a fish as long as I sat observing. Sunglasses were off, and the men strained their eyes across the water skewing their heads to negate the water's glare in the closing hour of dusk. Suddenly a rod flew up again, and the same man landed a hog which he guessed, and I quietly concurred, was in excess of 18 inches. He quietly advised the two other men to switch to a rusty spinner, as that was the only fly the bigger fish were keying on in the middle of a smorgasbord of aquatic offerings.

A rusty spinner, I thought to myself. Do I have one in my box? And then I remembered my first enthusiastic foray into the waters of Buffalo Ford over twenty years ago. I was teaching in Jackson, Wyoming, and joined to high school students on our first Yellowstone River initiation. The river was crowded that day, and it appeared that everyone was landing 14 to 16-inch fish all around me. I was so eager my hands were shaking in anticipation. After forty minutes of chasing rises like a dog chasing his tail, I was dejected. My two young companions, fortunately, had moved far down the river and were not witness to my dejection. Wading over to the bank humbled, I asked another fisherman what he had been using. He was leaving and looked on me in kindness. I had no idea what the fly pattern was that he handed me, but I caught fish for the next hour before it broke off. When I lost that fly, I went to my fly box and found a similar colored fly and trimmed it down to size. Although not as efficient as the first, it too caught fish. I joined my two young companions with a sigh of relief and a feeling of wonder having caught so many beautiful fish in a relatively short period of time. From Sulphur Caldron to Alum Creek the river is designated as a bird sanctuary and wildlife study area. Just above the falls lies a short section open to fishing, but the water speeds up in this section so wading is risky.

From there the river gathers speed and plunges 300 feet over Yellowstone Falls coursing its way through the Grand Canyon where angels fear to tread. Anglers seeking solitude, and who have the stamina to attain it, may once again ply the waters of the Yellowstone at the confluence with the Lamar River, through the Pleasant Valley area below the confluence and then in the Black Canyon region east of Gardiner.

(Calling home from a phone booth near Buffalo Ford on the Yellowstone River.) "Hi, Honey, I took a short-cut home through the park after the conference...uh huh, I miss you too...yeah, I threw in my 4 piece pack rod just in case...I wasn't even going to fish, but I just watched a guy land an 18-incher ... I was just wondering how you would feel if....")

The Big Hole River

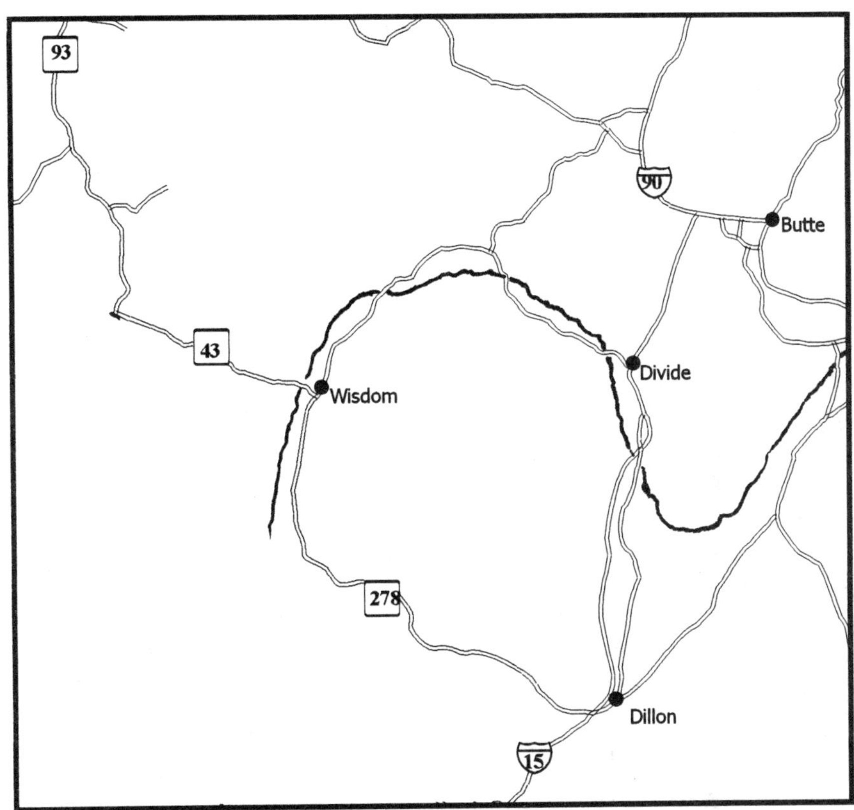

The natives first named the Big Hole Valley the Land of Big Snows and Ground Squirrel Valley. Captain Meriwether Lewis of the Lewis and Clark Expedition named the forks of the Jefferson River, Wisdom and Philanthropy, to honor President Jefferson's virtues. Later on the return trip, William Clark would name the present area of Jackson the Hot Spring Valley when they camped for the night near the hot springs. Fur trappers seeking valleys (holes) which were bounteous with beaver gave it its lasting name. With the passing of time, ranchers would sprinkle the valley with rich hay fields, producing some of the finest hay in the region. Ranchers nicknamed the valley 10,000 Stacks Valley with the invention in 1910 of the Beaverside Haystacker. But by the late 1930s and 40s, the Big Hole achieved piscatorial preeminence from local fly fishers and then by fishermen from around the country who came to pay homage to another one of Montana's fluvial wonders. From its headwaters down to Jackson, the river, more aptly described as a small meadow stream, meanders northwards to Wisdom, Montana and then to Sportsman Park. From there the river heads east and then south to Melrose and Glen. From Glen the river runs east for a short distance and then heads north again to meet the Beaverhead and form the Jefferson River. From the town of Wisdom to Twin Bridges, the river winds a little over a 100 miles. The most famous section, particularly during the Salmon Fly hatch in mid-June, stretches from Divide to Glen. From the second week in June through the end of the month, this section of river rivals the Madison in its hey days for boat traffic. The run-off, typically beginning in May, makes the Big Hole most difficult and perhaps dangerous to wade fish with the arrival of the Salmon Fly hatch in early June. The powerful current and half-submerged sweepers and rocks pose serious consequences for inexperienced rowers as well. Early July brings the arrival of the golden stoneflies, caddis and mayflies. With the arrival of mid-summer, irrigation drawdown and slow, heated water shuts the river down in some sections. In drought years the trout are barely able to survive in some sections of the river, and playing a fish to shore adds significant stress to their survival chances after release.

With the exception of the Salmon Fly hatch, the Big Hole River provides lots of elbow room for anglers seeking some solitude. During early summer the Big Hole fishes well with attractor patterns, particularly in the upper stretches above and below Wisdom where anglers also have the opportunity to catch Arctic Grayling. The Big Hole River holds the last survivors of river-dwelling grayling in the lower 48 states, and their numbers are growing under the careful protection of the state after the severe drought years during the 1980s. In addition to the grayling, the upper section holds high concentrations of brook trout and to a lesser extent cutthroats and rainbows.

With the discovery in recent years of Whirling Disease, the verdict is still out on the rainbow population, but recent research holds promise for securing a place for rainbows in the drainage. The mid section of the river below Wise River picks up both volume and gradient speed as the river flows through canyons offering floaters a mixture of riffles, rocks and pockets. Larger rainbows and browns are found from the Divide Bridge down to Melrose, the most popular float on the river. Some sections of the Big Hole River have produced shock-counts of over 3,000 trout per mile.

From Glen to the confluence at Twin Bridges, the river returns to pasture land and cottonwood bottoms and braided channels. Check with one of the shops before you float this section as it often contains many obstacles and impediments to safe and fun floating. The river holds mostly browns hidden under downed trees and undercut banks. The lower stretch may be accessed from a county road from Glen to Twin Bridges, but there are no public access points except bridges and non-posted private land. Access to the upper river, on the other hand, has improved greatly thanks to the efforts of the Big Hole River Foundation.

Fishing the Salmon Fly hatch requires patience, luck and good oaring skills. The greatest challenge to fishing this river is to wait for your turn to launch your boat. The last time I floated from Divide to Melrose, almost ten years ago, I was shocked at the number of people patiently waiting to take their launch turn. Fishermen were dropping drift boats in the water everywhere. As I drifted down the river, I was reminded of all those nature films I had seen through the years of crocodiles charging through the marsh grass and silently entering the water. I suppose the best attitude to embrace for this bevy of boats is to just enjoy the circus-like parade and be as generous as possible in sharing the river, as once the hatch is over the crowds disappear for another year.

The hatch moves typically four to five miles a day upstream from the confluence all the way up to Wisdom, although the heaviest concentrations are from Glen to Wise River. The Salmon Fly hatch on the Big Hole is generally earlier than the hatch on the Madison. As a result the Big Hole draws outfitters and guides from all over the region, including from the Missoula area which offers a good Salmon Fly hatch on the forks of the Bitterroot, Rock Creek and the Blackfoot about the same time.

Nymph fishermen like to get ahead of the hatch, but the bulk of the fishermen enjoy fishing right in the middle of the hatch. Most of them enter the river between 9 AM and 10 AM hoping to catch the first ovipositing females as they warm up. Timing and good luck determines whether or not you will have a memorable hatch experience. Most camping fishermen come to stay for a while knowing that cold, rainy June days are a reality in southwestern Montana. About 20 years ago I fished the hatch for the first time with a former principal of mine from Jackson, Wyoming.

Nick Holmes, who at the time was the principal in Whitehall, Montana, almost always fished with a nymph. He is an excellent fisherman, and he would softly chuckle every time he watched me tie on a dry fly. Invariably he would out fish me. Nick had no use for strike indicators or tapered leaders. He carried a few spools of monofilament in his vest and tied on short leaders. As I was his junior, coupled with the fact that he always out fished me, I generally took Nick's advice, including switching over to a nymph after watching Nick land three or four fish. The night before I had driven over from the Bitterroot Valley and camped at Divide Bridge where I would meet Nick in the morning. I spent that first evening talking to every fisherman who would answer my questions. The general consensus was that it was not worth getting out on the river early until the bugs were warmed up and landing on the water. Eager beavers, I was told, just pass up good water that would be productive water later in the morning. I had planned on meeting Nick at 6 AM the next morning!

When Nick arrived earlier than our scheduled time, I was groggy eyed. I told him of my findings, and he let out that soft chuckle which from past experience assured me he had some experience that I wasn't about to challenge. It was chilly, but the sun was coming up when we backed up to the launch and slipped into the river at 7 AM. I was on the oars first and ribbed Nick about using a nymph today. "No," he said, "I'll fish with drys today. Here, I tied up a couple for you as well."

Tied would be an overstatement. Nick was also a goose hunter, and he had carved magnum Salmon Fly bodies out of balsa wood and attached them to what I guessed to be shark hooks. Richly painted and finished off with bright feathers, they looked more like floating Rappalas. As I received the two gigantic flies in my hands, Nick good naturally said, "Be sure to cut off about half of that tapered leader of yours." It was good advice. Our agreement was two fish caught and you are on the oars. Within ten minutes, Nick had landed his first trout of the day over 20 inches. Within the hour I was on the oars, and although my first two fish weren't quite as large as Nick's, I was jubilant. As the day progressed, we both lost our two hand-carved Salmon Flies and the fish became progressively smaller and tougher to catch. I never fished the Big Hole River again with Nick, and I have never carved balsa wood Salmon Fly patterns although each spring I wonder if they would work on Rock Creek. The Big Hole Salmon Fly hatch is a great experience if you time it right, if the run-off is not severe, and if the sky is free from pounding rain.

March and April: During this pre-runoff period, the river is best fished with a variety of woolly bugger and streamer patterns along with stonefly nymphs.

May: The month of May begins the run-off season along with prolific hatches of caddis. Unlike many of Montana's other famous rivers, the Big Hole does not typically get blown out with mud. If the weather cooperates, the upper and mid section is certainly worth fishing using Elk Hair Caddis patterns as well as emerging nymphs.

June: The Big Hole's famous Salmon Fly hatch is usually in progress by mid-June and essentially over by the end of the month with the exception of some late bloomers. Followed closely on the heels of the Salmon Fly hatch, Golden Stones and a few Green Drakes appear along with PMDs.

July: Early July offers opportunities for standard attractor patterns such as Humpies, Wulffs, Trudes, and Parachute Adams

Late Summer: Hoppers, ants and tricos

Fall: Hoppers, tricos, blue-wing olives, streamers and buggers.

Big Hole River – Highway 43

The Big Hole River may be reached via Highway 93 from Salmon, Idaho or from Interstate 15 from Idaho Falls to Butte or at the junction with Interstate 90 and Interstate 15 west of Butte. The Big Hole River parallels Highway 43 which begins at the junction with Highway 93 at Chief Joseph Pass. From the junction to Wisdom is 27 miles. Dillon is 93 miles.

MM 16.5: Big Hole National Battlefield / North Fork: The Nez Perce, refusing to accept a re-negotiated treaty in which their people would lose 9/10 of their reservation, refused to move into the newly restricted reservation. Tensions mounted, deadlines were mandated and a few young warriors precipitated military reprisals when they killed some settlers. Thus began a journey of flight and a series of skirmishes. The Nez Perce elected Chief Joseph as their leader. At the Big Hole the 7th US Infantry, under the command of Col. John Gibbon, mounted a surprise attack. The Nez Perce tribe suffered the loss of almost ninety members, only a third of them were warriors. In military terms, the Indians had won the battle, but their loss of horses and provisions would soon exhaust them on their journey of escape. Thirteen hundred miles later, Chief Joseph would surrender to Col. Nelson A. Miles, just 40 miles south of the Canadian border.

"Hear me, my chiefs, I am tired; my heart is sick and sad. From where the sun now stands I will fight no more forever." Chief Joseph

The North Fork of the Big Hole River runs through the Battlefield and holds an abundance of brook trout.

MM 23: Lower North Fork Road / Mussigbrod Lake 18 miles, Pintler Lake 18: Mussigbrod Lake Campground (USFS) has 10 campsites. The lake fishes well for grayling and brook trout, but be prepared for ugly draw downs during the summer. **Pintler Lake** offers much more in scenery, good fishing from a boat and a small campground. The lake is between 30 and 40 acres and does not offer good fishing from the shoreline due to plant growth.

MM 26: Junction with Highway 278 to Dillon, Montana:

Highway 278 to Dillon

The route to Dillon leads to Jackson, Montana, which has a commercial hot springs. Seven miles south of Wisdom on Highway 278 is the turn off to Twin Lakes. **Twin Lakes** is sixteen miles from the highway. The lake, two lakes joined by a channel, is popular with locals and offers good fishing for rainbows and brook trout. Although large lake trout are present, their numbers seem to be in decline. Twin Lakes Campground has 21 camping sites and a boat launch.

From Wisdom to Jackson is 18 miles. Just out of Jackson a half of a mile is the turn off to **Lower Miner Lake**, which offers 18 campsites and a boat launch. The fishing, however, is only fair as the lake is shallow and suffers from oxygen depletion during the summer and periodic freeze-outs. **Upper Miner Lake**, along with **Rock Island Lakes**, offers good cutthroat and brook trout fishing for day hike fishing in the back-country. The hike is approximately four to five miles and well worth the hike for the scenery alone. My sons and I have fond memories of catching lots of 9" brookies in these lakes.

A half-mile further from the Lower Miner Lake turn-off on is the access road for **Van Houten Lake**, which is 10 miles from the highway. South Van Houten campground has three tent sites while North Van Houten has four tent campsites. The lake is barely 10 acres.

Bannack State Park and Campground: Located four miles on a county, dirt road off Highway 278 five miles south of Dillon, Bannack was Montana's first territorial state capital after a major gold discovery in 1862. A number of buildings remain on main street. The campground has 20 campsites for both tents and trailers. **Grasshopper Creek** runs through the campground and offers fishing for 14-to-16 inch brown trout. The creek runs through miles of ranchland. Take the time to ask for permission.

Returning to Highway 43 at Wisdom following the Big Hole River to Divide

MM 26: Wisdom, Montana

MM 42: Squaw Creek: Squaw Creek has a launch site and parking. This is also the junction with the Lower North Fork Road. Pintler Lake is 10 miles and Mussigbrod Lake is 22. (See MM 23.)

MM 48.7: Fishtrap Fishing Access: This access provides a boat launch, but there is no shade for a picnic.

MM 52. 5: Roadside tables

MM 54.4: Junction with Highway 274 to Anaconda: Anaconda is 25 miles.

MM 57.1: East Bank Campground: Eight miles west of Wise River, the East Bank Campground offers five camp sites with a boat launch.

MM 58: Dickie Bridge Recreation Area (campground): The campground has eight campsites. The first four have tables; the other four sites are primitive. The area also has a boat launch.

Wise River, Montana: Thirteen miles from Interstate 15, Wise River offers services and accommodations. The Wise River drys up as it reaches the Big Hole in its lower stretches. The upper reaches is fair fishing for smaller rainbows. Following Pioneer Mountains Scenic Byway along the Wise River will lead to many campgrounds.

MM 67.1: Jerry Creek Bridge Access and Launch

MM 71: Dewey Fishing Access and Launch

MM 74: Old Divide Bridge: If you are floating down to Old Divide Bridge, you must take out at this point as below the bridge is a dam. The next put-in site is a mile away at the new Divide Bridge.

MM 75: Divide Bridge Fishing Access and Boat Launch: From this point to Melrose and Glen is the most famous stretch of water on the Big Hole. Divide Bridge is 2.8 miles from Interstate 15, Exit 102. The site offers lots of parking and 25 campsites. (BLM)

Divide, Montana / Junction with Interstate 15 – Exit 102

Interstate 15 – Exit 99 – Moose Creek (river access) Moose Creek offers a primitive BLM camping site.

Interstate 15 – Exit 93 – Melrose, Montana: Melrose is a very small community. The launch site or take-out is right in Melrose at the **Salmon-Fly Campground.** The campground, if you can call it that, is a patch of grass, which is non-designated, close quarter camping ("parking"). Six miles further is **Maiden Rock Campground.** Maiden Rock Campground (FWP) has 30 campsites, which can accommodate 32' trailers, and it offers a boat launch. From Melrose you may follow the frontage road south to Browne's Bridge.

Beaverhead River

Throughout the many years of my guiding and teaching in the Bitterroot Valley, I would hear exciting tales of summer and fall trips to the Beaverhead by fellow guides. Regaled stories, combined with the "shocking" reports of Montana's fish biologists, heightened my desire to fish these fabled waters. But the culmination of each summer guide season, the arrival of a new school session and fall hunting kept me from sampling the Beaverhead.

Like the endless stories of gamblers who return from Las Vegas, no mention is ever made of losses. When pressed most recreational gamblers mutter that they broke even, or better yet their winnings paid all of their expenses. In twenty years of listening to river guides talk about their Beaverhead trips, no mention was ever made about a slow day in paradise.

And for the record, this paradise is verifiably evident with biologist proclaiming record populations and record size browns from their shocking studies even to this day. In the days when Blue Ribbon was bantered around so lightly, the Beaverhead studies reported astonishing numbers of trout per mile with record breaking browns waiting to enter the record books.

Today the numbers are only slightly down due to Whirling Disease, and anglers truly have the opportunity to catch "Five Pounders", which, in my mind, is another term lightly bantered about. No other river between Glacier and Yellowstone holds such promise for a catch-of-a-lifetime as this national treasure! But into this Garden of Eden reality meets heightened expectations (guides excluded).

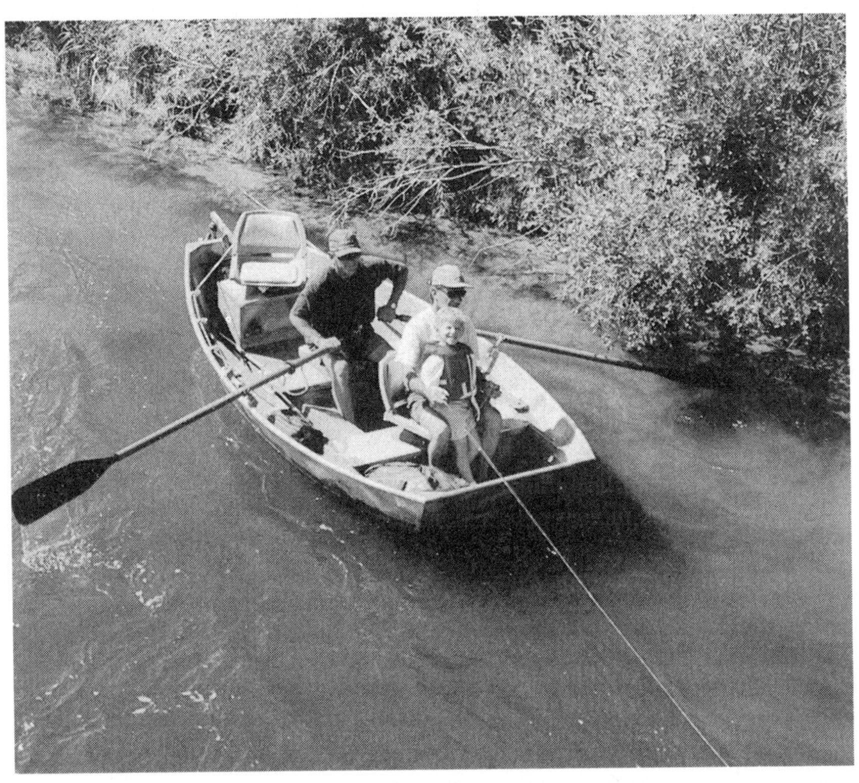

Three generations of Beaverhead fly fishermen: Alex Day, age 7 with Grandfather Robbie Garrett and Uncle Jeremy Garrett on the oars.

The Beaverhead hosts abundant insect life, half-submerged willows and a tailwater rich in nutrients. But by all standards this narrow river holds challenges for seasoned veterans. Yet each passing season innocents from abroad proudly photograph their "jackpot" reward. From the Clark Canyon Reservoir to Dillon is approximately 20 river miles of water, which races past a double-wall barrier of thick willow and undercut banks. Dangling willow arms greedily reach out to snatch offerings, and weighted nymph patterns and buggers stumble through underwater deadfalls. Shooting past a target, he who hesitates is lost, and lost flies mount up as the day progresses. Typical flows in mid-summer on a high water year reach in excess of 1,000 cfs making it tough on both guides and clients. The upper section from the dam to Barrett's Dam is the most famous stretch of water. Here wade fishers are even more challenged during high water releases. Optimum flows for floating this upper section are from 600 to 800 cfs. Compounding the aforementioned physical conditions is the simple fact that heightened pressure has produced some very educated browns. Whereas in the past heavily weighted buggers with incredibly short and stout leaders was the preferred method, realistic nymph patterns properly presented prevail today.

Rather than be intimidated, however, relish the prospect of fishing over 300 trophy size browns per mile after first taking a teaspoon of lowered expectations. If you can afford it, by all means hire a guide. During my last visit to the Beaverhead I sat in my truck outside a shop in Dillon arranging notes and brochures. I heard two out-of-state visitors debating the merits of hiring a guide. Money wasn't even a consideration. The men had pulled a drift boat behind them from another state and felt sheepish about hiring a guide on that basis alone. Sitting in my truck, I couldn't pretend to be oblivious to their dilemma so I hopped out and approached them. Within 60 seconds they returned to the shop to book a trip. Here is an almost word-for-word argument I gave them.

"Excuse me. I couldn't help but overhear your conversation. I am a former guide from out of the area, and I can tell you without hesitation I dearly wish I could afford to higher a guide. If money isn't the issue consider this. Only one of you will be able to fish at a time while the other person is on the oars. That's half the day watching your buddy fish. You are going to be speeding down the river 5 to 6 miles per hour not knowing what lies around the next bend. Before you can even react, your going to blow through a good pocket that you could have got out of the boat and fished. Even if you are an experienced oarsman, you are going to miss a lot of prime water, and hopefully you will miss rapping the top of that boat of yours on a low bridge. Lastly, you will probably doggedly cling to a non-productive pattern in the absence of a voice of authority."

The opener begins May 17, and the preferred fly patterns are small mayflies, small yellow stoneflies and caddis. Keep in mind that the first stretch down to Grasshopper Creek Access remains clear coming out of the dam. Grasshopper Creek muddies the water during run-off and during heavy rains, but this section above provides clear opportunities, albeit a short distance of a little over ten miles.

Early summer brings PMDs and then later tricos, but these hatches tend to be early and late in the day. The upper section lacks green pastureland for hoppers gradually working their way to the water's edge, but instead crane flies fill the void, and late summer and early fall find scattered hatches of Baetis. Throughout the river drainage, the Beaverhead is primarily known for fishing down and ugly versus sitting high and pretty. Floaters fishing below Dillon to Anderson Road will find conditions much better for dry fly fishing along with far fewer boats, and from Barrett's Bridge to the town of Dillon, wade fishers delight in catching smaller trout but in greater numbers.

Popular Sections and Access Points: The Beaverhead is easily accessed from Interstate 15 at Exit 44 at the dam; Exit 52 at Grasshopper Creek; Exit 59 with the junction to Highway 278 to Wisdom, and Exit 62 and 63 in the town of Dillon. For a quick preview of the river, follow the secondary road just past Poindexter Slough south of Dillon near the junction with Highway 278. This secondary road winds its way all the way up to the dam, crossing the river and at times under the Interstate. At times it joins with old highway 91. In some places it looks like a private ranch road. Wade fishers can travel this road to hop out and fish, and floaters new to the river should follow the road to check out each of the access points.

Clark Canyon Dam or High Bridge to Grasshopper Creek Access or Barrett's Park:

Built in 1965, the base of the dam provides a launch site and a picnic spot, along with a couple of camping sites. Less than a mile downstream, High Bridge offers an easier launch site. Wade fishers have a short stretch above and below the bridge to fish. This upper section is renown for its swift current and river bends. **Henneberry Bridge** is about six miles from the dam, and it too offers a good exit point or boat launch along with a picnic area. Henneberry Bridge is most easily found by following the secondary road south from Exit 52. **Grasshopper Creek Access** is the next access downstream, about ten miles from the dam. From Grasshopper Creek to Barrett's Park is the last floating stretch of the river. During high water the park take-out can be tricky as it is right in front of a low bridge, and there is no room for error. When you see the bridge, slip over and hug the left bank.

Tash to Cornell Park: Referred to as "Tash to Trash" by the local guides, the Tash access point is near the junction with Highway 278 by Poindexter Slough. A short float of about five miles, this popular evening float exits at the weir in Cornell Park in the town of Dillon, not too far from the dump. To find Cornell Park, follow North Montana Street past the museum and Depot until it comes to a T intersection. Turn west and follow the KOA signs. The park is about a half-mile further and offers a hand-launch site.

Cornell Park to Anderson Road: Be sure you take note of the low bridge and debris at the train trestle on Highway 91 at the north end of town. It could prove tricky during high water periods for a high bow drift boat. The exit point for this 12-14 mile float is Anderson Road, which may be reached at mile marker 7.4 north of Dillon on Highway 41 to Twin Bridges (28 miles from Dillon). The road is un-marked, but across the street is a ranch complex with silos. Turn west 1.3 miles. The access is small and next to a county bridge. Anderson Road may also be reached at mile marker 5.6 on Highway 91 north of town on the way to Butte.

Fly fishers should also consider fishing Poindexter Slough for good catches of browns in a spring creek environment as well as Clark Canyon

Reservoir, which produces exceptionally large rainbows. Stocked in the lake in the spring at four inches, these Eagle Lake strain rainbows grow in excess of twelve inches the first year and easily reach five pounder status in three years. Although popular with boat fishermen, the lake is likewise popular with float tubers prowling the shores for those lunkers.

Public Campgrounds

Dillon has a number of private campgrounds, and Barrett's Park has a few campsites. The best public campground facilities, however, are up on Clark Canyon Reservoir, which offers eight non-fee campgrounds provided by the U.S. Bureau of Reclamation. Most of the campgrounds are on the west side of the lake, and for the most part they lack any shade.

Fly Patterns and Hatches

Throughout my years of guiding, I was constantly surprised to discover the number of fishermen who would go to their local, out-of-state fly shop and buy flies for their trip out west to Montana. How could professional, well educated men, titans of industry and self-made millionaires dismiss local advice, especially since their guides are reporting to the shops each day on which patterns are working for a particular stretch or time of day. Never laboring under the pretension that I was the consummate guide, I always dropped by a fly shop, with or without a client, if I was away from my home waters. The price of bugs is the same, but the information is invaluable, and local experts often tie specialized patterns. Each day shops send out their guides with the simple goal of getting their clients into fish, and every day information is traded back and forth on what was working, where it was working and what time it was working. Shop owners and clerks readily pass on this information to first-time customers for a half a dozen flies or less!

Fly fishers debate the merits of fishing techniques, the dynamics of one rod manufacturer over another, preferences of leader material, nymphing techniques and a hundred other topics. But the one topic guaranteed to generate instant conversation is the mention of fly patterns. No other facet of fly fishing evokes so much enthusiasm and reverence

Through the years many surveys have asked prominent fly fishers to share their favorite fly patterns. Lefty Kreh, in an article published February, 1972, in Field and Stream, polled twelve expert fly fishers. The following list of dry flies, nymph flies and streamer flies represents a composite of the most frequently used flies for each category among these twelve experts.

Dry Flies: Light Cahill; Adams; Royal Wulff; Irresistible; Quill Gordon; Humpy

Nymphs: Trueblood Otter Shrimp; Quill Gordon; Ed Burk; Yellow Stone Fly; Muskrat; Woolly Worm

Streamers: Black Nose Dace; Spruce Fly; Muddler Minnow; Gray Ghost; Black Marabou; White Marabou

Dan Abrams, in a similar type survey published in Sports Afield, October 1975, polled thirty notable fly fishers regarding their top four fly patterns. Seven of the thirty were prominent Rocky Mountain fly fishers. A generalized list of the most popular patterns produced the following: Adams; Royal Wulff; Humpy; Muddler Minnow and Gold-ribbed Hare's Ear Nymph. Add the Woolly Bugger and a Light Cahill in varying sizes and I would be content for quite some time. Well, of course, I would need to add a hopper pattern and a PMD and maybe a ....

One of the great joys of fly fishing is sharing what works. If you are a beginner and meet a friendly fly fisherman, pull out your fly box and ask, "Which one should I use?" I fondly recall many occasions when someone took me under their guidance and shared their secret fly for the day. Through the years my own collection of fly patterns grew in direct proportion to my fly fishing budget. Like most of the fly fishermen I know, I can never have enough patterns. I have a number of match-the-hatch patterns for those special days, and I have my reliable stand-by attractor patterns and generic patterns which I started out with thirty years ago.

I have prioritized the following recommendations for the young beginner who has an empty fly box and a thin wallet. If you would like to begin tying your own flies, I highly recommend Jack Dennis' manual, Western Trout Fly Tying Manual. For a more in-depth approach to matching hatches, I would recommend The Complete Book of Western Hatches by Rick Hafele and Dave Hughs.

For those of you who are new to the sport of fly fishing and have never fished in Montana, I offer a “Baker's Dozen” of must have patterns that will cover about 90% of the fishing from Glacier to Yellowstone. Be observant of what the trout are feeding on and use a small aquarium net to scoop up the bugs and look at them closely. Purchase a fly box with a foam backing and sort your dry mayfly patterns by color and size. For example I start out with light, cream color Cahills and progressively move across in size to pale yellow, bright yellow, yellow-green, green, olive green and into the green-browns and finally mahogany and rust colors. I set up a separate row of gray and tan mayfly patterns. Personally, I am less concerned with Latin identification as I am with finding the right size imitation in as close to the natural color as possible. Organizing my fly box in this manner helps me to locate a pattern quickly. It also reminds me what colors I am missing or what sizes I am missing. The following 13 patterns are the ones "I never leave home without."

Dry Fly Attractor Patterns:

1. Royal Wulff: Sizes 10 – 16: The Royal Wulff is the definitive attractor pattern. Created by the famed Lee Wulff, it imitates nothing, and yet it offers to the trout an equivalent of an exquisite Julia Child masterpiece. Derisively called the "Dude Fly" because of its white calf tail wing, this extravaganza brings the fish up! Best of all, it is a fly the caster never fails to see. To digress for the beginner, keep in mind that you have to **set** the hook as the trout will spit the fly out on his dive back into the water. Most beginners miss the take because by the time they react, the fish is safely on its way. Wear Polaroid sun glasses so that you can begin to train your eyes for movement under the water. This early detection allows you to react more quickly.

Presentation: Classic, up stream dead drift

2. Humpy (Goofus Bug): Sizes 10 – 16: The Humpy's origin, according to Jack Dennis, is shrouded in controversy. Whether the fly originated in Jackson, Wyoming, or elsewhere is really unimportant. What is important to the beginner is that this fly works, and it is an indispensable pattern to have in your fly box. Although it is an attractor pattern, it may imitate a large caddis or stone fly in larger sizes. The fly is ideal for fast flowing waters because of its inherent buoyancy. When sparsely tied it works amazingly well on slow waters and can be used to imitate a Little Yellow Sonefly. The great advantage of this fly for the beginner is that it is almost unsinkable, and it offers great visibility in fast water for both the fisherman and the trout. It is, however, a most challenging pattern to tie. The best directions may be found in The Second Fly-Tyers Almanac by Robert H. Boyle and Dave Whitlock.

Presentation: Classic, up stream dead drift. However, since this pattern closely resembles a caddis fly and floats so well, try drifting the fly downstream under willows or overhanging branches. As the fly drifts to the targeted area, lift the rod tip up to create an erratic skipping motion on top of the water, and then lower the rod tip quickly to allow the fly to drift once again on top of the water. Await the strike!

Generic Patterns:

3. Adams / Parachute Adams: Sizes 12 – 22: The ubiquitous Adams is probably the most widely used dry fly pattern on the North American Continent. It imitates any number of gray mayflies. I highly recommend acquiring as many Adams in various sizes as possible. Because of the difficult visibility with this pattern, I have switched over exclusively to Parachute Adams for sizes 16- 22.

Although this is a generic type pattern, a #20 Parachute Adams performs quite well during a trico or baetis hatch on slow moving water with a 9' leader and 6X tippet.

The trico spinner imitation has a small black body with divided white poly wing in the spinner position. During the heat of summer, get out on a Rocky Mountain river between 7 to 9 AM (varies) for the tricorithodes or trico hatch followed by the spinner fall. Although one of the smallest of mayfly species, nonetheless, this is a staple for feeding trout primarily because of the preponderant numbers during the spinner fall. Generally found in slower waters, the trout settle into a sipping, rhythmic rise form. Do not be deceived by the small rings and the dark noses -- big fish! Fish in the morning during those dog days of August. I'm sure you will be delighted with the experience regardless of how many fish break off and get away. Because I have trouble seeing a small trico, I often add one on as a trailer behind a small parachute Adams.

Presentation: Classic, upstream dead drift

4. **Light Cahill or Light Variant:** Sizes 12 – 18: A light cream color Heptagenia mayfly imitation is another must have pattern. The Light Cahill pattern may also be used on slower waters and lakes to imitate Callibaetis. The Callibaetis dun body is olive-brown, however, so you may want to darken a few of your Light Cahills with a magic marker.

5. **PMD – Pale Morning Dun:** Hatches of Pale Morning Duns are probably the most prolific and reliable hatch from Glacier to Yellowstone. These Ephemerella drake patterns should be part of your must have patterns in sizes 16-22. PMD's hatch from June through October. Lighter in color from their cousins the Green Drakes, their bodies range from olive green to pale yellow and tan. The wings are generally slate gray to yellow. PMD cripples should be part of your collection. Nymph patterns such as the Zug Bug, Gray Nymph and the Hare's Ear generally work well. The darker green patterns will work well during a Baetis hatch. These blue-winged olive patterns should be available in your fly box in sizes 16-20. The Baetis hatches are more typical in the spring and fall, and they are generally smaller than a PMD. The body color for a Baetis pattern is olive brown with gray wings and light gray hackle. It is not uncommon for trout to be sipping the smaller Baetis during a hatch of PMD's.

The famous Green Drake hatches are typically from mid-June through mid July. If you are in an area with a Green Drake hatch, be sure to stock up on a number of these drake patterns at the nearest fly shop. The hatch is not heavy generally, but if they are out, the trout are looking for them. Reports from guides returning to the shop will determine if you should buy traditional drake patterns or Compara Duns or Green Paradrakes. All of the above patterns range in color from pale yellow to green to olive brown. Stock up.

6. Elk Hair Caddis: Sizes 10 – 18: Unlike the graceful rise and gliding fall of the mayfly, a caddis hatch looks like a burst of kindergartners swarming over a playground. An accompanying sound track for a mayfly would be a Viennese waltz. Conversely, the caddis dance would be a rap sound track by the Fat Boys. Generally, the caddis hatch in the evening. The most popular body colors are brown, olive, green, gray and tan.

The caddis are not easily missed, and they are an important part of the trout's diet in the pupa and winged stages. Look for them in the quiet pocket water under willow branches or overhangs, especially in the evening. You may also want to select a few patterns for the emergent phase such as a sparkle pupa. For larger caddis imitations use a Humpy, an X-Caddis or a Goddard Caddis for fast, heavy water.

Presentation: Classic, up stream dead drift or erratic action produced by rod tip action.

7. Hopper (Joe's, Dave's, Jay's, Dan's): Sizes 6 - 12 As you can see from the partial list, grasshopper imitations are recorded in the Who's Who of Terrestrials. Rarely, however, will you find such citation on the bins in a fly shop. I recommend for beginners a clipped deer hair head or collar. This feature adds stability and superior floatation. Although the grasshopper is meant to have a low silhouette, without the deer hair the buoyancy is drastically reduced and the caster generally struggles with a sinking pattern.

Presentation: The best source for learning how to fish a hopper imitation can be found in the September, 1985 issue of Fly Fisherman. In this issue Dave Whitlock, in his article "Hoppertunity", discusses hopper behavior, pattern characteristics and Hoppertunity Techniques. Here are a few of his suggestions:

1. Being a terrestrial insect, the grasshopper is on unfamiliar "ground" when he gets blown on the water. No gentle landings here. Make a splash with your cast. Strip the hopper in with intermittent twitches from rod tip action.
2. Use a heavy tippet, and use a twist piece of lead to sink the hopper in those promising pools.
3. Cast close to undercut banks and overhangs where trout hide during low water periods.
4. Fish during the heat of the day. Carefully pick your targeted area. Although a hopper smashing on top of the water will trigger a strike, it also quite often spooks fish in the outlying area. Keep moving.
5. Practice stealth and keep a low profile.

8. Muddler Minnow: Size 4 - 8 Popularized by Dan Bailey of Livingston, Montana, the Muddler Minnow should always be in your fly box. I have met fly fishers who fish almost exclusively with Muddler Minnow patterns. Along with its off shoot, the Marabou Muddler, this pattern has probably taken more large fish than any other fly. The Muddler may also be greased up and used as an effective hopper pattern, and I have used it both dry and wet on the same cast with great results.

Presentation: Fish the Muddler slightly upstream or downstream in a quartering action. Retrieve the Muddler by simultaneously pumping the rod tip and stripping in the line in quick, little jerks which imitates the darting action of a sculpin minnow. Allow for pauses, and add weight if necessary.

9. Hare's Ear Nymph: Sizes 12 – 16: In my opinion, this is the best of the small nymph patterns for spring creeks, beaver ponds and slow flat stretches of river. When I fish high elevation lakes, I always bring along the Hare's ear and a Zug Bug in smaller sizes. They work wonders. If you have someone along who is not an accomplished fly caster, use a plastic water-filled bubble with as long a leader as possible. Attach a Hare's Ear or Zug Bug and cast out as far as possible and retrieve with a spinning reel. If the fish are rising to the surface, be sure to cast way over them as the splash down with the water-filled bubble will spoke the fish in the near vicinity.

10. Bead-head Prince Nymph: This is perhaps the most popular nymph in the region! If you don't have any, go to the nearest fly shop. They work great as a dropper off a hopper pattern during the heat of August.

11. Woolly Bugger: Sizes 4 – 8: This pattern is a must for late spring and early summer when the water is high and off color and the hatches are sporadic. If you are fishing from shore, make short casts around all the rocks and boulders. Be sure the fly is actually sinking to the bottom. Add lead to your leader if necessary. Use a short 2X or 3X leader. Make short casts and keep the rod tip high so that you keep the Bugger bouncing along the bottom. Lift the rod tip when you feel a bump. Do not assume it is just a rock. If it is, lower the rod tip and let the bugger sink again.

12. Yuk Bug (similar to the Girdle Bug): Sizes 6 – 12: I love this bug! I have caught so many beautiful fish during early summer when the water is still high but with good visibility. I float along until I find a log jam or flooded backwater eddy. I usually select a size 10. The Yuk Bug has a dark body wrapped with grizzly hackle. Protruding from the body are white rubber legs. I find I generally have to cut back on the length of the rubber legs. I want them to pulse, but I also want them to flair out at the sides rather than collapsing backwards. I do not use weight. I fish it like a dry fly allowing it to gradually sink. Most important, I cast from a knelling position. I am always amazed how adept large trout are in hiding. As the Yuk Bug sinks slowly into the quiet water, the trout slowly emerges from its hiding spot. I have had large trout appear from under a small tree trunk in shallow water. They never rush to the Yuk. They take their time. I love this bug!

13. Beetle Patterns – OK Ant Patterns too!

Well, there you have it, the fly patterns "I'd never leave home without!"

Author with his two sons – always on the oars!

Tips for Hiring a Fishing Guide

Let me begin by saying that after fifteen years of being a fly fishing guide in western Montana, I offended a party of fly fishermen on my first spring trip a few years ago. They had come to fish the Blackfoot River; a little early I might add. After three days with this very large party, their complaint against me was awkwardly relayed to me by the guide in charge. I was shocked. I must be honest in telling you I was hurt and angry, but then I had to realistically appraise my guiding skills and etiquette.

Had I become complacent and sloppy through the years? After much reflection, I had to shoulder most of the blame. We were fishing in coffee colored water. Our Woolly Buggers, shackled and weighted down with lead, resembled some primordial serpent. The run-off was late and especially heavy. As a school teacher, I was unaccustomed to fishing in the manner that all of us were forced to fish. Generally the run off is usually over by the time school is out. Although I was never significantly out fished by the other boats, I failed to be assertive and take charge according to one of the clients.

On one of the days, I was encouraged into a friendly conversation on incompetent teachers and tenure laws. I threw caution to the wind and lay the blame on the shoulders of lazy administrators who fail to follow due process procedures and document. This conversation followed a request by the client to exchange political views with a Democrat. The man had promised his wife he would yearly hold at least one civil conversation with a Democrat, and I was his man.

I thought to myself, don't get pulled into a political debate. In spite of the slow fishing, everyone seemed in jovial spirits so I threw caution to the wind, again! I had broken another rule: Don't discuss your personal life, your politics or your religion. Apparently my views were brought up at the round table that night. On the third day I broke from the pact (nine guides) and headed for the upper Clark Fork. That was the day the fishing improved dramatically on the Blackfoot, and you can guess "the rest of the story".

My worst offense, however, was reserved for the last day when I gave casting advice to an elderly gentlemen who had been fly fishing for forty years and loved to either encroach on his partner's water or cast out in the middle of the river. I had become critical. I heard it in my voice. I drove home from the Blackfoot that fourth morning reflecting on the qualities that I admired in the top guides who I worked with through the years, and I took stock of myself as a guide.

The following year, at age 52 I retired myself as a guide knowing I could no longer keep up with the younger, more passionate guides. Let me share with you the responsibilities of both the guide and the client. Hopefully, this will help you communicate with your outfitter in selecting a guide who is best suited for you.

Guide Responsibilities:

1. Be an accomplished fly fisher, a cautious rower and an enthusiastic teacher.
2. Hold a state guide license and be trained in first aid and CPR.
3. Work hard to have your client catch fish. Never give up or become discouraged.
4. Be friendly and honest. Never inflate the fishing prospects, and allow a client to cancel a trip due to inclement weather or poor fishing conditions.
5. Be punctual. Be organized, and carry extra equipment and supplies.
6. Provide a classy lunch!

7. If you are with a large group and you are having good luck on a particular pattern, share with your fellow guides.
8. Know when to join in conversations and when to withdraw and allow privacy or just quiet time.
9. Ask the clients how much instruction they want. Gauge their response. Many clients find themselves invited on trips, and yet they are really not interested in learning a new skill, not to mention feeling the pressure from a guide. Many of these clients are content to enjoy the float trip in the company of their friends.
10. Never take for granted the natural beauty that surrounds us. Share in the wonders of nature and the catching and releasing of wild Montana trout.

Responsibilities of the Client

Be realistic in your expectations and your fishing skills. As a guide of many years, I would just cringe when I had a client who booked a trip in the heat of August, had little or no rudimentary casting skills and fully expected to catch a trophy trout that day. A few years back I heard a guide good naturally say to a client who was denigrating the river, "Well, the fish are here all right, but like a lot of folks, they're not hungry all the time. That's why they call it fishing, not catching."

If a guide tells you he wants you to cast no more than 6 inches from the shore, he's serious! If you didn't have the skills to do so he wouldn't ask you. A client who spends a fortune to come to fish in Montana and then winces when he looses a few bucks worth of flies always puzzles me. If you're not loosing flies, you're not fishing hard.

Also, dress appropriately. If you do not have waders, wear an old pair of pants and a pair of tennis shoes. At least once a year I would have a client who would show up with dress pants and Gucci loafers. Realistically, this limits the guide's opportunities to stop the boat and let clients wade fish favorite hot spots.

Speaking of flies. Please ask the guide ahead of time if you are expected to pay for the flies. Some shop guides merely add the flies onto your total bill and deduct any flies you didn't use that day. Some outfitters and guides make it a policy to provide the flies free in the hopes that the tip they receive will compensate their loss of flies for the day. Other outfitters and guides bill the client for each fly and leader used. I have worked under both systems. I will tell you honestly that many times I will have given up twenty dollars worth of flies and leaders. As an independent guide, I paid retail prices for flies and leaders most of the time.

Regarding tips (No objectivity here!) Did you enjoy your day? Did the guide work hard at getting you over fish? Did you have a gourmet or lavish lunch? Was the trip well organized? I won't share trade secrets about how much the outfitter pays the guides, but I will tell you that the guide is responsible for all of his equipment and insurance. With few exceptions, the lunches are made by the guide or paid for by the guide. Shuttling the guide's rig usually costs $25 a trip. Boats and rafts are usually replaced within six or seven years at around $2-4,000. Trailers are forever breaking down. The season is very short. Up front yearly start-up costs translate to three guide trips before you make a profit. OK -- guides do have a great job, but tips are greatly appreciated.

What type of guide do you want? Most people rarely make requests of the outfitter in selecting a guide. Are you new to the sport? Do you really want a day's worth of concentrated instruction? Some of the guides do poorly with beginners; others never know when to let up. Good communication between the guide and client easily resolves this dilemma. I generally push and demand a great deal up until lunch. After lunch I let my beginner's just have fun. When they need instruction, I wait for them to ask for it. Ask your outfitter for the best instructor for a beginner.

Do you want a young guide who bursts with enthusiasm, rows the boat with a fierce macho pride, and jumps up and down like a cheerleader? Your outfitter has them. (God, I am getting old.) Be open with the outfitter regarding what you want in a guide. And finally, I would like to close with some advice to novices. Take a class before you book a trip. Check out a fly casting VCR tape. I recommend Doug Swisher's casting instruction tape as well as his book. But if you want to learn on your vacation, ask for a walk-in trip instead of a float trip. Trust me, you will learn more in one day of instruction on a creek catching dozens of 7 inch trout than a couple of days casting from a boat with no previous experience.